DATE DUE

MAR 2 1 2011	

WORK,
FAMILY,
AND
FAITH

WORK, FAMILY, AND FAITH

Rural Southern Women in the Twentieth Century

edited with an
introduction by

Melissa Walker
and
Rebecca Sharpless

University of Missouri Press   Columbia and London

Copyright © 2006 by
The Curators of the University of Missouri
University of Missouri Press, Columbia, Missouri 65201
Printed and bound in the United States of America
5 4 3 2 1   10 09 08 07 06

Library of Congress Cataloging-in-Publication Data

Work, family, and faith : rural southern women in the twentieth century /
edited by Melissa Walker and Rebecca Sharpless.
      p.   cm.
   Summary: "Collection of essays capturing the transformation of the American
South from agrarian to industrial/commercial over the course of the twentieth
century from the perspective of women struggling against poverty by relying on
tradition and inner strength"—Provided by publisher.
   Includes bibliographical references and index.
   ISBN-13: 978-0-8262-1629-8 (alk. paper)
   ISBN-10: 0-8262-1629-3 (alk. paper)
   1. Rural women—Southern States—History—20th century.   2. Social
change—Southern States.   3. Southern States—Rural conditions.   I. Walker,
Melissa, 1962–   II. Sharpless, Rebecca.
   HQ1438.S63W68   2006
   305.40975'0917340904—dc22   2005028714

♾ ™ This paper meets the requirements of the
American National Standard for Permanence of Paper
for Printed Library Materials, Z39.48, 1984.

Designer: Foley Design
Typesetter: Phoenix Type, Inc.
Printer and Binder: Thomson-Shore, Inc.
Typefaces: Adobe Caslon and Chevalier

Contents

III. Town and Country Come Together

Acknowledgments

This book has been a marvelous collaboration throughout. Not only have we thoroughly enjoyed the process of grappling with ideas through the process of writing our own essay and editing the volume, but we have also reveled in our exchanges with these fine authors. This volume owes its existence to the incisive work being done by scholars devoted to deepening and complicating our understanding of rural women's lives, and we thank them.

New scholarship is built on earlier work, and we happily acknowledge our scholarly debts. We name in the Introduction many of the scholars whose work has been influential in shaping our understanding of rural women's lives, but two historians deserve special thanks. We both were profoundly influenced by the work of Pete Daniel and Jack Temple Kirby, work that is inspiring not only for its careful scholarship but also for the way both of them put ordinary people at the center of the stories they tell about the rural South. As the series editor for Rebecca's first book, Jack was extremely encouraging. Likewise, Pete was the series editor for Melissa's first book. She is enormously grateful for his supportive words and continuing encouragement. We also thank our colleagues in the Southern Association for Women Historians and the Rural Women's Studies Association, who have provided nurture for us and feedback for our work for well over a decade now.

Beverly Jarrett, director of the University of Missouri Press, has been a great fan of this project from our first overture, and we are grateful for her enthusiasm as well as her administrative know-how. Jane Lago has been wonderful as managing editor for the press.

Rebecca's thanks:

First, many thanks to Melissa Walker for dreaming up this project and for thinking I would be a worthy partner. This project has been a time of deepening a friendship, of discovering what an astonishing amount we have in common. The e-mails between South Carolina and Texas have been voluminous and just plain fun. I am grateful, as always, to my incomparable colleagues in the Institute for Oral History at Baylor University: Lois E. Myers, Elinor Mazé, Becky Shulda, and Leslie Roy Ballard. The four of them, individually and collectively, provide much to me and my work, including encyclopedic knowledge of *The Chicago Manual of Style*. Tom Charlton, my husband, simply makes everything in my life possible.

Melissa's thanks:

Buckets of thanks go to Rebecca Sharpless for making this project such a joy! Thanks to all my colleagues at Converse College, including Jeff Barker, vice president for academic affairs, and the faculty development committee who granted me the sabbatical leave during which I completed much of the work for this volume. Thanks also to my departmental colleagues who had to pick up the slack while I was gone. I am grateful to History and Politics Department chair Joe P. Dunn for his enthusiastic support of my scholarship and to John Theilmann who cheerfully offers helpful comments on my work on rural southern women, work far afield from his own work on medieval Britain and on southern politics. The women in my writers' group—Anita Rose, Suzanne Schuweiler-Daab, Laura Brown, and Cathy West—though they have not read pieces of this particular book, are sustaining friends, repeatedly sharing my ideas, critiquing my prose, and providing a monthly dose of female companionship and support. Thanks to my students for their endless curiosity and warm interest in my scholarship. Most of all, thanks to my husband, Chuck Reback, for his patient toleration of my perpetual distraction and interminable conversations about "my farm women."

We dedicate this volume to the scholar whose work has influenced it most strongly: Lu Ann Jones. Lu Ann was the first scholar of southern rural women that either of us met. Over the years, she has proved to be a warm and generous colleague, always encouraging, always willing to share. She remains an example of the kind of scholar we both strive to be in her commitment to telling the stories of ordinary people from their own perspectives—perspectives that are often competing and contested, but always central to understanding the past.

WORK, FAMILY, AND FAITH

Rebecca Sharpless and
Melissa Walker

Introduction

I know that this world is built up on strong women, built up and
kept up by them too, kneeling, stooping, pulling, bending, and rising
up when they need to go and do what needs to get done.

—KAYE GIBBONS, *A Virtuous Woman*

Like Ruby Stokes, the sharecropper's wife in Kaye Gibbons's
novel *A Virtuous Woman*, women who lived on the land in the
twentieth-century South had to be strong to survive, and they knew
it. Rural women—the majority of the South's female population until
midcentury—faced enormous challenges in a region beset by rapid
economic change and uncertain agricultural markets. Making do and
doing without; working endless hours in the house, the fields, and off
the farm; and organizing to improve rural life, farm women were
essential to their families, their rural communities, and the larger southern economy. Our goal for this volume is not to glorify or glamorize
the stories of rural women. It is, rather, to expand the discussion on
rural women in the American South that has begun in the past fifteen
years. The nine essays in this volume continue to document southern
rural women's lives, but they also complicate, deepen, and broaden
the topics of discussion and the analysis.

1

The editors of this book came to the study of rural southern women from different places. Melissa grew up on a dairy farm in East Tennessee, and grandparents on both sides of her family had spent at least part of their lives on farms. She spent her childhood listening to stories about early-twentieth-century farm life. In college, she looked for works about southern farm life but found very little scholarship that incorporated the perspectives of farm people themselves and none that considered farm women. In an attempt to fill some of this void, she focused her own scholarship on farm women in the upcountry South. Rebecca, on the other hand, was a city girl whose family filled her head with stories of life on Texas cotton farms. She did not consciously set out to study rural women, but one graduate-school encounter with Margaret Jarman Hagood's 1939 study *Mothers of the South: Portraiture of the White Tenant Farm Woman* was enough to set her on the path to learn about women like her grandmother. Both of us wrote our dissertations (later published as our first books) on rural women, and our fascination with the subject has not wavered.

The idea for this joint project emerged gradually. In the spring of 2000, historian R. Douglas Hurt asked each of us to contribute an essay to a collection he was editing on African American life in the rural South. At the time, Melissa was a visiting scholar at Baylor University's Institute for Oral History, the research center that Rebecca directs. Melissa spent her days in Waco reading transcripts of rich oral history interviews with Texas farm people, and on the weekends, we drove around the Central Texas farmland that provided the backdrop for most of these narratives. As we rode across the prairie, we talked about the Hurt book and about the state of scholarship on the rural South. We also talked about our frustrating search for suitable works on rural southern women to assign in our own classes. We realized that a growing body of research on rural southern women existed but that a good deal of it remained unpublished and that other work was in the form of dissertations, journal articles, and monographs—inaccessible or unaffordable forms for students. Over the course of the next year, the two of us worked on some other projects together, and we discovered that we collaborated well, with similar approaches to rural women's history and similar work ethics. We batted around some ideas for further collaboration, returning at last to the challenge of providing students, scholars, and even general readers with an accessible introduction to scholarship on twentieth-century southern rural women. Eventually, the plan for this project took shape. We issued a general call for proposals for essays, and we received numerous interesting proposals—evidence of the increasing sophistication in southern rural women's studies. The essays in this volume represent our choice for work best representing the spectrum of southern rural women's lives. Had we chosen other essays, we would undoubtedly have had a book of equal quality.

❧

No work exists in a vacuum, of course, and we owe a debt of gratitude to the scholars who broke the ground, as it were, for this volume. In the past twenty-five years, scholars have gathered a wealth of information about rural women in all parts of the United States, and three of them, in particular, set the standard for subsequent work on rural women's history. Historian Joan Jensen was the first to call on scholars to turn their attention to the lives of rural women. In 1981, she published a pathbreaking anthology, *With These Hands: Women Working on the Land,* that mapped out a research agenda on rural women. She followed up with *Loosening the Bonds: Mid-Atlantic Farm Women, 1750–1835,* a monograph that examined the central role of nineteenth-century women in mid-Atlantic dairy production and provided a valuable model of how to reconstruct farm women's work lives. Around the same time, historian Jacqueline Jones charted a similar course for the study of African American farm women. In *Labor of Love, Labor of Sorrow: Black Women, Work and the Family from Slavery to the Present,* she examined African American women's farm work in the context of the family labor system. Exploring the ways that the South's racial caste system limited the options available to rural black women, she found that black women nonetheless struggled to sustain family and community ties in the face of overwhelming pressures. Jones raised important questions about the intersections among race, class, and gender in shaping privilege, oppression, and resistance, questions that continue to engage scholars. Third, Lu Ann Jones designed and conducted a massive oral history project for the Smithsonian Institution's National Museum of American History. She traversed the South interviewing more than two hundred people—men and women, black and white, landowning, yeoman, and tenant—for An Oral History of Southern Agriculture. Through this project, Jones charted the experiences of a watershed generation of southern farm people who experienced the transition to capitalist agriculture. She provided an invaluable archive for scholars of southern agriculture and a fine model for oral history projects that considered ordinary people's work and community lives.[1] With her work, later studies, including those of Michelle Haberland, Ann McCleary, Karen Utz, and Melissa Walker and Rebecca Sharpless in this volume, demonstrate amply the crucial importance of oral history in understanding the lives of rural women.

In addition to the groundbreaking work of these three scholars, historians of rural southern women build on four streams of scholarship. First, we draw on the work of New Deal–era sociologists and anthropologists who plowed the rough ground of the poverty-stricken, racially segregated southern countryside to record conditions of life and labor there. Margaret Jarman Hagood, Arthur F. Raper, Charles Johnson, Rupert Vance, and Howard W. Odom all produced important studies of southern rural life and delineated the fault lines of race and class. These scholars, Hagood and Raper in particular, were among the first to pay attention to the lives of farm women, and they shared important insights about the gap between the South's rigid gender ideologies and the realities of most black and white farm women's lives. Photographers employed by New Deal agencies, most

1. Jensen, *With These Hands* (Old Westbury, NY: Feminist Press, 1981); Jensen, *Loosening the Bonds* (New Haven, CT: Yale University Press, 1986); J. Jones, *Labor of Love, Labor of Sorrow* (New York: Vintage Books, 1985); L. A. Jones, "Voices of Southern Agricultural History," in *International Annual of Oral History, 1990: Subjectivity and Multiculturalism in Oral History,* edited by Ronald J. Grele (New York: Greenwood Press, 1992), 134–44.

notably Dorothea Lange, supplemented these textual accounts with unforgettable visual images of the people who lived on the land.[2]

The second stream of scholarship that informs the study of rural southern women is work on southern agriculture and rural social history that began to appear in the mid-1980s. Pete Daniel, Jack Temple Kirby, and Gilbert C. Fite initiated the study of the protracted transition to capitalist agriculture in the South and the impact of that transition on rural people.[3] Daniel and Kirby, in particular, discussed the effects of rural southern transformation on ordinary people and communities.

Work on rural women in other parts of the United States has built on the example set by Joan Jensen to provide a third stream of influential scholarship. Historians Sally Ann McMurray and Nancy Grey Osterud in the northeastern United States and Deborah Fink, Mary Neth, and Katherine Jellison in the Midwest, in particular, have focused on the ways that the transition to mechanized, specialized

2. Hagood, *Mothers of the South: Portraiture of the White Tenant Farm Woman* (1939; repr., New York: W. W. Norton, 1977); Raper, *Preface to Peasantry: A Tale of Two Black Belt Counties* (Chapel Hill: University of North Carolina Press, 1936) and *Tenants of the Almighty* (New York: Macmillan, 1943); Johnson, Edwin R. Embree, and W. W. Alexander, *The Collapse of Cotton Tenancy: Summary of Field Studies and Statistical Surveys, 1933–35* (Chapel Hill: University of North Carolina Press, 1935); Johnson, *Growing Up in the Black Belt: Negro Youth in the Rural South* (1941; repr., New York: Schocken Books, 1967); Vance, *Human Factors in Cotton Culture: A Study in the Social Geography of the American South* (Chapel Hill: University of North Carolina Press, 1929); Odum for the southern regional committee of the Social Science Research Council, *Southern Regions of the United States* (Chapel Hill: University of North Carolina Press, 1936); Odum, *Race and Rumors of Race: The American South in the Early Forties* (Baltimore: Johns Hopkins University Press, 1997); Lange and Paul Schuster Taylor, *An American Exodus: A Record of Human Erosion* (New York: Reynal and Hitchcock, 1939).

3. Daniel, *Breaking the Land: The Transformation of Cotton, Tobacco, and Rice Cultures since 1880* (Urbana: University of Illinois Press, 1986) and *Lost Revolutions: The South in the 1950s* (Chapel Hill: University of North Carolina Press, 2000); Kirby, *Rural Worlds Lost: The American South, 1920–1960* (Baton Rouge: Louisiana State University Press, 1987); Fite, *Cotton Fields No More: Southern Agriculture, 1865–1980* (Lexington: University Press of Kentucky, 1984).

commercial agriculture transformed the lives of farm women and rural communities. Essay collections from the conferences on Rural and Farm Women in Historical Perspective also examined aspects of farm women's work and rural family life across the country.[4]

Finally, scholars of rural southern women have emulated studies of middle-class urban women by examining reform in the rural South. Much early work on southern rural women emphasized home demonstration work, in part because the records were plentiful and readily accessible. Pioneering investigations by three historians included in this collection, Lynne A. Rieff, Ann McCleary, and Lu Ann Jones, focused on home demonstration agents' efforts to assist rural women in improving their lives, work done within the confines of notions about appropriate racial and gender roles. Mary Hoffschwelle cast a wider net in studying rural reform, focusing on the efforts of Progressive Era reformers to improve rural schools and communities.[5]

❦

At a 1992 Rural Women in Historical Perspective conference, a participant came up to Rebecca, who had just given a paper titled "Southern Women and the Land," breathlessly thanked her for her presentation, and said, "I just hate to think about the South!" South-

4. McMurry, *Transforming Rural Life: Dairying Families and Agricultural Change, 1820–1885* (Baltimore: Johns Hopkins University Press, 1995); Osterud, *Bonds of Community: The Lives of Farm Women in Nineteenth-Century New York* (Ithaca, NY: Cornell University Press, 1991); Fink, *Open Country, Iowa: Rural Women, Tradition, and Change* (Albany: State University Press of New York, 1986) and *Agrarian Women: Wives and Mothers in Rural Nebraska, 1880–1940* (Chapel Hill: University of North Carolina Press, 1996); Neth, *Preserving the Family Farm: Women, Community, and the Foundations of Agribusiness in the Midwest, 1900–1940* (Baltimore: Johns Hopkins University Press, 1995); Jellison, *Entitled to Power: Farm Women and Technology, 1919–1939* (Chapel Hill: University of North Carolina Press, 1993); Wava G. Haney and Jane B. Knowles, eds., *Women and Farming: Changing Roles, Changing Structures* (Boulder, CO: Westview Press, 1988); Jensen and Osterud, eds., "American Rural and Farm Women in Historical Perspective," special issue, *Agricultural History* 67:2 (Spring 1993); Fink, Valerie Grim, and Dorothy Schwieder, eds., "Special Symposium Issue on Rural and Farm Women in Historical Perspective," *Agricultural History* 73:2 (Spring 1999).

5. Rieff, "'Go Ahead and Do All You Can': Southern Progressives and Alabama Home Demonstration Clubs, 1914–1940," in *Hidden Histories of Women*

ern farms seldom conformed to the rural stereotype of red-painted barns and contented Holsteins chewing their cuds. The lives of southern farm women varied from those of their counterparts in other regions in at least three ways. First, they were poorer, coming from a region noted for its widespread poverty. In 1900, 36 percent of southern whites and 75 percent of African Americans farmed land owned by someone else. The agricultural downturn of the 1920s and 1930s only exacerbated the poverty of the region. By 1930, 47 percent of whites and 79 percent of African Americans were tenants. Landlessness destroyed the control of most farm people over their own lives, and minimal industrialization guaranteed few opportunities to leave the land. Poverty became a relentless and endless cycle for many rural southern families, both African American and white, until the economic changes wrought by World War II.[6]

Second, the population of the South divided along racial lines, with an African American population of seven million composing more than one-third of the region's people in 1900. The legacy of slavery created relationships of extraordinary complexity. Legal and economic discrimination constrained the economic opportunities of African Americans, while the capricious practices of segregation forced them to negotiate daily lives filled with unpredictability, humiliation, and often danger. As the tenancy figures above suggest, poverty was often linked to race in the rural South. Although not all poor people were African American, most African American people were poor. Most

_____

in the New South, edited by Virginia Bernhard, Betty Brandon, Elizabeth Fox-Genovese, Theda Perdue, and Elizabeth H. Turner (Columbia: University of Missouri Press, 1994), 134–49, and "'Rousing the People of the Land': Home Demonstration Work in the Deep South, 1914–1950" (PhD diss., Auburn University, 1995); McCleary, "Shaping a New Role for the Rural Women: Home Demonstration Work in Augusta County, Virginia, 1917–1940" (PhD diss., Brown University, 1996); L. A. Jones, "Re-visioning the Countryside: Southern Women, Rural Reform, and the Farm Economy in the Twentieth Century" (PhD diss., University of North Carolina, 1996), chaps. 4–5; Hoffschwelle, *Rebuilding the Rural Southern Community: Reformers, Schools, and Homes in Tennessee, 1914–1929* (Knoxville: University of Tennessee Press, 1998).

6. U.S. Bureau of the Census, *Statistical Abstract of the United States*, Bicentennial Edition (Washington, DC: Government Printing Office, 1976), 465.

white people were poor as well, but almost all the well-to-do people were white. As a result, African American farm women found only limited opportunities for autonomy and choice with regard to their work roles, while white women found their choices about work shaped by racial ideology.[7]

Third, southern white women labored under gender constraints unlike those elsewhere in the United States, codified in the myth of the southern lady, and African American women often realized those limitations as well. Farm women recognized the impact of these three factors, and they constructed their work lives and their thoughts about themselves accordingly. The way that farm women describe their lives and their work illuminates much about race, class, and gender in the American South between 1900 and 1940. Despite significant divisions by race and class, they shared core experiences as women. To paraphrase David Roediger, women were concerned with issues of race and class even as they fashioned their gender identities.[8]

Even more than females in other regions, southern women were rural. The American South had been an agrarian region even before the arrival of the first colonists from England. With generally humid conditions and a long growing season, the region lent itself to commercial agriculture, first with tobacco and rice, then cotton and sugar cane. Subsistence farms in many locations gave way to the exigencies of the world market. By the turn of the twentieth century, most families raised either tobacco or cotton as cash crops, depending on their location. Ironically, neither of these crops is edible, and farm families sometimes concentrated on these cash crops to the detriment of raising food for their families.[9]

Cotton and tobacco cultivation both involved enormous amounts of labor. Cotton growing provides a good example. Planting com-

7. Historical U.S. Census Data Browser, available online at http://fisher .lib.virginia.edu/census.

8. Roediger, "Race and the Working-Class Past in the United States: Multiple Identities and the Future of Labor History," *International Review of Social History* 38 (1993): S134.

9. Gavin Wright, *The Political Economy of the Cotton South: Households, Markets, and Wealth in the Nineteenth Century* (New York: W. W. Norton, 1978), 181.

menced in early spring, followed by a long round of thinning (a process known as "chopping") and cultivation with hoes and plows. By early July, the crop was "laid by," meaning that field work ceased until harvest time. In late summer, as the bolls started to open, workers moved through the fields, pulling cotton from its sharp shells and filling sacks with the fiber. As more bolls opened, workers passed through the same fields again and again. Harvest was often not completed until early December. The ripe cotton was taken to cotton gins where seed was separated from the lint and the cotton was baled and sold. Because of the endless hours required to cultivate cash crops for market, all but the wealthiest farmers relied on family labor, including the work of women and children. As a result, field work figured prominently in the lives of most southern farm women.

Farm women performed their work in the context of the southern agricultural economy, which swung wildly between 1900 and 1920 depending on markets, weather, and disease, then after World War I began its inexorable slide toward the Great Depression. Poverty shaped women's lives, and the land-tenure status of a woman's male relatives determined much about the nature of her work—indeed, almost every physical aspect of a southern farm woman's life. Much historiographical debate still surrounds the rise of the system after the Civil War, but by 1900 it was so well developed that its rules had attained the status of common wisdom. A landless farmer who owned nothing— no work stock, no tools—was a sharecropper, who split the crop with the landowner fifty-fifty. A tenant farmer had no land but owned his own work stock and tools, and he paid the landowner one-third of the corn crop and one-fourth of the cotton or tobacco crop. The landowner or a nearby merchant supplied the landless farmer with credit during the growing season and at harvest totaled up the credit plus interest and subtracted that amount from the tenant's or sharecropper's portion of the harvest. This system worked to keep landless farmers in debt year after relentless year, with little means of advancement. A few landless farmers were able to accumulate some savings as well as work stock and tools; these farmers often became cash renters, paying a regular rent for the use of land and keeping all of the proceeds from their crops. But cash renters could easily slip into sharecropping or tenant-farming status if they suffered a bad year due to drought, blight, insects, or low commodity prices. As a result of these factors, a few southern farmers were wealthy, some were comfortable, and many lived in fairly deep poverty. Most farm families lived on razor-thin margins of sufficiency.

One of the features of rural life that most distinguished it from urban situations was the family economy, in which all members of a family labored together to produce a single wage. If a family worked as a unit to bring in the cash crop, whether it be cotton, tobacco, or rice, they received payment in a lump sum irrespective of who had contributed how much labor. For a woman, this so-called family wage had at least two ramifications. First, it meant that all of her work was on behalf of her family and so might be socially acceptable. Second, she had no money to call her own, and in many families the wife had to negotiate with the husband for any spending money. This situation appalled reformers, who believed that such a system particularly exploited women. But the family economy included much more than the cash crop. A woman marshaled the resources of the farm, particularly food and clothing, and her skill in doing so made a notable difference in her family's well-being. Her ability to preserve food could mean a more varied diet for her children, and her ability to sew feed sacks into clothing could create a change or two of dresses for her daughters. A woman's petty-commodity production, furthermore, could significantly widen her family's options as consumers, as she traded eggs, butter, and other goods for everything from medicine to curtain fabric. As transportation increased, a woman could travel farther to sell her goods, and she might even receive cash for her petty commodities. The family economy depended heavily on the input of women, whether or not other family members acknowledged it.[10]

10. L. A. Jones, *Mama Learned Us to Work: Farm Women in the New South* (Chapel Hill: University of North Carolina Press, 2002), 12, 14, 50, 52, 70, 73–79, 98, 171–83; R. Sharpless, *Fertile Ground, Narrow Choices: Women on Texas Cotton Farms, 1900–1940* (Chapel Hill: University of North Carolina Press, 1999), 3, 186–87; M. Walker, *All We Knew Was to Farm: Rural Women in the Upcountry South, 1919–1941* (Baltimore: Johns Hopkins University Press, 2000), 33–34.

One of the emphases in this volume is the degree to which women's lives on southern farms changed during the twentieth century. Technology, particularly transportation, significantly altered rural women's lives. As roads improved, from mud to gravel to blacktop, and as springboard wagons gave way to cars, a woman could go to town to sell her goods and buy things with cash. Her children could attend consolidated schools. The vision of the world began to widen, and rural families realized the limitations of life on the farm. At the same time, women saw increased opportunities for employment. In the southern upcountry, for example, women took jobs in manufacturing plants of various descriptions, worked in government installations, or became domestic workers. In some cases, they moved to town; in others, however, they continued to live on farms and commute to town. Farm people sometimes moved to large regional market centers, but on other occasions they went to the nearest town that would provide work. As the Utz and Haberland essays in this volume demonstrate, rural people brought their country ways to town, and parts of the towns and cities resembled country neighborhoods, complete with cows and chickens.[11]

Opportunities in town provided the "pull" factors for rural people leaving the farm. Government policies, beginning in the 1930s, provided some of the "push" factors. New Deal agricultural policy encouraged landowners to get rid of their tenants, and the U.S. Department of Agriculture encouraged farmers to buy increasingly sophisticated equipment. More and more, farmers "got big" or got out. By 1960, the majority of the people in the South lived in town, and by 1980, that number had risen to 75 percent. The lives of those who stayed little resembled the way they had been in the first half of the twentieth century.[12]

☙

11. Walker, *All We Knew Was to Farm,* 21, 23–24, 35, 43, 70–71, 86–93, 262–63, 278–80, 284–85, 287–88.

12. Daniel, *Breaking the Land,* 237–98; R. Douglas Hurt, introduction to *The Rural South since World War II,* edited by Hurt (Baton Rouge: Louisiana State University Press, 1998), 1–4.

The organization of this volume reflects the major categories of research on twentieth-century rural women. The first two essays acquaint the reader with women's daily lives on the farm. Using an edited oral history interview, Lu Ann Jones introduces us to Nellie Stancil Langley, a North Carolina yeoman farm woman—one of a group of farm women often ignored by historians intent on exploring the lives of landowning planters or the landless. Langley's life illuminates the broad range of activities that occupied a farm woman's day and shows how yeomen women, through their petty-commodity production and field work, played an important role in the larger agricultural economy. Rebecca Sharpless and Melissa Walker focus on the least-studied aspect of farm women's endless round of labors: their field work. They probe the complex interactions between ideology and necessity that guided women's decisions about whether to engage in field work and how to talk about such work.

The second group of essays looks beyond the farm woman, her family, and the farm to explore the work of rural reformers. Appropriately, this is the largest group of essays on the topic that represents the bulk of research on farm women to date. Evan Bennett argues that not only was women's work critical to successful tobacco cultivation but women also bore a heavy load from southern rural poverty. Their support was essential to efforts to organize tobacco farmer cooperatives, which ultimately failed for numerous reasons. Home demonstration was a reform movement that has enjoyed considerable attention by scholars, and two essays bring increasing analysis to the work of earnest young demonstrating agents and their followers. Ann McCleary traces the history of a home demonstration curb market, revealing how it helped white farm women temporarily regain a measure of control over the marketing of their products, control that was eroding as men came to dominate the marketing of all types of farm products. Lynne Rieff places the work of home demonstration agents like those who organized curb markets in the larger context, arguing that as home demonstration work became more professionalized, the help it provided to farm women became more specialized, less practical, and more individualized. In addition, black home demonstration agents found many of their efforts to help farm families stymied by poverty and by the obstacles imposed by the racial caste system.

The Christian church also provided a locus for rural reform efforts. Lois Myers explores the work of Southern Methodist deaconesses who served farming communities. Like many rural reformers, most deaconesses came from rural backgrounds and tended to devise practical and effective strategies for addressing the spiritual as well as the material needs of the rural poor, people often ignored by the church and the larger society. Similarly, Connie Rice shows us how Cecil Brown developed a successful Salvation Army ministry in the mountains of North Carolina. Although the Salvationists mainly emphasized urban ministries, Brown was able to transcend the traditional rural gender boundaries because she herself grew up in the mountains and because she adapted her ministry to the needs of the local people.

The final pair of essays explores the blurring of boundaries between town and country and the resulting widening of opportunities for farm women. Karen Utz examines the experiences of African American farm women who moved to Sloss Quarters, a steel company–owned village in Birmingham. At Sloss Quarters, women drew on rural subsistence practices and on traditional mutual aid networks to sustain community ties, but they also took advantage of new employment opportunities and leisure activities offered by town life. Finally, Michelle Haberland examines how the arrival of the apparel industry in southern Alabama redefined the social, economic, gender, and racial dynamics of rural communities. She demonstrates the way low-wage apparel manufacturing jobs improved the local standard of living but failed to provide permanent opportunities for rural women.

These essays hint at aspects of twentieth-century rural life that scholars have yet to explore. Although we have learned a good bit about farm women's work lives early in the century, we need to uncover more about the work and family lives of black and white women who persisted on the land after World War II. Another promising area for further study is found in the lives of farm women who took off-farm jobs, their salaries serving to subsidize the farming operation and help the family attain a middle-class lifestyle. Much work remains to be done on women's roles in most twentieth-century farm organizations, particularly the United Farm Organization, the American Agriculture Movement, and Women in Farm Economics and in cooperative movements. Similarly, scholars have yet to give much attention to twentieth-century rural churches and the roles of women within them. Mechanization played an increasingly significant part in farm families' lives, and we should discover more about its impact on southern women. Southern aspects of farm economics after World War II merit further investigation. And, following Haberland and Utz, the transformation of the rural landscape into a suburban one merits significant study. There remains much to be done to understand the important and dwindling segment of the population that is farm women. We are grateful to the authors in this volume who continue to expand the horizons of studies on southern rural women.

I.

*Life on
the Farm*

Lu Ann Jones

"Work Was My Pleasure"
An Oral History of Nellie Stancil Langley

Because southern farm women's voices are often muted in written records, many scholars have used oral history to document women's work on behalf of families, farms, and communities. A new generation of oral historians has picked up where New Deal–era interviewers and photographers left off in order to chronicle changes in southern agriculture and rural life since the 1930s. Between 1986 and 1991, I joined these documentary efforts when I directed An Oral History of Southern Agriculture, sponsored by the Smithsonian Institution's National Museum of American History.[1]

The rural elders I interviewed belong to a watershed generation. They came of age during the Great Depression and witnessed how tractors and harvesters, chemical herbicides and pesticides, and federal farm programs that regulated crop acreage and prices transformed the southern countryside during the middle of the twentieth century. My task was to help people describe the interplay among broad economic and social changes and personal, family, and community life. The emerging literature on American farm women also encouraged me to consider the farm family economy in all of its dimensions and to observe women closely as they rushed between kitchens, barnyards, and fields. As narrators and I collaborated to create new evidence and

---

1. For more on An Oral History of Southern Agriculture, see Jones, *Mama Learned Us to Work: Farm Women in the New South* (Chapel Hill: University of North Carolina Press, 2002).

17

determine its meanings, we challenged and complicated the received scholarly wisdom.[2]

Nellie Stancil Langley was among the two hundred farm women and men who turned their lives into stories, and her narrative exemplifies how interviews with rural women enhance our understanding of southern agriculture. Born in 1918, Langley grew up in Wilson County, North Carolina, in the heart of the South's flue-cured tobacco economy. She describes the work culture of one of the region's major cash crops and how its seasonal demands shaped women's farm and household labor. She leaves no doubt about why farmers dubbed tobacco the "thirteen month a year" crop. There was always something to do when the golden leaf was planted and tended by hand, cultivated with mules, cured with wood-burning fires, and carefully graded for sale at warehouse auctions.[3]

Just as farmwork changed over time, household labor and domestic technologies have a history, too. Until the Rural Electrification Administration was established in 1935 and began subsidizing energy costs, few southern farm families enjoyed the benefits of electricity. Langley reminds us of the skills, stamina, and artistry required to cook and preserve food, wash and iron clothes, and clean house in the days before modern appliances—and that farm women practiced those skills long after their urban sisters had forgotten them. It was 1952 when power lines reached her farm.[4]

Langley's narrative also illustrates the complicated ways that class and race shaped experiences of rural life. As a white woman from a

2. On oral history as a collaborative process, see Michael Frisch, *A Shared Authority: Essays on the Craft and Meaning of Oral and Public History* (Albany: State University of New York Press, 1990).

3. Langley, interview by Jones, December 5, 1986, Stantonsburg, NC, An Oral History of Southern Agriculture, Archives Center, National Museum of American History, Smithsonian Institution, Washington, DC. On the tobacco culture, see Pete Daniel, *Breaking the Land: The Transformation of Cotton, Tobacco, and Rice Cultures since 1880* (Urbana: University of Illinois Press, 1985).

4. Excellent descriptions of farm women's domestic work and technologies are found in Rebecca Sharpless, *Fertile Ground, Narrow Choices: Women on Texas Cotton Farms, 1900–1940* (Chapel Hill: University of North Carolina Press, 1999).

Nellie Stancil Langley. Photograph courtesy of the Southern Agriculture Oral History Project Records, Archives Center, National Museum of American History, Behring Center, Smithsonian Institution, Washington, D.C.

middling family, she represents a group of rural southerners who have remained hidden in plain sight—a twentieth-century yeomanry who owned and operated their own farms. Scholars have tended to dichotomize the South's farmers and focused either on the poorest of the poor, sharecropping families who owned few productive resources and received a portion of the crop as payment, or on planter landlords who managed other people's labor. Langley's family, in contrast, occupied a middle ground as owners of a modest farm. When Nellie was growing up, sharecroppers and tenants predominated in Wilson County, but owners like her parents were typical of a slim majority of the state's farmers. Although her family was poor, they nonetheless benefited from the labor of a black tenant family for years. Whereas more prosperous large landowners rarely worked alongside tenants, Langley notes that small farmers and tenants, black and white alike, often shared similar work routines, credit arrangements, and standards of living—and those commonalities of class could mute hierarchies of race and build bridges of respect, buttressed by paternalism, across the color line.[5]

Oral history interviews with women like Nellie Langley illuminate a portion of the farm economy that has escaped serious analysis: women's subsistence strategies and their production for market. While male farmers placed their bets on cash crops, Langley makes clear that, like many southern farm women, she and her mother remained diversified farmers. Ownership provided a measure of control over the land's use and allowed them to put a "live at home" philosophy into practice. To meet as many of the family's needs as possible, they grew a good garden and preserved vegetables and fruits, they kept a cow for milk and butter, they butchered hogs and canned and smoked their meat, and they raised chickens to put food on the table. Production for home use shaded into production for exchange. The chickens that Langley's mother raised provided eggs for sale and trade— and a small margin of safety in a volatile market economy. She was not alone. Throughout the South, farm women sold dairy and poultry products to traveling buyers known as hucksters, to storekeepers, and to regular retail customers, and sale of these products was part of a larger economic strategy that guaranteed the survival of the family. In the 1950s, as federal farm programs cut tobacco acreage and farm income fell, Langley turned the household economy into a commercial enterprise when she began selling produce at a curb market in Wilson sponsored by the agricultural extension service. Like other farm mothers before her, she invested in the future when she used profits to underwrite her son's education.[6]

5. On the tenure status of farmers in Wilson County and North Carolina, see *Wilson, North Carolina: A Pictorial History* (Wilson, NC: Wilson Chamber of Commerce, 1993, prepared under the direction of the History Book Committee, Wilson Chamber of Commerce), 66; and U.S. Department of Commerce, Bureau of the Census, *Fifteenth Census of the United States: 1930, Agriculture,* vol. 2, *Part 2: The Southern States* (Washington, DC: Government Printing Office, 1932), 30–31.

6. Jones, *Mama Learned Us to Work,* chap. 2; Lu Ann Jones, "Taking What She Had and Turning It into Money: The Female Farm Economy," in *Cornbread Nation 1: The Best of Southern Food Writing,* edited by John Egerton

Several characteristics of Langley's interview stand out. Her un-adorned narrative of hard work interweaves the tobacco crop cycle and the female life cycle. Time and again, she notes continuity as well as change as she draws comparisons between her life and that of her mother. Like many members of her generation of farmers, Langley laments the demise of an ethic of sharing and trust that she believes once characterized her rural community. The labor demands of the traditional tobacco culture had encouraged mutual aid, and families routinely swapped work during harvest time. But her jeremiads do not invoke a naive nostalgia for the "good old days." Rather, implicit in her comments is a thoughtful critique of capital-intensive agricul-ture and rural modernization and changes that have come in their wake. When machines reduced the need for human labor, farmers had fewer neighbors. As private forms of entertainment replaced vis-iting, people felt more isolated. Chemicals and pesticides promised greater crop yields, but they created hazards to the environment and public health.[7]

My interview with Nellie Langley also contained contradictions and silences that I had failed to notice and probe in 1986. Because she died in 1996, when I began editing her narrative I turned to fam-ily members for help in reconciling them. On a sunny spring morn-ing in 2003, one of her brothers, her son and daughter, and a grand-daughter joined me at a Wilson restaurant to pay tribute to a woman who had worked hard to ensure their success against even longer odds than I had originally imagined. Nellie Stancil, as it turned out, was unmarried when she gave birth to her son in 1942. She bore what-ever stigma accrued to a single mother then without self-pity or com-plaint and remained a respected, albeit quiet, member of her commu-nity. Her brothers helped her farm before and after their stints in the military and after she married a farmer in 1952 who still suffered the

---

(Chapel Hill: University of North Carolina Press, 2002), 223–34; "Home Prod-ucts Help Off-Set Tobacco Cut," *Wilson Daily Times*, February 27, 1957.

7. This interpretation of the history and memory of community is inspired by Melissa Walker, "Mythologies of Community in Oral History Narratives of Rural Southerners," unpublished paper in author's possession.

crippling effects of childhood polio. Through it all, no one pulled a heavier load than Nellie Stancil Langley—or had higher ambitions for a son who became a certified public accountant and a daughter who became a pharmacist.[8]

Oral histories remind us that while we collaborate with narrators to create primary sources for scholars to interpret we are also entrusted with the stories of a mother, a sister, a grandmother. Now treasured parts of the family archives, the tapes and transcript of my interview with Nellie Stancil Langley continue to inspire and preserve memories of a woman who had no tolerance for laziness, did a day's work in the garden before most folks crawled out of bed, graciously prepared a granddaughter's favorite dish of mouthwatering chicken and pastry upon request, and always welcomed her brothers on Sundays when they decided, "Let's go down home." Only after her death did her family learn that she had made the final payment on a farm note in 1960, just as her son left for college. "How did she do it alone?" Jack Stancil pondered after reviewing the edited narrative. "Being a single parent during that time was not socially acceptable. How did she keep the small family farm together and make a life for herself and me?"[9] The son who had joined her in the fields at the age of five could find answers in stories of the woman for whom work was her pleasure.

"If We Didn't Raise It, We Didn't Eat It"

My daddy's name was Jack Stancil. [In 1918] Daddy had to go off to World War I, and Mama was pregnant with me. When Daddy got to Raleigh, they let him know I was being born [and] they let him come home. Daddy was afraid he was going to have to go back to

8. Howard Stancil, Jack Stancil, Mary Langley Baker, and Loree Stancil Brown, conversation with Jones, March 24, 2003, Wilson, NC, in author's possession; "Mrs. Langley Is Selected July's Cook-of-the-Month," *Wilson Daily Times,* July 20, 1983.

9. Jack Stancil, letter to author, May 7, 2003. Corrections and additions suggested by the family have been incorporated into the edited narrative.

war, so he wanted somebody named after him so they put Nellie Jack to my name. The war ended and Daddy didn't never really have to go, and after he come back he had five boys. Just about a year's difference in every one of us. I was the oldest one, and I got stuck with the name Nellie Jack.

[When I was growing up, Mama was pregnant] all the time. You know back then there won't no hospitals, there won't no doctors. The babies were born at home with a grannie lady. She was a black lady that just come and stayed till the baby was born, then left. All of us were born right here and my first child was born February 11, 1942, right here in this house.

[Mama and Daddy owned] about sixty-five or seventy acres, with the woodland, too. We won't rich people; we were poor people. They raised tobacco, cotton, and corn. Back then, if you sold a pound of tobacco for nine cents you thought you were rich. And we'd make a bale or two of cotton. We didn't never sell our corn. We'd put it in the barn, and if we needed something we couldn't raise Daddy'd take a bag full or two and go sell it, or I would or Mama would. There was a mill in Stantonsburg we'd haul it to. We used to take our corn and make our cornmeal. Make chicken feed out of it. We also had a cotton mill in Stantonsburg where we baled our cotton. See, there's nothing there like that now. There's no corn mill, no cotton mill, or nothing. It don't even look like the same town.

We had chickens all over the back yard. You couldn't walk out there without getting in chicken stuff. The hog pen come right up there next to the house. We had mule stables out here. We had a log corn barn, and we had two log tobacco barns. We had a milk cow and a place out for the cow to stay. Okay, we'd milk the cow, we'd put the milk in pans and then let the cream come on top. We'd skim that cream off, shake it in a big gallon fruit jar and make butter. Then if you wanted to keep the milk till the next day, we'd have to let it down in that open well on a rope and it hung down in that cold water all day long.

We used to kill a lot of hogs. Back then we had no freezer, we couldn't freeze anything. We would can it. I don't know why in the world it didn't kill us. We'd fry us a sausage and put it in big quart jars and fill it full of the sausage grease. We done lean meat the same way. And sometimes when we'd kill hogs we would put a bunch of the fresh sausage at the bottom of a lard stand and then fill it up with lard. And sometimes we would hang sausage up in the smokehouse to dry so it wouldn't spoil.

We raised everything. We used to raise our popcorn. We did. We didn't have to buy nothing. You know, we didn't have to buy Christmas trees or Christmas decorations. We made 'em. Mama used to go in the woods and cut a lot of holly, string it and put it all over the windows and decorate with holly. If we couldn't find a decent Christmas tree, she'd just get the top out of a pine tree and decorate it.

I know this sounds crazy, but we used to have to loop tobacco on a stick. When we'd take that tobacco off dry to grade it and tie it, we'd save them tobacco twines and make round balls. About a week before Christmas we'd soak those balls in kerosene. We would strike a match to them and throw them to each other. It's a wonder we didn't hurt ourselves. We called them fireballs. That was our Christmas.

If we didn't raise it, we didn't eat it. I know we used to dry apples and we used to pick peas and we'd hang them up in the top of the barn in a sack down on a string where the rats couldn't climb down that string. What peas we couldn't eat green and can green, we would pick them and sheet them up in cotton sheets, and when we got caught up on the farm we'd beat them peas out and put them in bags and hang them up in a barn. But now you can't; when I dry my apples I have to put them in the freezer.

I still got some of the pea seeds that Mama died and left here in 1940 hanging in a barn. I save them every year, from one year to the next. That's her same peas. You can't hang them out in the barn, now, like we used to. If you put them in a plastic container now with a lid on them, bugs still get in them. They do. You shell your peas and stick them in the freezer dried because the bugs'll eat them up. Several years ago I strung some red pepper and the bugs got in that. Hot red pepper. So now I have to pick that and put it in a Zip bag in the freezer.

I know used to that we didn't have to poison our butter beans, we didn't have to poison our collards. Like in the fall of the year if we had a few worms, Mama would make us take the tobacco dirt off of our lugs [the bottom, poorest quality leaves on the stalk] and go put on the collard bud to get rid of those collard worms. And now it costs us a fortune to raise collards buying this expensive poison— worm dust and Sevin dust. But sometimes that don't get them. I think [the bugs] get immuned to it. It just stays there so long, they get to the place they can eat it and it don't even bother them. I just wonder if it's good for us.

"Farming Was a Year-Round Job"

The land that we tend is about a mile from here back across that woods. We'd get up early and fix breakfast. Cooked biscuits three times a day—there won't no bread back then; we didn't have no money to buy it if they had it. I learned how to cook, to make biscuits, standing on a fifty-pound lard stand bucket.

We'd be at the field ready to go to work at six o'clock. We rode on a two-horse mule and wagon. And we would come back at dinner time on that two-horse mule and wagon, eat a bite of dinner, feed the mules and water them and go right back over there to work until it got dark and come home again. Some mornings [Mama'd] get up and cook a big pot of dried peas and Irish potatoes and biscuit and we'd carry them over on the wagon and eat right over there so we wouldn't have to come home at lunchtime and then turn around and go back.

Back then you had nothing but mules so farming was a year-round job. In the winter months when it was so cold you couldn't do nothing else, you had to go in the woods and cut wood to cure that tobacco with. Haul it to the house and get it to the tobacco barn. Then in January and February when you were doing that, you'd get your plant bed sowed. After you'd get the plant beds sowed, you've got to go there with some canvas cloths and cover them, then go back and check them right steady. When you started seeing the weeds, you'd start picking. Back then they had nothing to put on the plant beds to kill the weeds. So I've been out there many a day in March and picked plant bed all day long and near 'bout freeze. We'd have to build a fire around the plant bed. We'd go up and warm our hands. But see, now they put something on the plant bed that kills the weeds. They don't have to pick them no more.

Then the latter part of April, first of May, you'd start setting out the tobacco plants, and it was work from then on. We had to sucker it with our hands; we had to chop it with our hands; we had to pick the worms off with our hands. Back then, we didn't have nothing to kill worms; we had nothing to kill the suckers [small, superfluous leaves that drain nutrition from the rest of the plant]. So it was a continuous job.

Lord, you'd have to plow it about every week to keep the weeds down. And you'd chop it three or four times, 'cause the plow couldn't get up there on the tobacco ridge and cover up the high weeds. The ones up around the stalk, you'd have to pull the weeds up with your hands. You'd have to sucker it and top it. You'd have to go through it every week after you got it going to keep the suckers and tops out. 'Cause if you didn't keep them suckers and tops [the plant's flowers that drain nutrition from the rest of the plant] out, that kept the weight out of the leaf.

Back then my daddy and mama grew around fifteen or twenty acres of tobacco. [Before the 1930s and the federal farm programs] there won't no allotment [federally mandated limit on how much tobacco could be grown]. You could plant all you wanted to, if you had the barn room and somebody to help you house it. You didn't hire nobody. I would help our neighbors harvest theirs for nothing, then they'd come help me put in mine for nothing. That's the way we worked it. No money. We didn't swap money, we just helped each other.

We usually had five or six acres of cotton, and the balance of our land—fifteen or twenty acres—in corn. See, what we done then, we pulled corn by hand. We'd also pull the fodder off and tie it up and stack it, and that's what we'd give to the mules. We had four [mules]. Four-horse farm they called it. I remember we had one [mule] we called Blackie and one we called Red and one we called Old Ada. I forgot what the other one was.

I always wanted Mama and Daddy and everybody to be good to the mules, feed 'em good and water 'em good. Used to, you know, you couldn't turn a spigot on and get water. We had to tote the water in washtubs and buckets from way out here to the mule stables. A lot of folks would bring the mules home at dinner time and not give them no water, because there was nowhere to get water unless you carried it to them. We were always taught to feed the mules whether we eat or not.

We usually got through, at least we'd try to be through [harvesting tobacco] by August the first. Because back then we'd have a storm. We'd call it August gusts; now they call it hurricanes. And Mama would say, "August gusts is coming. We'd better get the rest of that tobacco in." If we'd get that tobacco in the pack house where it wouldn't get wet and the cotton needed picking, we'd go pick the cotton. If the cotton won't ready to pick, we'd grade some of the tobacco. You know, you used to have to put tobacco in piles, grade it and tie it, and stick it up on a stick. Now, they just take it out of the barn and put it in sheets and tie it up. Used to it was a lot of hard work to tobacco.

We didn't ever have to stay out of school much to grade tobacco, but we did have to stay out to pick cotton. Tobacco come off at a time when there won't no school. But we did have to stay out and pick that cotton.

They were hard times back then. We raised our own flour, our own meal, our own molasses. We growed cane. Daddy was dead, and the colored man lived on the farm and we would cut the cane and he would carry it to Stantonsburg and have molasses made out of it. And they had big wood barrels they would carry with them and bring the molasses back in.

We lived good back then. People were closer; they were more friendlier. If somebody got sick, everybody was there. It was just better than it is now. I mean, it's more convenient and we got lights and all that stuff now, but seems like the closeness is not there like it used to be.

The houses were closer than they are now. Back then, you know, one man would tend an acre of tobacco. There were a lot of tenant houses. And if somebody got sick or somebody's crop got behind, everybody'd go there and help. Like if this man got sick and his corn won't harvested, all the neighbors would go and help get his corn up. If he got sick and won't able to cut wood, everybody went and helped cut his wood. But it's not like that no more. Now you don't even know what your next-door neighbor's doing.

"He Got Half and I Got Half"

We had one tenant family. The man and his wife, Willie and Linnie Pender, are still over there now. They were over there when I was born. All their children are gone now. He's eighty-some years old, and I'll be sixty-nine my next birthday. See, what we would do, we'd give him part of the crop. We'd help him put in his, and he and his family would come and help us put in ours. He tended on shares; he got half and I got half. He furnished the labor and done all the work, and I furnished the land and the mules and the plows [and] a house to live in. He got half and we got half. I think that's the way it was with everybody.

Back then during the winter, spring, and early summer you'd get about fifteen dollars a month to eat off of [from a merchant who furnished supplies and credit]. We got fifteen and the tenant family got fifteen. We went to a store in Stantonsburg. W. R. Rogers [was the merchant's name]. We didn't get the money, we got a book with coupons in it. The reason that man let us have that was so we wouldn't go nowhere else to spend the money. We'd have to go back there, and he'd tear those tickets out—twenty-five-cent and fifty-cent ones. He wouldn't let us have the money. But when that fifteen dollars give out, you couldn't get nothing else until the next month. The interest rate back then wasn't too much different from what it is now. Ten percent.

You could buy anything in the world you wanted in there, from shoes to fatback, flour, fertilizer. Plows, harnesses for the mules, plow lines, salt block. You could buy mules, you could buy lumber, shoes, yard cloth, thread, needles, rat traps, meat, lard, flour, cheese. Anything except fresh meat. You name it, he had it. There's no stores like that no more.

Yes, you had to go there and sign over everything you had to him until you sold your crop and paid him off. I remember one time I signed over a two-horse wagon and two mules. Everwhat kind of farm equipment you had, you had to give him a note on all of that for him to furnish you that money.

You usually settled up when you'd sell your tobacco and would go give him the check for selling it, until you got him paid up. I never remember having no tobacco money left over. If we had a wagonload of corn we thought we were rich. We'd always go sell that at Christmas, get us a few dollars for Christmas. It took that little tobacco we had and what little corn we had to pay the bills with.

Well, see, I started doing that after Mama died in 1940. Daddy died in [1930]. I reckon Daddy worked himself to death trying to get this house built. He lost everything he had. What little bit of money he had saved up, which won't much but it was a whole lot to him. Back then, if you had a hundred dollars, you were a rich person. That was Depression years in 1930. And then Mama was left here with all of us. Then in 1940 my mama died, and I was left here with my brothers. I raised every one of them, sent them to school.

"Women Did Work Back Yonder"

[Mama] worked in the field just like Daddy did. She could do the same work my daddy done. After Daddy died, yes [she plowed]; before he died, no. After Daddy died, she had to. She had to. We had those two old log barns I was telling you about. I've looked out the window a many a night, and she'd be laying out there on a tobacco truck—you know, you used to cure tobacco with wood, and you had to sit up all night long. She'd be laying on a tobacco truck [a wooden sled used to haul the leaves from the field to the barn], and she'd get up and down to keep wood in that furnace to keep the tobacco curing. Yes, women did work back yonder. They don't work now like they used to.

She worked hard. I sit back there and look at television and cry because Mama never saw a television and she never saw electric lights;

she never had an electric iron. She never had a radio. No refrigerator. I just don't hardly know how they made it back then. When I started coming along, we had an old icebox. There was a store about two miles down that road. We'd get the boys at dinnertime to take the mule and tobacco truck and go down there and get a piece of ice, wrap it up in guano bags. And we had a hole dug in the ground with sawdust in it. And we'd put that ice in that hole. If we got a little piece of ice, that's the way we had it. Back then, a piece of ice was so good. We don't even appreciate the things now that we've got that we didn't have back then. You don't remember it, but I do.

The way we canned back then, it's a wonder it hadn't killed us. We had no pressure cookers. We canned in the wash pot. And sometimes when we were curing tobacco we would can tomatoes and peaches and things like that in the tobacco barn. Just put them in the tobacco barn and let them cook while the tobacco was curing. That's the way we done it. Mama done that and I did it, too.

Some weeks we didn't put in tobacco every day to the week. And if we could harvest the tobacco in the daytime we'd can at night. Sometimes we'd take three to four days in the tobacco field, then we'd have the rest of the week to do our canning and cleaning. We'd try to get all the canning done, then, say, on Saturday we cleaned.

Houses won't hard to clean then. You didn't have no carpets; you had wood floors. Didn't buy nothing back then! We would cut broom straw to make brooms with. We'd make our own soap. We even made our own scouring mop. It was made out of corn shucks. You haven't never heard of that? It's a great big board and holes bored in that board. And you'd put a big wad of corn shucks in there, and it had a handle on it and you'd scrub. You could scrub these floors just as pretty and white. Seems like it won't as hard to keep clean as it is now. You had an open fireplace and you swept the stuff right in the fireplace. You won't as particular then as you are now.

I remember back when Mama was living we didn't have floor wax; we were lucky to have a linoleum rug on the floor. And Mama would put kerosene in the water after she mopped it and rinsed it and mop over it. She said it would make it shine. Look like that would have made it smell, but that's what she done.

Every Monday you got to wash. That's what you done on Monday, unless you had to put in tobacco. In tobacco time you'd do it when you got time. We had three wash pots. We'd first scrub 'em on a washboard; then we'd put them in the wash pot with box lye soap and boil them; then we'd take them out and scrub them again. Then we'd rinse them three times and hang them on the line. There was some clean clothes back then. We never had no help to help wash. I never had no help; [Mama] didn't either.

"Biddies in the House"

Back then when Mama was living, you didn't buy biddies [baby chicks]. You raised them. You'd save your prettiest, biggest eggs and set them under a chicken hen. You'd have nests, you know. You started out mostly in the spring of the year to set your hens. I don't know why, but you could always tell when one set on a nest two or three days you felt like she'd be a good mama so you'd put fifteen or sixteen eggs under her. I think it took twenty-one days [for the eggs to hatch]. Sometimes she'd hatch them all, and then again there'd be two or three under there no good. And she'd come off the nest with the biddies. You'd see them all in the yard, a chicken hen with fifteen or sixteen little biddies going behind her. If it rained, she'd run and get under a shelter or bush or something.

If Mama had a hen hatch in the wintertime, you couldn't leave them out there so she'd bring the biddies in the house. We had a great big fireplace in our living room. She'd get a big pasteboard box and put paper or a big old rag at the bottom. You'd have to clean it out every day. We'd raise them in here in boxes until they got maybe half a pound or a pound. You can imagine how this house smelled. I mean, biddies in pasteboard boxes in the house. People wouldn't do it no more. Sometimes at night you'd wake up and they'd be running all over the floor. (I've done it, too, so we'd have some early chickens to eat, some fryers.)

Then Mama built little chicken houses out of tobacco sticks and put a piece of tin or a plank across the top so when it rained it wouldn't rain on them. They just raised theirself in the yards. Sometimes she'd have corn shelled and cracked [to feed them]. And scraps, pour the scraps out. They'd eat up your collards or what turnips you didn't have covered up or anything green that was growing in a garden. They more or less looked after theirselves.

On Sunday is when we had fried chicken. She'd get up that morning and kill two and clean them. She had a big bucket full of boiling water. She'd kill the chicken—just wring its neck. She'd stick the chicken down in that hot boiling water and you could stand right there and pull all the feathers off. Then take a piece of paper and get the paper on fire and hold the chicken and get the yellow fuzz off. Swinge [singe] them, they called it. Swinge them. Clean it good on the outside and cut the head off and the feet. I used to love the feet; don't ever see a chicken foot no more. Clean the feet and then you put it in another bucket of clean water and scrape it and gut it and go all over it again. You got good, clean chicken then.

Yes, chickens were a whole lot better back then. You didn't see no black bones then. Can't you buy chickens now that you see the bones turned a little bit dark? But they say that's because of being raised so quick. Back then it took a long while. They say you can do it now in six to eight weeks, but back then it used to take us six months, 'cause they won't on a floored pen and they just picked up what they could find out in the yard to eat. They just had a better taste.

You had them coming off all during the year. All different sizes. You'd see some just been hatched; you'd see some about like a big ball, and then you'd have some just right to eat and some too big to eat. We always tried to make chicken salad out of the big roosters. Then we'd have the pretty hens we were saving, you know, to lay and hatch.

We got more eggs in the summertime, because in the wintertime it would get cold. Seems like chickens didn't lay good when it got cold back then. But I guess since they've got them in houses they lay about all the time. In the wintertime we'd kind of have to save the eggs up for Christmas or Thanksgiving so we'd be sure to have enough to make cakes with. The cakes turned out prettier. They were more yellow than they are now. Egg yolks made the cake more yellow. A long time ago there used to be men selling fish traveling up and down the road. We'd trade them three eggs for a piece of ice or three eggs and a salted-down hog head for a mess of fish. Or if we had enough eggs we could get us a cold drink. They'd put them in there and carry them to where they could sell them. That's the first [soft] drink we ever had; a man come by selling drinks. The [fish man] that used to come by here so much used to come from Wilson. There used to be a lot of that up and down the road, but it's not anymore. And our mail-man would stop here and buy eggs.

We'd carry them to the store we traded at, we sure did. But we didn't get nothing for them. We'd carry ten or twelve dozen up there at a time and try to pay on our bill, so we could get us at least a piece of cheese to eat. It was Christmas if we could get a piece of cheese; we thought that was something.

"Farming Took All of Us"

[My brothers and I went to school] about a year after Mama died. I didn't ever finish high school. Back then you could finish in the eleventh grade. I was promoted to the tenth, but trying to get five boys off to school and me, too, we had to farm and I had to cook and look after them. I just had to quit.

All of [my brothers] got in service gradually, one at the time. They didn't want to live on the farm; there won't enough here for us. You know, we could barely eat. So they would get in service and then they'd get married. They finally left one at the time.

I got married in 1952. And I was here farming at that time. [My husband] had a farm over here at Saratoga. But he lived in a rented house. The house on his farm won't much good and this one was better, so we lived here.

We raised corn and tobacco. We didn't raise no cotton. [We stopped raising cotton] pretty soon after Mama died, 'cause there won't no money in it. And it was hard work to pick it with your hands. It got so cheap so we more or less just switched to corn and tobacco.

We tended this farm for a long time with just mules, but then my husband bought a tractor about '56 or '57. It was a Ford. I thought that was the biggest thing that ever happened to us because they could get out there and turn so much land where used to you turned just a little bit with a mule. He got out there with that tractor and done a lot of work. You could work all night with a tractor [because it had headlights], but you couldn't with a mule.

See, when Daddy died he left [the farm] to Mama, and when Mama died it automatically went to all of us. Okay, there was six of us. Well, on this little, bitty farm there was no dividing to it. So my brothers wanted to get out of the country—they didn't like the country—so they wanted me to buy it. Well, I rode everywhere in the world trying to borrow money. I couldn't hardly borrow no money. I went to Stantonsburg at the bank, finally my last point. So Mr. Will Rogers, this man that had W. H. Applewhite and Company, was the president of the bank. So he told the man at the bank to let me have the money because he felt like he was going to get the farm in foreclosure. He got a lot of farmland that way. I borrowed the money from the bank to pay each one of my brothers off. I borrowed nine thousand dollars in '48. I borrowed that money in my name by myself.

Well, Mr. Will Rogers—the one we were just talking about—he knew me and he knew how hard I worked. So he told the man at the bank, "Go ahead and let her have the money. I'm going to get the farm anyway." He owns just about all this whole area in here. But he didn't get mine. I paid for it. Lord, it took me a long time.

Every year I'd go pay every penny I had left to him. Every penny that that crop brought that year, I'd go pay it and he knew it. He treated me nice. If I'd missed a year, I really don't think he'd have foreclosed on me because he knew I was doing everything I could to pay that money back. He'd come out here and look and see if your crop was clean, see if you had a good stand of tobacco, if you were working. Sure, he'd come out and check on it.

My husband got money from Production Credit Association [a federal lending agency]. He started with the Production Credit Association, and I started with the bank in Stantonsburg. I couldn't borrow nothing from Production Credit Association. Because I was a woman.

No, they didn't tell me that. But I knew that was the reason. They didn't approve my loan. People in Stantonsburg knew me and they knew I would work and they knew I was smart, so the bank just took a chance on me.

We wound up with two tractors and a little bit of equipment. [My husband] was the type that would go around to sales and try to buy something secondhanded and fix it up so he could use it. He couldn't go out and buy the best and the newest. He'd have to buy something somebody else wanted to trade off. We'd try to fix it up and use it. We didn't have a lot. Like, we didn't have no corn pickers or nothing like that. We just had two tractors with a disc harrow and plows.

[My husband] would help somebody do something, and they'd come help him do something. If somebody would get behind, he'd go help them catch up. Then if he needed a little help, they'd come help him. They might have something he didn't have. Like I know one of his friends one time had a tobacco sprayer on a tractor and we didn't have one. So my husband went and helped him break up land, and he come sprayed our tobacco.

We had to [make decisions together] because it'd take both of us to get [equipment]. Because he had a little farm and I had one, and so we had to kind of get together and see how much each one of us could do to help pay for it. I purchased my first vehicle, a pickup truck, in 1952. I remember the first car we ever had. It was a little Ford Falcon station wagon. We made a deal when we bought it: I'd pay three hundred dollars a year on it, and he'd pay three hundred. Ain't that something? Yeah, we'd get together on tractors and things. I mean, we had to.

On my farm I had a little tenant house. On [my husband's] farm there was a little house and he had a colored man and a family in there. So we all worked together. We'd go over to my farm and put in that tobacco, then we'd go to Saratoga and put in his. We kind of worked so we wouldn't have to pay nobody any money. See, if each one of them'd hired any help on their little crop, they'd've had to paid it. So each one would help each other so there wouldn't be no money passed.

I didn't ever go to the [tobacco] market much. The colored man done that. Somehow or 'nother it just won't like a woman's place at tobacco market. After we got married and my husband got too disabled to haul it, we had a pickup truck then, I would haul it to the market, and the colored man would get it unloaded. That was his and ours together.

I don't know where all this racial stuff started at. It won't like that way back yonder with us. I respect them people that helped us farm just as much as they respected me. Back there when times was real tight, I would always buy them a little Christmas gift. It won't much; maybe something ten cents. But I'd always carry this man and woman that lives over there now, all their children, a little gift wrapped up. We treated each other like family.

I didn't make them do nothing that I didn't do myself. If my tobacco patch needed discing or water out of it, we'd get a shovel and we'd go out there. I was out there right with them. I didn't say, "You go get the suckers out of my tobacco today." Now, I think the bigger farmers more or less let them do the work, but now I didn't. I worked with them. It's still that way. Before we got a tractor we would dig in the fields to try to eliminate the Johnson grass. We called it wire grass because the roots were two or three feet beneath the surface. A lot of whites wouldn't go out and work with the blacks, but I couldn't tell no difference. We worked together.

We got along good. If I was at their house and they had something I wanted I'd go sit down at their table to eat. They were clean. And if the colored man come up here to do a little work in the yard for me and I had something I felt like he wanted to eat, I'd ask him right in here to my table to eat. What was so funny about it, two or three years ago his wife was in New York and he's eighty-some years old. I asked him to come up here and eat Thanksgiving dinner with us. You know, he didn't want to sit down at that table with us. He didn't want to, but we made him. He still thinks, you know—I don't know what he thinks. But I just won't never like that. They respected me and I respected them.

[His children are] all gone. They've all moved off, doing good.

He's got some that's finished college; he's got some of them teaching at colleges. I carried his youngest daughter to Raleigh and got her in a college and signed a paper so that she could get in and borrow the money. Yeah, they're all doing good. They have more than sixty grand- and great-grandchildren now.

"The First Real Money I Ever Had"

Way back yonder, if we didn't raise our food we didn't have anything to eat. I'd just raise and can and raise and can and raise and can. Mrs. [Ona P.] Humphrey, our county home demonstration agent, come out here to see me one day around in the fifties. She said, "Mrs. Langley, why don't you go up to the curb market and all these excess vegetables you got, you can sell?" I said, "Well, nobody'd want to buy them." She said, "Yes, they do." We had an old pickup truck, and I started going up to the curb market. That's the first real money I ever had.

I went for eight years every Tuesday and Friday. And you know, sometimes I'd sell a hundred dollars' worth. We had eggs, all kinds of vegetables. I carried cured meat. We'd pick butter beans and I'd carry four and five bushels of butter beans shelled. Four and five bushels of peas shelled. Bushels of snap beans. Fifteen, twenty dozen eggs, and cleaned chicken hens and cleaned fryers. In the fall and winter you'd go out there with a shovel and get up frozen onions and clean them and sell them. You didn't have a lot to sell this time of the year. If you could make good chicken salad and make good cakes and pies you could afford to go; you could always have collards and turnip salet [salad] this time of year. But we went twelve months a year.

If I hadn't sold it, it would have all been throwed away or some- body else would have come by and picked it up. And we give it away; back then, you give away what you didn't want. I just sold what we didn't need and didn't want. My husband was good at gardens so we had a good garden. And we started raising a little bit more and tried to take better care of it, to keep it longer. You were lucky if you could have tomatoes early or either have them late—you got a good price for your vegetables. We'd try to have something real early and try to have some real late.

I had an aunt that helped me shell butter beans. She and my husband won't able to pick. He was kind of feeble and my aunt had cancer. We had a lot of shade trees then, and they'd sit out there and shell everything for me. I'd pick them and they'd shell them. We had pecan trees then; I'd keep a fifty-pound lard stand full of pecans shelled all the time.

The extension agent or the secretaries would go by the grocery stores when they'd leave the office and check the price on stuff. When we'd get out there, they would already be out there and they'd have the prices, and we'd have to sell for the same price they sold at the stores. But people'd rather have ours because they knew it was fresh; we got up early and brought it right in. So I never had no problem selling anything.

And [the extension service] sold us a wooden container—I still got it—to measure and be sure we got the right amount in a quart. Like if we sold a quart of butter beans or a quart of pecans or a quart of peas, we couldn't sell them out of a glass quart jar, we had to have a wooden measure container so it would be correct. They had great, big long tables for us to display our stuff on. We had to pay them three cents on the dollar, I think, for using the table. And we had to pay tax.

We'd have oodles of customers to come in. After I got a telephone, some of them would even call me up and give me their order before I left home, and I'd have it packed for them. Like one woman would want a chicken hen for her and a chicken hen for her son. She'd want two dozen eggs for her and two dozen for him. "If you kill hogs, Mrs. Langley," [she'd say and then] she'd tell you how much of each thing she wanted, and we could pack it here and have the price on it. They'd order cakes—"I want two pecan pies." I could sell all the chicken salad I could make. And you could sell soup; you could sell applejacks, cakes, cupcakes, candies. That's what we sold.

I was the biggest seller at the curb market for a lot of years. You got a prize if you sold the most that year at the curb market. Sometimes it'd be a great big plate, or I got a card table one time. Different things. It won't money, now. We'd all rush to see who could sell the most.

I didn't never fall under fifty dollars on a Tuesday or a Friday either one. It'd go from fifty to a hundred. We'd never had any money like that before. That was our spending money, and that's the way I sent my son through college. Jack just happened to come home one day and said, "Mama, I want to go to college." I said, "You can't go to college. We don't have no money." He said, "Well, I'm not going to work like you have. I'm going to college." By that time I had started going up to the curb market. So when you want to do something, you can do it. The first money I ever had, really had in my hand, was going to the curb market. I give the agricultural extension service a lot of credit for what's happened in my life.

"Work Was My Pleasure"

My husband died, and I farmed two or three years here right by myself with my daughter. My son was married and gone. We tried to farm. And I just got tired, and I said, "I'm going to quit." The extension service found out about it and called me up and asked me would I like a job. I said, "Yeah, if I can do it." So I worked up there twelve years as an extension program aide. We had to teach the low-income families about having a garden, try to encourage them to have a garden. At that time they were getting this commodity food [distributed by the U.S. Department of Agriculture], and they didn't know how to use plain flour; they didn't know nothing about oatmeal. We tried to teach them what a balanced meal was. How to prepare it different ways. So I went to work with extension the day I was fifty, and I worked there until I was sixty-two.

When I started working as a program aide with the extension service, I didn't have any dresses to wear. So I had to buy some cotton dresses to wear. I was trying to pay for the farm and I was trying to keep everything paid up, so I didn't spend no money. I wore tennis shoes. If I had a dress, it was made out of feed bags. I wore pure old pants.

My folks always told me work was my pleasure, and I believe it was. Now I've gotten old and I can't do it, it just worries me to death. I can't do like I used to. My leg's been operated on for no circulation and varicose veins, and the doctor thought I had a cancer here a while back and I was operated on. It won't cancer. But my health is bad now. Work, work, work, I reckon.

My brother used to tell me I couldn't sleep from the time I planted my plant-bed seed until I sold the last leaf. Lord, you'd worry. You could start farming that year, and at the end of that year you didn't know whether you'd have a farm or not. And I was always scared of losing it. Lord, yes. Not have nowhere to stay when you got old. Sure. You didn't sleep at night; you were scared to death, worried. I reckon they're still that same way today. But back then when I farmed we just tended a small amount. Everybody had a little bit. But now, like on this road, one man tends just about everything on this road, he's got so much equipment.

Right now, I lease my farm out for sure rent the first of every year. The man gives you so much, and it's his problems. As long as I can do it that way, that's what I'm going to do. I have a garden. For two years in a row we haven't had much garden because we had such dry weather. But we get all I can eat. And years and years ago the [Raleigh] *News and Observer* gave me a prize for having the best garden in Wilson County. I got fifty dollars. I think that's what I put in that drain pipe to carry off dishwater from the house. Yeah, I love a garden. Used to, I did. I do now, but I just can't hold out. I still love to can and freeze.

You know, used to, we didn't go to town. The only time when we saw anybody they'd walk to see us or we'd walk to see them. Seems like it's not as friendly; there's not a closeness like there used to be. It could be, but that's just the way I feel about it. People would sleep on the front porch at night, and we never locked a door. We didn't lock our smokehouse, and we killed seven, eight, ten hogs a year. No, we didn't even have screen doors, no screen windows, no locks on the door. Now my house has been broke into two times. I was working each time.

I don't know, seems like it was a lot friendlier way back yonder. People were a little bit closer. They got cars now and the highways are paved and they go more. Used to, people didn't go that much. Used to, there won't no television. People sit now and look at television all the evening. Before TV I guess to keep company or to have something to do, they'd walk and visit. But see, now they don't do it. They look at those stories on TV all afternoon, and they're just not neighborly like they used to be.

REBECCA SHARPLESS AND
MELISSA WALKER

"Pretty Near Every Woman Done a Man's Work"

Women and Field Work in the Rural South

Etta Carroll, who lived on Texas cotton farms most of her long life, observed, "Well, if it hadn't have been for the women, the men couldn't have gotten to work. They did housework and helped with the farmwork, too. They did both."[1] Carroll succinctly summed up one of the most important realities of southern farm women's lives before World War II. Virtually all southern farm women worked in the house, fulfilling the domestic needs of their families—cooking, cleaning, sewing, and caring for children. A significant number also produced petty commodities for local markets. Most controversially, many women helped raise cash crops. They labored in the cotton and tobacco crops, very much a part of the national marketplace that women were supposed to avoid according to the cultural principles of the time. The labor of southern farm women—in the house, in the garden, and for the market—was absolutely crucial on at least two levels. It was essential to their families' well-being, and it played a major role in the economy of the region.

The most complicated aspect of southern women's work is that of field work, which carried great social and emotional significance for many rural people. In the rural South during the first half of the

1. Dovie Lee Carroll and Etta Lillian Hardy Carroll, interview by Sharpless, July 11, 1991, Waxahachie, TX, interview no. 7, Baylor University Institute for Oral History, Waco, TX (hereafter IOH).

42

twentieth century, the practical need for women's labor in the fields collided with a social norm that dictated separate spheres for white men and women. African American farm families, too, struggled to balance the desire to free the family's women from the arduous conditions of field work with the need for their labor. In this essay we will examine the work of women in the cotton and tobacco fields, looking at what it meant for individual women as well as southern society at large. We pay special attention to the ways that southern farm women, especially white women, negotiated the paradox of a cultural ideal that dictated that women stay in the house and an economic imperative that required the majority of them to work in the fields.

Some women were compelled to work outside by necessity or the expectations of their families, while others deliberately chose to. Some women avoided field work completely. For many farm women, the separation of gender roles carried much cultural weight, heavily laden with the notions of class and race that formed much of the foundation of white southerners' sense of self. Such women often believed that they were upholding their status as members of a certain class or a certain race by avoiding outside work, and they vigorously defended their right to remain inside the house. But others, often less privileged, simply took the practical approach, doing what was necessary for the well-being of their families.[2]

For several decades, women's and labor historians have struggled to understand how women's domestic and workplace lives interact, how they complement or compete with one another. Southern farm women in the early twentieth century further complicate an already complex picture of women at work. The physical location of their work could not be easily classified as either "public" or "private." Women worked, for the most part, in the places where they lived. Not even the house or the yard could be labeled as exclusively private space; although many of the activities that occurred there benefited the family, women performed some market-oriented work in both

2. Anne Goodwyn Jones, *Tomorrow Is Another Day: The Woman Writer in the South, 1859–1936* (Baton Rouge: Louisiana State University Press, 1981), 5.

locations. For example, they processed cream and churned butter in the house and tended chickens in the yard. The fields, too, occupied an ambiguous place, not private but not necessarily completely public, particularly when the family did not own its own land and the landlord had significant authority over what occurred on his property. For farm families, home was not a "haven" from the public world or the world of production; it *was* the location of production. The public-private dichotomy that has characterized many studies of work does not apply to the majority of southern agricultural families.[3]

Understanding the place of work in farm women's lives is complicated by varying family dynamics and by overlapping and often contradictory ideological viewpoints. As Elizabeth Faue and others have noted, women make decisions about their work lives in the context of highly complex family systems and of various forms of class, gender, and racial ideology. Farm women, like other women, often focused their identities on home and family, seeing their work as primarily directed at the welfare of those families. Although farm women may have sometimes seemed to be complicit in their own exploitation because they did not receive wages of their own or because they did not challenge gender boundaries, they often chose to perform field work because they believed it would improve the lives of their families over the long term. But women also actively chose to work in the fields, taking pleasure in the work itself and in their abilities to do it well. Southerners, and southern women in particular, had mixed feelings about women's field work. In complex ways, gender norms shaped the way in which southern women incorporated work into their thinking. For reasons both ideological and pragmatic, southerners in the early twentieth century felt deeply about and debated loudly the subject of women's work in the fields.[4]

The dilemma of women's field work had its roots in the antebellum American South, where slave owners commonly assumed that en-

3. Micaela di Leonardo, "Women's Work, Work Culture, and Consciousness," *Feminist Studies* 11 (Fall 1985): 491–95.

4. Faue, *Community of Suffering and Struggle: Women, Men, and the Labor Movement in Minneapolis, 1915–1945* (Chapel Hill: University of North Carolina Press, 1991), 159–211.

slaved women would perform the same jobs as men. By contrast, the ideal white woman was expected to stay completely within her world of family and traditional homemaking tasks. Carefully distinguished from the slaves, a lady would never dirty her hands in the fields. The type of work performed by women became a key marker of racial difference. Yet the distinction between the work of white women and the work of African American women was never as absolute as antebellum white southerners wanted to believe. Because of the labor required for southern crops, and because their families could not afford to buy slaves, wives of small landowners routinely worked in the fields. Therefore, according to historian Stephanie McCurry, white "women's work in the fields, although customary, was customarily ignored and even denied." The idea of white women picking cotton was too threatening to the southern ideal to be acknowledged.[5]

The ideology that deemed field work unsuitable for women persisted and was adopted by African American families even as the deterioration of the southern farm economy in the aftermath of the Civil War rendered that ideal increasingly unreachable. Some sources indicate that African American women withdrew from the fields following the end of slavery, wanting to devote full time to the well-being of their families. By the early twentieth century, however, African American women performed prodigious amounts of field work. White women, too, became increasingly involved in field work. Dozens of studies exist on the transition from slavery to sharecropping, but none of them examines the impact of the shift on white women. As the agricultural economy worsened, many white sharecroppers and small landowners became more dependent than ever on the labor of all family members to make a crop or to hold on to their land. In his

5. Deborah Gray White, *Ar'n't I a Woman? Female Slaves in the Plantation South* (New York: W. W. Norton, 1985), 66–67, 120–21; Bertram Wyatt-Brown, *Southern Honor: Ethics and Behavior in the Old South* (New York: Oxford University Press, 1982), 200; Christie Ann Farnham, *The Education of the Southern Belle: Higher Education and Student Socialization in the Antebellum South* (New York: New York University Press, 1994), 2, 28–29, 127, 145; McCurry, *Masters of Small Worlds: Yeoman Households, Gender Relations, and the Political Culture of the Antebellum South Carolina Low Country* (New York: Oxford University Press, 1995), 62, 72, 74, 78, 79, 80, 81–82.

1936 study of two Georgia Black Belt counties, Arthur F. Raper noted that, like the black farmwife, "the mother in the white tenant household, and even in that of the small owner, is usually the chief burden carrier, frequently working in the fields in addition to doing her housework. In the planter family, the mother nearly always has heavy responsibilities. Scarcely any farm mother leads an idle or sheltered life." By the early twentieth century, the majority of white farm women in the South performed at least some field labor. Ironically, as economic lines between the races blurred, ideological lines hardened, resulting in the virulent racism of the late nineteenth century and the continued, and sometimes increased, idealization of the white lady. The less whites were able to distinguish themselves from African Americans in economic terms, the more they sought to do so in cultural terms. A Central Texas woman, when asked about picking cotton, drew herself up to her entire height and vehemently declared that she had never picked cotton. It was extremely important to her to affirm her privileged status.[6]

By the early twentieth century, the issue of women's field work, particularly that of white women, had become a battlefield on which economic necessity met cultural imperatives head-on. Many people paid close attention to the gap between the ideal and the reality, and African Americans and whites alike entered into vigorous discussions of the proper role for women. Some women adhered strictly to the idea of separate spaces for the sexes. Writing to the *Semi-Weekly*

6. Roger L. Ransom and Richard Sutch, *One Kind of Freedom: The Economic Consequences of Emancipation* (Cambridge: Cambridge University Press, 1977), 6–7; Ruth Allen, *The Labor of Women in the Production of Cotton,* University of Texas Bulletin no. 3134, September 8, 1931, 134, 191, 231; Ellen Nathalie Matthews and Helen Maretta Dart, *The Welfare of Children in Cotton-Growing Areas of Texas,* U.S. Department of Labor, Children's Bureau Publication no. 134 (Washington, DC: Government Printing Office, 1924), 44–45; Neil R. McMillen, *Dark Journey: Black Mississippians in the Age of Jim Crow* (Urbana: University of Illinois Press, 1989), 128–30; Raper, *Preface to Peasantry: A Tale of Two Black Belt Counties* (Chapel Hill: University of North Carolina Press, 1936), 75; Farnham, *Education of the Southern Belle,* 181; Genevieve Westbrook Charlton, conversation with Sharpless, December 1990, Corsicana, TX.

Farm News, a newspaper based in Dallas, in 1910, Mrs. Vina Cochran of Collin County, Texas, put the argument into simplest terms: "I believe God made man to till the soil and woman to care for the house." While Cochran based her views on theology, others relied on biology, believing that appropriate work roles were embedded in the biological differences between women and men. When asked how it was decided what tasks boys and girls would do on the Central Texas farm of her childhood, Myrtle Irene Calvert Dodd replied, "I guess it just kind of came natural . . . for the boys to help out at the barn and milk."[7] Her testimony suggests that she had never considered why some tasks were assigned to men and some to women; to Dodd, the division of labor was simply the way things were.

West Virginian America Jarrell, the daughter of a poor mountain landowner, described her mother's hard work to an interviewer in great detail. As a young woman, she decided that she would not follow in her mother's footsteps, and she laid the conditions unequivocally before her husband-to-be: "Before I was married I said [to my husband], 'I'm going to ask you one thing. . . . You are going to stay out of my kitchen. . . . You keep your horses at the barn and I'll never go about them. . . . My place is in here; that is your place out there with the horses.'"[8] Jarrell was determined not to replicate her mother's life, and she confidently used the concept of separate spaces to distribute her work with her new husband.

ᘉᖋ

Women who objected to field work often did so because they believed that the work done in the house was equally valuable and time consuming. Historians have documented the ways in which wider availability of household labor-saving devices resulted in increasingly

7. Cochran, *Semi-Weekly Farm News,* February 8, 1910; Dodd, *Oral Memoirs of Myrtle Irene Calvert Dodd,* interview by Sharpless on four occasions, August 14–September 1990, Waco, TX, Texas Collection, Baylor University (heratfer TC), 32.

8. Jarrell, interview by Gary Miller, ca. 1975, Oral History of Appalachia, Marshall University, Huntington, WV (hereafter OHA).

exacting standards of domesticity. In the early twentieth century, Americans also expected mothers to become more intensely involved in the educational and emotional as well as the physical aspects of child rearing. In the face of rising standards, caring for a home and small children could take all of a woman's time if she did it well. "M. S. B." declared in a letter to *Farm and Ranch* in 1919: "I think it is a sin for women who have babies to go to the field. To be sure it is ambition that causes many of them to do this, but children need a mother more than anything else. A poor, tired, worked-down woman can't be a good mother." In trying to meet these multiple demands, a woman might wreck her health by working to exhaustion. A writer named "Mrs. Joe" observed:

> I think there is a great deal of farm work that women and girls can do as well as a man—if—this is a mighty big "if" too—if they have nothing else to do. There is a limit to human strength and endurance and beyond that we are not expected to go. There never was a mother with small children who had any time or strength to work in the field. They may think they have and think they are doing their duty to help, but they are robbing themselves by using up energy that should be conserved . . . [W]hatever help (?) they render in the field will have to be paid for in doctor bills with compound interest; if not soon, maybe years later.[9]

A wealthy family might even consider the husband's needs great enough to warrant his wife staying in the house full-time. Virginia McIntyre of Franklin Parish, Louisiana, voiced her opinion as an elite farm woman. She recalled that her landowning husband had twenty-two tenant farm families on his place. She described her own role on the farm: "Well, I had to be around to fix his lunch, get him off in the morning, then at night when he came in, he was tired. . . . I felt like I had to be home to take care of him. I felt like he was my first

9. "M. S. B.," *Farm and Ranch*, August 23, 1919; "Mrs. Joe," *Farm and Ranch*, February 1, 1919.

responsibility, and I still do. . . . He didn't exactly demand it, but he kind of expected me to be there and provide for him. And I felt like if he was the breadwinner, the least I could do was to be the home-maker."[10] In return for supporting his wife financially, McIntyre's husband received her undivided caregiving, which almost surely made his life more pleasant and comfortable.

For some women, the decision not to work in the fields was carefully calculated. In 1937, North Carolina–based *Progressive Farmer* held a "Home Income Contest" for readers. The contest, subtitled "Shall Women Work in the Field?" invited female readers to send in letters describing the most effective way they had found to contribute to farm income. The first-prize winner, Mrs. H. M. Milford of Hart County, Georgia, reported that she had tried working in the field "every day that there was any work that women could do." She reported that she neglected her house, garden, laundry, and her family's diet in order to work the fields but that "year after year there would be some obstacle to prevent our prospering." She went on to explain that she had been more successful in contributing to her family's economic well-being once she began producing eggs, chickens, milk, and butter for the market. Her earnings from petty-commodity production had enabled her to send her son to school, refurnish four rooms of the family house, and buy a kerosene refrigerator.[11] Milford's prizewinning argument neatly meshed with the editorial stance of *Progressive Farmer*, which firmly espoused the woman's place in the home and extolled the glories of their petty-commodity production. Yet Milford criticized women's field work not from a philosophical standpoint but from a purely practical one. In her view, there was nothing inherently wrong with women doing field work, but, rather, women simply did not have enough time to do all of the tasks, and the more womanly tasks involved in petty-commodity production were more profitable.

10. McIntyre, interview by Doris Ashley, May 3, 1982, Franklin Parish, LA, Extension Homemakers Oral History Project, copies in Special Collections, Dacus Library, Winthrop University, Rock Hill, SC (hereafter EHOHP).
11. "Home Income Contest Winners," *Progressive Farmer*, March 1937.

Another *Progressive Farmer* prizewinner, Mrs. Fannie Ray from Cook County, Georgia, highlighted the tension between women who worked in the fields and women who did not. In her view, the larger society expected women to work outside, and she railed against the criticism of her field-working neighbors: "I have been considered a poor wife by these women, although I always set a better table and we had better clothes and lived generally better.... No woman can keep house and go to the field too."[12] Many of these arguments carry the ring of a bourgeois ideal of housekeeping and child rearing such as that being promulgated by home demonstration agents working for the Department of Agriculture, where the husband raised the living ("the breadwinner") and the woman kept the house ("the homemaker"). Twenty-first-century scholars may be inclined to dismiss these arguments as women accepting too easily culturally dictated limitations. Yet stories abound of women working a full day in the blazing sun and still cooking two hot meals, of babies left with siblings who were little more than babies themselves, of damaged uteruses and strained backs. One can scarcely blame a woman for electing not to go into the fields.

But work in the fields they did, irrespective of the rhetoric or the standards of domesticity. Across the South, women spent day after day in the tobacco patch or the cotton field. Even families in which women were expected to work outside followed their own sets of taboos as to what was suitable field work and what was not. Alice Hardin's mother hoed and picked cotton on their South Carolina sharecropping plot. She recalled that local folk considered hoeing and picking "women's work," while the heavier task of plowing was "men's work." In Texas, at least one out of ten white women plowed, yet this continued to be considered men's work; people referred to "plowing just like a man." In the late 1920s, sociologist Ruth Allen found that even Anglo women who chopped and picked cotton for long periods of time referred to cultivating and plowing as "men's work." Families sometimes guarded their womenfolk from certain outside tasks. A daughter of white South Carolina sharecroppers Mar-

12. Ibid.

shall and Edna Webb explained that her parents strictly limited the types of work the girls could do. Like Alice Hardin, they could hoe or pick cotton but never plow.[13]

For many families, the ability to spare women from some types of field work was a source of pride, symbolic of a certain level of prosperity, and for the men part of their definition of masculinity. By keeping women from certain types of work, men or other women in the family were sheltering them. Alleyne Holliman Ward recalled that her father worked his sons hard in the fields but that "he sort of protected" his daughters. If children could substitute for their mother's labor in the fields, they could take pride in shielding her from toil under the wicked summer sun. Some farm families tried to free mothers from the burden of field work, even if it meant that daughters put in long hours swinging a hoe or dragging a cotton sack. Black North Carolinian Susie Weathersbee, the daughter of sharecroppers, told an interviewer that her mother "didn't work as hard as I worked, 'cause when, after us got up some size, us didn't like her to work. Us let her stay to the house."[14]

Families who could not shelter their women from field work were often embarrassed by their inability, according to reformers. Sociologist Ruth Allen observed that women were reluctant to give her information about the amount of plowing and cultivating that they performed, for they were "rather ashamed of having to do" those tasks. "The woman who plows seems to feel, and others feel, that she has lost something real but indefinable," Allen wrote.[15]

---

13. Allen, *Labor of Women,* 142; Hardin, interview by Allen Tullos, quoted in Tullos, *Habits of Industry: White Culture and the Transformation of the Carolina Piedmont* (Chapel Hill: University of North Carolina Press, 1989), 259–63; J. W. Joseph, Mary Beth Reed, and Charles Cantley, *Agrarian Life, Romantic Death: Archaeological and Historical Testing and Data Recovery for the I-85 Northern Alternative, Spartanburg County, South Carolina* (Stone Mountain, GA: New South Associates, 1991), 109–11.

14. Ward, *Oral Memoirs of Alleyne Holliman Ward,* interview by Patricia Wallace, July 2, 1983, Waco, TX, TC; Weathersbee, interview by Leslie Brown, June 30, 1993, Halifax, NC, Behind the Veil, box UT5, tray B, Center for Documentary Studies, Duke University, Durham, NC.

15. Allen, *Labor of Women,* 142.

Part of the stigma of plowing came from the widespread belief that working with mules was unsuitable for women; another line of reasoning asserted that women were not physically strong enough to handle the plow or that mules were too dangerous for women. Dorothy Woods Moore, whose family sharecropped in northeastern Texas, picked and chopped but was not allowed to plow because her father said that girls were not strong enough. She remarked that she never understood the distinction because picking was such heavy work. Whether they knew the reasoning behind the taboo or not, families of Anglo women avoided putting their women at the plow whenever possible. African American families also sometimes observed the social constraints on women plowing. Alice Owens Caufield recalled that neither she nor her sister ever plowed, nor did they know any women who did in their neighborhood of African American and German farms: "They were using mules, and the mules pulled the plow, the middle buster. No woman was going to be struggling. That wasn't her job. Men did that. Women didn't have nothing to do with the stock. Her place was in the home."[16]

But women did plow, especially if too few males were available to perform the work. In the Folley family of Limestone County, Texas, the father was too feeble to plow, and the older brothers left to farm on their own. Under these circumstances, young Inez Folley plowed along with her brothers, despite her poor eyesight that led her to create crooked rows. She did not complain, however, nor did she seem ashamed.[17] For families such as the Folleys, need rather than social conventions dictated the work of the female members.

Some women hated working outside and made it plain that they did so from sheer necessity, not choice. Ernestine Anderson, the daughter of a Texas African American tenant-farming family, recalled her

16. Moore, conversation with Sharpless, July 18, 1991, Commerce, TX; Caufield, interview by Sharpless, February 9, 1993, Waco, TX, interview no. 4, IOH.
17. Della Inez Folley, interview by Sharpless, September 4, 1990, Mart, TX, interview no. 1, IOH.

field work: "Those are what I called my dark days. I did not like that at all. I did it because, as I say, it was necessary to survive." Given a choice, Anderson would have withdrawn from field work. Lacking that choice, she remembered the labor with distaste. Amy Stella Barrington Marshall was married to an ailing white Central Texas sharecropper. Between giving birth to six children and caring for the members of her household, Marshall picked cotton. She told an interviewer: "There didn't too many other women, back then, work in the field. . . . It was just because my husband wasn't in good health, and it just took, you know, more work to keep us going. You didn't get much for your work then."[18] Marshall believed that she was different from other women, who were excused from field work. She wanted the interviewer to understand that she performed field work out of necessity. But she did it nonetheless.

Other women viewed field work as completely positive. In direct contrast to Fannie Ray, who thought that a woman could not possibly balance housework and field work, a writer with the nom de plume "Working Lass" voiced her opinion to *Farm and Ranch* in 1919. "Working Lass" equated the value of work with life itself: "Any work that is honorable is worth while and it gives me an indescribable feeling to hear some one boast 'I never had to work' while her hands are soft and so well kept and she shows that she has lived in an atmosphere of luxury. Now, that woman has unconsciously suffered a misfortune. She knows not work, nor life, for in real life we get a taste of work and it makes better boys and girls, men and women of us."[19] Tellingly, a woman saying she "never had to work" likely did not count housework as "work."

A number of women acknowledged the tension that differences of opinion regarding field work created but nonetheless told of their willingness to work outside. Frances Freeman, in the *Semi-Weekly Farm News,* noted the value of her work in tandem with that of her husband: "Move over sisters, please, and give me a seat by the sisters who help

18. Anderson, interview by Lois E. Myers, February 17, 1999, Riesel, TX, interview no. 1, IOH; Marshall, interview by Anne Radford Phillips, January 22, 1992, Weir, TX, IOH.
19. "Working Lass," *Farm and Ranch,* October 4, 1919.

their Johns in the field. I do, and do not think it is a disgrace." "Happy Belle" from Central Texas shrugged off the people who decried her field work. She, like many women, took to the fields in the absence of available males, in this case her father: "My father died when I was small and I had to work for a living." But she refused to let social mores dictate how she thought of herself, remarking, "I will tell you what I have done in life, and I am still a lady, thank God. I have plowed and hoed and built fences and have done almost everything on a farm a man has done.... I worked everywhere, and I am still a lady. If a girl is going to be anything, she will be it anywhere you put her."[20] While Happy Belle validated the image of the lady as a proper cultural icon, she made ladyhood a state of being rather than one of actions.

Like Happy Belle, many women went to the fields when men were not available. Although they clearly indicated that they were directly substituting for male labor, many of the women did not seem to feel any shame about performing "men's work." On the contrary, they were very matter-of-fact: they were needed, and they went, with a minimum of angst. At a time before antibiotics, when a scratch on the arm could result in a fatal case of blood poisoning, husbands might die or fall ill. Essie Simmons's father died in 1913 when she was twelve. At that point Simmons, an Anglo, began to learn to cook when her mother left the house for field work. According to Simmons, her mother went to the fields to show her teenage sons "how to farm." The mother must have done farmwork at some point in her life to be able to instruct her sons. The daughter, however, was surprised at her mother's knowledge of field work, having apparently never before witnessed her mother working outside. The mother's status changed drastically when she became a widow. Without a husband, she had to raise the cash crop, and housework became secondary. Maggie Langham Washington, an African American from Texas, recalled that her hardworking mother, Leta Langham, combined household responsibilities with field work beside her landowning husband. Later he entered the ministry, and Leta Langham continued

20. Freeman, *Semi-Weekly Farm News,* August 30, 1910; "Happy Belle," *Farm and Ranch,* March 19, 1910.

her farmwork. As Washington observed, "She worked side-by-side with Daddy until he started in the ministry, and then she carried on the work on the farm." Washington added, "You see, when I was six years old, I was keeping house like a woman. I had the babies to care for, the food to cook, clothes to wash and iron the hard way."[21] Both Simmons's mother and Leta Langham were relieved of domestic labor by their daughters, who picked up the household work in their mothers' stead. The families made the choice for the younger women (girls, really) to remain in the house and the adults to go to the fields—just the opposite of the Weathersbee family who put the girls outside and the mother in the kitchen. Simmons's mother and Langham may have been too effective as field workers to be spared.

Women who had grown up on farms often possessed superior knowledge of farming processes than did their husbands. Lizzie Broyles, from East Tennessee, married a man who had inherited a small farm, making farming a logical source of livelihood. Unlike her husband, Broyles had grown up on a farm and obviously knew how farming was done. She told her interviewer that her husband, by contrast, "didn't know anything about farming. He didn't. He couldn't do nothing. He couldn't go set out tobacco. He couldn't haul in the wheat and everything that was to do. I had to go to the field and do it."[22] Broyles seemed proud of her ability to work like a man and did not hesitate to talk about it. In fact, the tone of her language suggests her scorn, decades later, for her husband's ignorance of farming.

Ida Mae Gambrell and her husband farmed on fifteen acres that they owned near Honea Path, South Carolina, beginning in the 1920s. She told an interviewer that when she married her husband, he knew very little about farming. As she put it, "He was a dummy about farming. I knew more about farming than he did." After several years

21. Simmons, interview by M. Houser, April 19, 1982, Mulberry, AR, EHOHP; Washington, *Oral Memoirs of Maggie Langham Washington*, interview by Doni Van Ryswyk on three occasions, March 10–May 19, 1988, Waco, TX, TC.

22. Broyles, interview by Lon Broyles, November 16, 1975, Limestone, TN, Charles Gunter Collection, Archives of Appalachia, East Tennessee State University, Johnson City, TN.

of farming full-time, her husband accepted a position on the night shift at the Ware Shoals textile mill. Gambrell took on the farmwork in addition to her household responsibilities. She said, "I've plowed mules and horses and plowed as much or more than he did on the farm." Later she purchased a tractor. Gambrell bragged, "I could use that tractor and work it better that Elbert could. You'd be surprised! [H]e'd go in [to work], and I could take the tractor—I knew more about farming than he did—I'd take the tractor and plow."[23] Ida Mae Gambrell felt no need to apologize to anyone for working in the fields.

Relationships with the men in her family sometimes affected a woman's attitude toward field work. Housework fell completely under a farm woman's control, but because farm men exercised most authority over field work, performing field work could limit a woman's control over her own labor. Perhaps women like America Jarrell who refused to do field work were rejecting work over which they had little authority—work that reduced them to little more than hired hands. Peggy Delozier Jones of Loudon, Tennessee, seemed to find working under her husband's supervision particularly galling. Jones noted, "My husband wasn't a farmer when I promised to marry him; I always said I wouldn't marry a farmer, but I did." Homer Jones's father purchased a farm for the young couple after they had been married several years, and Peggy Jones indicated that she devoted the early years on the farm to housekeeping, child rearing, and petty-commodity production. Peggy Jones was a college graduate, and once her sons were in high school, she obtained a position with the county welfare department. At several points in the interview, she alluded to tensions in her marriage, and she indicated that she rarely did field work while her husband ran the farm. Things changed, however, after her son took over management of the family farm, an event that coincided with Peggy Jones's retirement. She explained, "I didn't do too much out in the fields [when my husband ran the farm]. But after I retired from my job, I helped my son. [The grandsons] and Homer Vaughn and I filled four siloes that fall. I'd drive the empty wagon to the field

23. Gambrell, interview by Kristin Oates, ca. 2003, Honea Path, SC, copy of tape in Melissa Walker's possession.

and bring a full one back, and the other son would unload it. And I'd work from daylight to dark with him. I like to drive a tractor, and I'd help him. I'd even load the hay and drove a tractor to pull a mower and haul the hay."[24] Jones also had more time after her retirement, but her strained relationship with her husband may have been the most salient factor in her avoiding labor with or for him.

The ways in which women recall their field work indicates much about the experience of southern farm women. Some women, rather than being embarrassed, actually took pride in their work, and they expressed that pride in their oral history interviews and in letters to editors of farm magazines. Some embraced various types of field work and rejected or minimized others based on their enjoyment of the work. Enjoyable work is always more desirable for workers, and they maintain a stronger sense of choice and autonomy when doing work they like than work they dislike. Often farm women's pleasure in a particular type of work went hand in hand with pride in their skill at performing that task. Texan Marie London had strong preferences for a specific type of field work: "I didn't mind chopping, but I couldn't pick no cotton. But now I'd go to the fields and chop. I could chop all day long." Etta Carroll preferred chopping over plowing, mostly because of her remarkable ability as a chopper: "Well, I plowed one round, and I went up there, and I said, 'You just have the plow; I'll take the hoe.' . . . I can chop left-handed or right-handed, either one." Lessie Shiveley, a white woman from Kanawha County, West Virginia, avoided the dreaded plowing but bragged about the rest of her labors: "Pretty near every woman . . . done a man's work. I've done everything but plowing. I've worked in hay, I've binded oats, I've shucked corn. Done everything in the world that a man could do but plow."[25] Shiveley, unlike Amy Marshall of Texas, believed that she was in the majority as a field-working woman. She was the rule, not the exception.

24. Jones, interview by Walker, July 21, 1994, Loudon County, TN, McClung Historical Collection, Lawson-McGhee Public Library, Knoxville, TN (hereafter MHC).

25. London, interview by Anne R. Phillips and Jacquelyn Johnson, April 2, 1992, Waco, TX, IOH; Carroll and Carroll, interview no. 1; Shiveley, interview by Gary A. Jarrett, ca. 1972–1974, OHA.

Picking cotton was an activity at which women often excelled. Harvest time was exciting, if difficult, with many hands needed to bring in the crop quickly. The entire family focused on gathering the crop and often worked in groups, knowing that successful picking was absolutely critical for the family's annual income. Many women expressed pride in their abilities as cotton pickers, sometimes even setting goals for themselves. Marguerite Cooper, whose greatest daily cotton-picking weight was 315 pounds, remembered, "It was something if a girl could pick five hundred. And they tried, just a lot of them." At other times, women might compete among themselves. Inez Folley remembered her mother as

> a good cotton picker. My greatest delight was trying to beat her picking cotton, but I never did. She could always—we'd go to the scales to weigh the cotton, she'd always have two or three or four pounds more than I did, and I just picked myself to death, I thought, trying to beat her. But I never did. One time, I was able to pick over two hundred pounds of cotton, and she could pick two hundred pounds without even thinking about getting tired. She was just used to working. She was a strong woman.[26]

Even women who plowed could revel in their prowess at the much disparaged task. Rowena Weatherly Keatts, who had no brothers, thus became her father's chief assistant. The daughter of an African American landowner in Texas, Keatts recalled that she learned to pick cotton before any of her four sisters: "They'd stay at the house with Momma. I was with my daddy. I could plow just as good as he could. Plowed with mules and horses." Keatts marked the contrast between herself and her sisters, as she alone equaled her father's ability in plowing and working with the livestock. White Texan Laura Belle Holley Bateman took readily to technology, and she recalled that she drove the first tractor that she and her husband bought around 1940: "Yeah, I plowed. Sure did. Plowed corn and maize and cotton [laughs] and broke land. Yeah, I was right in there doing a little of all

26. Cooper, *Oral Memoirs of Marguerite Ethel Webb Cooper*, interview by Kay Clifton, March 25, 1977, Waco, TX, TC, 20; Folley, interview no. 1.

of it."[27] Women who were forthcoming about having done field work often believed they were good at that type of work. By extension, they would have seen their work as important to the family economy because they were highly skilled.

But the ambivalence remained for some southern farm women. Some emphasized the intermittent nature of their labor, going into the fields only when they had satisfied the need for their housework. Alma Stewart Hale explained that, at cotton-picking time, on her childhood farm outside Temple, Texas, her mother came to the field to join their father and the children in picking "when she wasn't home cooking." Even many women who participated actively in the most labor-intensive farming activities sometimes deprecated their labor. Etta Carroll, who could chop cotton as fast as anyone in the vicinity, commented, "I helped some. I never did just go to the field and make a hand all the time, but I'd go to the field and help out as I needed to be."[28] Carroll clearly made the distinction between being a "regular hand" and an occasional laborer. A regular hand was a full-time laborer, but occasional work may have carried the implication that the woman's work was done during times of peak need and largely of her own volition and was therefore more socially acceptable. In reality, the intermittent work of women enabled many families to get their crops harvested without hiring outside labor. In sheer quantity, intermittent work apparently represented the largest contribution of women to agricultural labor. It was far more than merely "helping."

In addition to downplaying the importance of their work, some women simply did not talk about the aspects of their work that they found unpleasant or socially undesirable. Landowning farmwives who had done field work were sometimes silent about it, suggesting that they didn't find this work acceptable or perhaps that they didn't expect listeners to approve. Scholars Alexander Freund and Laura Quilici

27. Keatts, *Oral Memoirs of Rowena Weatherly Keatts,* interview by Sharpless on five occasions, May 5, 1986–April 15, 1987, Waco, TX, TC, 105; Bateman, interview by Sharon Siske Crunk, January 20, 1994, Meridian, TX, IOH.

28. Hale, *Oral Memoirs of Alma Stewart Hale,* interview by Doni Van Ryswyk on eight occasions, January 27–March 28, 1988, Waco, TX, TC, 15; Carroll and Carroll interview, September 29, 1990, interview no. 2.

have noted that "women's perspectives often combine two separate consciousnesses: one emerges out of their practical activities in the world, and the other is rooted in an assumption of women's role in society." When women's experiences do not conform to the ideal of womanhood, they often reconstruct narratives to make sense of this tension. As Freund and Quilici put it, "Women may mute their own thoughts and feelings by describing their lives in ways that outwardly conform to acceptable behavior." When an interviewer asked Annie Lee Barr of Loudon County, Tennessee, about her work on the family's dairy in the 1930s, she talked about housework, caring for chickens and cows, and selling eggs. She readily admitted her participation in milking: "That's the way we started [the farm]. It's a lot easier now than when I did it. . . . Can you imagine me sitting in there milking all those cows by hand?" Her testimony almost mythologizes the work of milking. To this tenant farmer's daughter, married to a man who inherited part of a small farm, milking the cows herself was part of the process of overcoming great odds to build a large commercial dairy. Then the interviewer asked her about her contributions during busy times on the farm. She spun elaborate stories about cooking for threshing teams. Clearly, this activity evoked nostalgic memories of community mutual aid. Finally, the interviewer pressed her: "Did you work in the fields?" Yes, she admitted, seeming reluctant. She did sometimes work in the fields. Then she changed the subject and returned to stories about feeding men at threshing time. This exchange was revealing. Barr had been a partner in the family farm. She spoke of decisions to buy land or invest in new equipment as joint decisions, and neighbors confirmed that her business acumen was important in developing the large Barr dairy.[29] Her reluctance to talk about her field work suggests that she was uncomfortable with having worked in the fields. Perhaps she believed the interviewer wouldn't approve. Or perhaps field work violated her own notions about the work a prosperous farm woman of her status should do. Her telling and retelling of

29. Freund and Quilici, "Exploring Myths in Women's Narratives: Italian and German Immigrant Women in Vancouver, 1947–1961," *Oral History Review* 23 (Winter 1996): 10; Barr, interview by Walker, July 19, 1994, Loudon County, TN, MHC.

the story of cooking for threshing parties, an important and more so-cially acceptable part of her life, also seems to be a way of avoiding talking about her field work.

Most farm families operated according to the "family wage," wherein all of the income came in a lump sum, usually controlled by the husband. Whether a woman worked in the fields of her own accord, whether she liked it or detested it, she almost never earned money to call her own. Instead, women's work mingled, indistin-guishably, with that of other family members, and they received no special credit for their efforts in making the crop. Julia Hardeman recalled that her father controlled the earnings of his entire family, doling funds out to those who had earned them: "Our father was over it [the family money]. He was the one, you see. He'd collect the money, but he was always good and kind enough to give us a per-centage to spend." This lack of remuneration appalled reformers such as sociologist Ruth Allen, who declared that only through the exploita-tion of women's labor could the cotton industry continue to produce a profit. But the family wage may have helped justify women's labor in the eyes of society. Work done on behalf of one's family may have been more acceptable than work performed for oneself.[30]

Many years after the end of the old-fashioned southern farm econ-omy, women told of their relationships to work on the farms. The breadth of their choices and the control over the choice of tasks shaped the way women talked about field work. Southern farm women could view their work in the fields positively, either as something they enjoyed or as critical to the family economy. They could also see field work negatively, as drudge work usually controlled by men and forced upon them by poverty or male authority.

Some women defined themselves primarily as "homemakers." They either rejected field work and other tasks that could be defined as "men's work," or they denied having done that work when in fact they had toiled in the fields, at least occasionally. These women rejected

30. Jones, *Tomorrow Is Another Day*, 13; Hardeman, interview by Corrinne Crow, May 15, 1975, Commerce, TX, James Gee Library, Texas A&M Univer-sity, Commerce, TX.

field work because it was seen as drudgery, hot and boring and miserable; because it distracted them from valuable and important work in the home; or because it was seen as something that respectable women did not do. The farm women most likely to define themselves as "homemakers" were those like Virginia McIntyre, the wives of prosperous white landowners who had the financial wherewithal to remain in the spheres that mainstream society defined as "feminine."

Occupying a middle ground were the women who described their roles as "helpers" rather than as primary field workers. Like Etta Carroll, they readily admitted performing field work, but they minimized the importance and scope of this work, seeing their efforts as "helping" with the family economy. These women took a practical view, acknowledging the superior role of men in decision making and financial matters but also seeing their field work as essential for the family's well-being.

The third group of women included those who were active decision makers, with superior knowledge of and skill at farmwork. In many cases, the women served in place of an ill, dead, or ignorant husband or father. Such women were most likely to acknowledge their talents and to take pride in their abilities as field workers and in their contributions to the family's well-being. As black North Carolina sharecropper Susie Weathersbee told an interviewer, "And when I come up, I was a farmer. . . . Was a farmer. And that's all I ever done, any work on a farm."[31] Although few women might use Weathersbee's title of "farmer," they knew that their work in the fields carried great importance. As testimony from women such as Laura Bateman suggests, women who *chose* to work in the fields were more likely to talk about that work and even to show pride in that work. Indeed, moderately prosperous farm women like Bateman could afford *not* to do field work; thus, they could probably exercise more control over the work and more choice about when and what types of field work they would perform when they did work in the fields. Some embraced field work as something they were proud of doing, even as something they *chose* to do, as a way of rejecting the label of "drudge." Although it is

31. Weathersbee interview.

clear that African American women performed more field work and more difficult work, the ways they discuss that work in their narratives is not significantly different from their white counterparts. Some rejected field work or minimized the fact that they had performed it, while others embraced it and expressed a preference for it.

The way that people think about themselves affects the range of acceptable options and behaviors available, and thus it shapes the choices they make. Yet the reverse is also true. People take the options available to them and mold their self-images around those options. Looking back on their lives, few southern farm women lamented the opportunities that were never available to them. Instead, they described how they had fashioned a life around the available options. Southern farm women sometimes embraced field work, sometimes tolerated it, and sometimes rejected it outright. The way they talked about that work reveals much about the complex interaction between autonomy and necessity. In the early twentieth century, southern farm women exercised the limited freedom of action available to them to choose their lives to the greatest extent possible.

II.

Rural Reformers at Work

EVAN P. BENNETT

"A Responsibility on Women That Cannot Be Delegated to Father, Husband, or Son"

Farm Women and Cooperation in the Tobacco South

In January 1921, as stump speakers, extension service agents, and other organizers fanned out across Virginia and the Carolinas to enroll farmers in the newly formed Tobacco Growers' Cooperative Association, Clarence Poe aimed his editor's pen at the farm women of the tobacco South. "Now the fight is on to see how many farmers are willing to stand with their brother farmers in this contest, and how many are going to be slackers," he wrote in the pages of the *Progressive Farmer*, the region's leading agricultural journal. "If the farm women of the three states become thoroughly aroused there will be but few slackers. Without their help there may be a great many." A native North Carolinian, a director of the cooperative, and a tobacco planter himself, Poe believed that the new organization would fail without women's participation, and he challenged farm women to become "missionar[ies] for cooperative marketing," saying, "You must learn about the plans and talk them not only to other farm women, but to your husbands, sons, and farmer neighbors."[1]

At first glance, it may seem odd that Poe sought support for the cooperative among the farm women of the Tobacco Belt. After all, membership in the cooperative was limited to those selling tobacco, which, in most families, was the male head of household. But Poe

1. Poe, *Progressive Farmer*, January 29, 1921.

knew exactly what he was doing. Farm women's work was central to both the production of bright tobacco and the household economies of the families that grew it. At the same time, women were integral to the family and community networks that interlaced the rural countryside. By appealing to the women of the Tobacco Belt, Poe hoped to build support for the cooperative among entire farm families and communities, not just among individual farmers.

The most ambitious and far-reaching effort to correct the abuses of the tobacco auction system in the years before the New Deal, the Tobacco Growers' Cooperative (also known as the Tri-State Cooperative) attracted thousands of farmers from Virginia and the Carolinas who hoped to make tobacco farming pay. Begun in the wake of a disastrous harvest in 1920, the cooperative promised to bypass the traditional auction system by offering farmers the opportunity to pool their tobacco and sell it directly to manufacturers as a group. Unfortunately for farmers, the plan never worked; by 1926, the cooperative was in receivership, a victim of grower apathy, internal mismanagement, and powerful enemies.

Historians by and large have focused their attention on the Tri-State's inability to fulfill its promise to provide farmers fair prices for their crops. They have documented the rise and fall of the organization and judged the Tri-State to be another in a line of abysmal, if well-intentioned, failures to reform the system. The purpose of this essay is not to quibble with this assessment; the organization indeed fell terribly short of its goal to reform the tobacco auction system. Instead, this essay uses the brief history of the Tri-State to explore the centrality of farm women's experience in the culture of bright tobacco. Farm women's work placed them in the nexus of domestic and market production. Because most tobacco never would have come to market without women's work at every step, and low prices placed the burden of maintaining the household squarely on farm women's shoulders, the farm women of the Bright Tobacco Belt necessarily had an interest in how well the crop sold at market. Organizers like Poe believed this put them in a position to determine the organization's ultimate success or failure, and thus appealed for their help.

Women's Work

There was nothing easy about raising bright tobacco in the years before World War II. Requiring upwards of 430 hours of arduous labor per acre, growing the golden leaves demanded farm families' energy, resources, and time. Most tobacco grown in the flue-cured belt that stretched from Virginia to Georgia was grown by individual families, and, as a 1922 study of Virginia tobacco farms found, "the size of the tobacco crop is largely determined by the amount of family labor available." Every member had a stake in the family's crop and a responsibility to work in the fields. Male and female children alike were brought up to work in tobacco. "When I was a girl, I helped plant tobacco, sucker it, pick off the worms, and everything else," remembered one Virginia woman. As these children became men and women, tasks became increasingly sex segregated, but women remained key actors in the production of the golden leaf. Indeed, in her 1939 study of white tenant farm women, sociologist Margaret Jarman Hagood found that women worked tobacco in every season and that most preferred working in the fields to working in the house.[2]

Farm families began the year by burning a new seedbed for the tiny tobacco seeds that took about two months to germinate and grow to transplanting size. During this time, farmers turned their attention to the fields and began plowing and fertilizing for the coming season. From April to early June, the entire family toiled at moving the plants from the seedbed to the fields, a backbreaking task that often served as a child's introduction into the world of tobacco farming. "The whole family... took to the fields at planting time," one

2. "Resume of the Attached Preliminary Report on Cost of Virginia Dark Fire-Cured and Bright Tobacco for 1922," General Correspondence of the Office of the Secretary of Agriculture, Records of the Office of the Secretary of Agriculture, Record Group 16, National Archives and Records Administration, College Park, MD (hereafter RG 16); Pamela Barefoot with Burt Kornegay, *Mules and Memories: A Photo Documentary of the Tobacco Farmer* (Winston-Salem, NC: John F. Blair, 1978), 36; Hagood, *Mothers of the South: Portraiture of the White Tenant Farm Woman* (Chapel Hill: University of North Carolina Press, 1939), 89.

son of tobacco farmers recalled. "Mama, who seldom worked outside the house, presided over the plantbed, pulling the plants carefully, and stacking them into the neat piles to be carried to the fields. There Papa took over, doing most of the planting himself. The smaller children dropped the plants, carefully placing one plant after another, about three feet apart."[3]

The end of planting opened a hot summer's worth of work for everyone on the farm. Plants that did not survive transplanting had to be replaced with viable seedlings, a daunting task considering the thousands of plants required to cover even a small number of acres. More grueling was the nearly constant cultivation required by the fields throughout the early summer. Everyone old enough to handle a hoe chopped weeds until the plants grew large enough to shade the ground. Cultivating season did not end the work, however, as caring for the plants absorbed the rest of the summer. Once the plants reached sufficient height, farmers removed the terminal bud of each plant— "topping," in the vernacular of tobacco—in order to concentrate growth in the leaves. Removing the terminal bud, however, spurred the plants to sprout ancillary buds, commonly known as "suckers," that had to be removed by hand. Horn worms were also regular, if unwelcome, summer visitors that were best eliminated manually. "The arduous task of worming & suckering in a crop of much size is never finished until the crop is saved," remarked one nineteenth-century planter. Since these tasks required little physical strength or experience and other chores often demanded the attention of older male family members, these tasks often fell to women and children. "One real nasty thing I had to do was worm tobacco," North Carolinian Betty Jackson remembered. "I could not pull the heads off of the big worms. Aunt Millie gave me a jar and told me to put the worms in it, and she'd kill them at the end of the row."[4]

3. Elmer D. Johnson, "Life on a North Carolina Tobacco Farm in the 1920s," ms. dated 1990, 13, North Carolina Collection, University of North Carolina, Chapel Hill.

4. "Treatise on the Cultivation and Curing of Bright Tobacco in Pittsylvania County, Virginia," Leftwich-Shepherd-Bowles Families Papers, Accession no. 27988h, Personal Manuscripts, Library of Virginia, Richmond; Bob Lasley and

Harvesting season, which began as early as August and could run into October, required the labor of everyone in the family. "The urgency of this crucial time demands every hand from the youngest child who is able to hand leaves to the oldest grandparent who because of age might be relieved from other field duties," explained Margaret Jarman Hagood. Getting the tobacco from the field to the warehouse floor consisted of a number of tasks, many of which were often, though not always, divided along lines of age and gender. Grown men and older boys took on the task of picking the leaves, while younger boys were charged with driving the leaves to the curing barn on wooden sleds. At the barn, women prepared the leaves for curing by tying them in groups and hanging the strings on tobacco sticks. "This part of the labor was often done by the women of the family," Elmer D. Johnson remembered, "since it involved a little dexterity without too much back-bending labor." Whether it fell to women because of some innate agility is unclear, but many girls learned the skill at the feet of their mothers, aunts, and older sisters. "We'd hand up tobacco leaves, three at a time, to be strung on a stick," one woman recalled of her years growing up on a tobacco farm. Betty Jackson similarly remembered rising before daybreak to hand leaves before rushing to catch the school bus.[5]

After enough leaves had been picked and strung, the men came from the fields to hang the sticks in the barn and cure the tobacco. To make their tobacco turn the yellow color that would bring the highest prices, farm families cured the leaves by forcing hot air through a series of flues attached to fireplaces on the side of the barn. Following formulas handed down from earlier generations, growers slowly raised the temperature in the barn to effect a chemical change that turned the leaves yellow before driving all the moisture from the leaves. A barn of tobacco took about three days to cure and required a family's constant attention. Left unattended, curing fires could grow

---

Sallie Holt, comps., *A Prayer for the Baby Goat and Other Alamance County Tales* (Hickory, NC: Hometown Memories, 2001), 42.

5. Hagood, *Mothers of the South*, 86; Johnson, "North Carolina Tobacco Farm," 15–16; Lasley and Holt, *Prayer for the Baby Goat*, 42, 105.

cold and ruin the tobacco or rage out of control and set the barn on fire. Although older male family members usually assumed oversight of the curing process, curing time was a communal event and entire families might sleep next to the barn and take shifts watching the fires. "Once the tobacco was in the barn ready for curing," Shirley Underwood Troll remembered, "I would spend some nights there with my great-uncle who was the person responsible for seeing that the leaves turned out a golden flue-cured color. The fun part of this time was roasting potatoes and ears of corn in the fire used to cure the tobacco."[6]

Preparations for the auction floor followed curing. Because tobacco buyers based their bids on the quality of the tobacco, farm families had to grade and group leaves of similar quality. Here, again, the entire family worked together, and farm women were indispensable. "In the striphouse where the processes [of grading tobacco] are carried on," Hagood found, "the mother is the star performer, the chief grader." Although the husband might direct the activities, she continued, "he is usually somewhat respectful of his wife's ability." As with stringing, some claimed women were better suited to these tasks on the basis of biological assumptions—better dexterity or more discerning vision— but it is just as likely that farm families saw assigning this work to women as a commonsense solution to the family's labor needs. For many tobacco farmers, the end of curing season meant it was time to sow winter wheat or harvest other crops. While the time-consuming work of grading would pull men away from this work, women could more readily combine it with their housework. "I'd grade tobacco all day long and pack it down," recalled one North Carolina woman. "Then we'd tie it at night. You see, the pack house was right here at us, and the young'uns could stay at the house. That's the way we made our living."[7]

6. Lasley and Holt, *Prayer for the Baby Goat*, 57.
7. Hagood, *Mothers of the South*, 88; Anne Radford Phillips, "Farm Women of Stokes County, North Carolina and Production of Flue-Cured Tobacco, 1925–1955: Continuity and Change" (PhD diss., University of Maryland, 1990), 134.

Whereas farm families relied largely on their own labor to raise their tobacco, neighbors usually shared labor to bring in the crops. Once picked, the leaves had to be cured as quickly as possible, and since it usually took several acres' worth of leaves to fill a barn, those picking and stringing the leaves had to work as quickly as possible. "Priming the tobacco, hauling it to the barn on sleds, tying the leaves to tobacco sticks and hanging the sticks in the barn, as well as the actual curing, often make it necessary to hire help or exchange labor with neighboring farmers," explained a North Carolina Writers Project guide to tobacco farming. "When at the end of the season the plants matured and a motley yellow came over the green leaves, cutting was scheduled," one North Carolina woman recalled. "Such a day was a great event. The Boone family, with whom we exchanged work, came over to help."[8]

Work swaps and seasonal hiring were critical to the production of bright tobacco, but farm families got much more than a few extra hands when neighbors came to help. Sharing labor was a social occasion that offered neighbors opportunities to strengthen the bonds of community. As men, women, and children worked in the fields and at the barns, they told jokes, talked over local politics, and traded gossip. In so doing, they reinforced neighborhood communication networks that pulled them together. Margaret Jarman Hagood found that tasks done around the curing barns most easily facilitated such interaction. "To work in the striphouse is favorable to conversation and tall tale telling," she wrote, detailing her experiences visiting tenant farmers in North Carolina's Piedmont. "One daughter yelled 'You all shut up!' to several women working inside as the visitor approached a striphouse. They later confessed they had been telling 'mighty rough

8. Federal Writers Project, "Gamblers All: The Story of North Carolina Tobacco with Life Histories of the People Who Grow, Market, and Manufacture It," 108–9, Charles Horace Hamilton Papers, Collection MC 159, Special Collections, North Carolina State University, Raleigh; Sallie Walker Stockard, "Daughter of the Piedmont: Chapel Hill's First Co-ed Graduate," Southern Historical Collection no. 3704, Wilson Library, University of North Carolina, Chapel Hill.

jokes.'"[9] While conversation regularly flowed across lines of gender and age, the general sex segregation of many tasks helped to build relationships between farm women.

From spring to fall, husbands, wives, sons and daughters, extended family, and neighbors worked together to get the crop ready for market. After sorting and grading, families loaded their bundles of leaves into wagons and automobiles and carried them to the towns that dotted the landscape. Farmers sold their tobacco by putting it up for auction on the floor of one of the several warehouses that dominated the towns. Large brick buildings with vast selling floors lit by skylights, these warehouses often vied with one another for farmers' business by promising the lowest auction fees, the fairest scales, or the best selling environment. At the time of sale, the farmer lined up his piles of tobacco on the auction floor with hundreds of other farmers, and waited for the auctioneer to reach him. One contemporary wrote that the "auction sale of tobacco is one of hustle and motion." A small cadre of buyers followed the auctioneer from pile to pile, handling the leaves and answering his singsongy chant with winks, nods, and other signs to indicate their bids. Once sold, the tobacco was tagged with the winning bid and moved off the floor by the black warehouse employees who kept the markets moving. The auctioneer by then had moved on, dispatching the other piles at upwards of three to four hundred per hour. Within seconds, the auction was over, and the farmer knew how much he would get for his year's work.[10]

The auction system had some benefits for farmers. Most important, buyers paid farmers cash on the spot for their crops. In a region dependent on credit and plagued by a chronic lack of currency, the benefits of immediate cash payments cannot be overlooked. Warehouses also provided competitive sales, which, in theory, should have benefited farmers. It was here, however, that farmers' complaints about the system began. Some accused buyers, who represented both manufacturers and independent leaf dealers who hoped to resell the

9. Hagood, *Mothers of the South*, 90.
10. A. B. Bradsher, "Tobacco Culture and Manufacture in North Carolina, Part 2," *Trinity Archive* 18 (May 1905): 380.

tobacco, of colluding to keep prices low. Many also expressed frustration at the speed of the auctions. With auctioneers selling hundreds of piles every hour, they questioned their ability to get the best prices. At the same time, many complained that buyers purposefully downgraded the value of their leaves by using secret grading scales that differed from buyer to buyer. Secret grading, they argued, made it impossible for farmers to know how to arrange their tobacco to get the best prices. Even more infuriating to farmers were "pinhookers," individuals who bought tobacco from farmers and used their knowledge of the markets to get higher prices. The pinhookers' ability to work the system made farmers painfully aware of their own vulnerability in the markets.

Growers, of course, had some recourse. If a farmer believed the winning bid was too low, he could refuse the bid and seek to auction his tobacco at another warehouse. Refusing a bid, however, could be costly. Warehouse owners made their money by charging sellers a percentage of the sale price and a number of other warehouse and storage fees. If a farmer refused a bid, he still had to pay the warehouse fees out of his pocket. In addition, offering the tobacco at another sale guaranteed only another set of warehouse fees, not a higher price. Add this to the costs of moving the tobacco again and the potential costs of staying in town an extra day, and it is clear why many farmers simply took what buyers offered. Walking away with money in hand, no matter how little, was better than losing more on a long shot.

Although farm families relied heavily on women's work to produce a crop of tobacco, the propriety of women coming to the market was the subject of some debate. In the minds of many, tobacco market towns were no place for a lady, especially at night. Male farmers who traveled great distances to town often slept in bunk rooms over the warehouse floors. These men filled the streets after the markets closed, giving places like Durham's Rigsbee Street a distinctive masculine atmosphere. Most entertained themselves by listening to street-corner musicians, testing their aim in makeshift shooting galleries, or dining in bustling cafés filled with other farmers in town for the sales. Others, however, found more fun in illicit pursuits. Bootleggers and prostitutes found plenty of business in the market towns and sometimes traveled from market to market as the season progressed. In Kinston, North Carolina, male farmers in search of female company found it in Sugar Hill, "an old and established section with some attractive dwellings among its several dozen houses in the warehouse district." Stories of manly debauchery were common in tobacco lore, leading many to shield their wives and daughters from going to market. North Carolina native Nevada Jane Hall "never went to the tobacco market when her father took the crop to be sold, because women who went to the market were sometimes considered huzzies."[11]

Despite this image, there is considerable evidence that women were common, if not regular, visitors to the markets. Market openings were great social occasions, and much of the fanfare that followed them was aimed at entire farm families, not just male farmers. Community leaders used the occasion to tout the golden leaf's economic benefits, while shop owners held sales to entice farmers to prove them. Meanwhile, politicians and itinerant clergy alike pleaded with farmers for their votes and their souls. While some farm women came to town for the social events, others came with business on their minds. It was fairly common for a wife to have claim over a certain portion of the family's crop that she could sell for her own money. "The mother gets all except the landlord's fourth from her patch, which brought over a hundred dollars this year," Margaret Jarman Hagood reported of one tenant farm woman. Similarly, many parents allotted their children portions of the crop to teach them the economics of tobacco, and boys and girls alike went to town to sell their tobacco. "Misses Bettie and Helen's six lots ranged from 22½ to 46, bringing them an all around price of $31.05," one Virginia newspaper reported in 1929. "The young ladies claim they did all the work except, of course, the plowing."[12] Clearly, men, women, and children all inhabited the space created by the tobacco markets.

Whether or not a farm woman actually came to the market, she clearly had an interest in the outcome of the sale of her family's

11. Federal Writers Project, "Gamblers All," 254; Phillips, "Farm Women of Stokes County," 69.
12. Hagood, *Mothers of the South,* 15; "New Orders Boost Tobacco Prices," *South Hill (VA) Enterprise,* November 7, 1929.

tobacco. If tobacco failed to bring remunerative prices, women's enterprises became more critical to the family's survival, placing a greater burden on farm women. In many, if not most, farm families, the mother served as manager of the household. Hagood expressed surprise at tenant farm women's knowledge of farming matters, which extended "not only to the immediate condition of the current crop but to details of renting, credit, the sequence of operations, and to the basic data for making an estimate of how they will 'come out this year.'" Most farm women, even many tenants, tended gardens and potato patches to provide for their family's needs. Additionally, women regularly raised livestock (especially chickens) or cultivated truck gardens for market. One North Carolina woman explained her many jobs to a Federal Writers Project interviewer:

> 'Course I tend the garden, do all the picklin', cannin', preservin', an' get the eggs, butter an' garden truck ready for market. . . . We go to our smoke house for meat; to the hen house for chickens an' eggs; to the cows for milk an' butter; send our own wheat an' corn to the mill for flour an' meal; have gardens an' orchards for vegetables an' fruit; in winter there's canned stuff, potatoes, plenty of cabbage, collards, an' turnips, an' our fire wood grows all 'round us.[13]

The significance of women's work to the production of bright tobacco and, more important, farm women's position at the center of the home economy made their participation critical to the success of any attempt to organize tobacco farmers. Organizers of the Tri-State understood this and sought women's support for the organization from the start. While some promoters of cooperation used the image of women working the fields to chide male tobacco farmers for failing to work for higher prices, others understood that reaching out to those women in the fields could make or break the Tri-State. With a sense of women's management of the home and an understanding of

13. Hagood, *Mothers of the South*, 77; "Bud Taylor, Tenant Farmer," Durham County, November 14, 1938, Federal Writers Project Papers, Southern Historical Collection no. 3709, Wilson Library, University of North Carolina, Chapel Hill.

the communal nature of much farmwork, the largely male leadership of the Tri-State consciously enlisted women in the fight for agricultural cooperation. Farm women, they believed, could argue their interest in the crop to convince their husbands to join and sell with the cooperative while exploiting their connections with other farm women to spread the gospel of cooperation. According to Tri-State leaders, their ability to do both tasks made farm women critical, indeed invaluable, to the cause of cooperative marketing.

Farm Women and the "Co-ops"

The Great War brought boom times to farming families across the tobacco South. Sales on the market floors of Danville, Virginia, the premier market in the northernmost bright tobacco–growing area known as the Old Belt, are indicative of the increasing prices. In the years between 1900 and 1914, prices averaged just over eleven cents per pound. Between 1917 and 1919, this average price rose to nearly forty-one cents per pound. Driven by wartime demand for cigarettes, tobacco prices skyrocketed to previously unseen highs, and farm families who relied on bright tobacco for their incomes celebrated their newfound prosperity. "Farmers can be seen hugging each other over the amazing prices they are getting, and pinch themselves quite frequently to see if they have been dreaming," one observer reported from the markets in 1917.[14] Having finally received prices worthy of their labor, farm families rushed to catch up with the burgeoning consumer age, buying everything from automobiles to indoor plumbing.

Bright tobacco's golden days were brief, however. In 1920, despite warnings from buyers, warehousemen, and extension agents, farmers carried record amounts of tobacco to market at the very moment demand evaporated and prices plummeted. Discontent flowed north

14. Annual Market Statistics, Danville, VA, President's Report, 1984, Danville Tobacco Association Records, 1878–1984, reel 2, Accession no. 32168, Library of Virginia, Richmond; *Southern Tobacco Journal*, September 11, 1917, quoted in Nannie May Tilley, *The Bright-Tobacco Industry, 1860–1929* (Chapel Hill: University of North Carolina Press, 1948), 389.

from South Carolina to Virginia as the markets opened. In early December, one North Carolina official reported that tobacco prices had declined between five and ten dollars on the Oxford market during the week, creating "some local agitation" for the markets to be closed. In Virginia, one observer reported that farmers were "very much wrought up over the low price of tobacco." Although prices were higher than before the war, they were much lower than farmers had anticipated and got only worse as the marketing season wore on. The amount of tobacco marketed in the Danville warehouses increased almost 84 percent between 1919 and 1920, while the average price per pound fell by more than half, from fifty-five cents to twenty-six cents.[15]

The shock of the postwar plunge renewed calls for farmers to band together in marketing their crops. Over the years, many voices had commended cooperation as the solution to the problem of low prices. The Grange, the Farmers' Alliance, and the Farmers' Union had all opened cooperative-sales warehouses in the late nineteenth and early twentieth centuries, only to see the mass of farmers continue to take their crops to commercial floors where warehousemen and buyers, hoping to silence calls for cooperation, waited with ready cash and easy terms. The repeated failure of farmers' organizations to compete with commercial warehouses turned many farmers against the notion of beating the warehousemen and tobacco buyers at their own game. On the eve of the disastrous 1920 harvest, one extension agent reported that he found it "very hard to talk cooperative warehouses to these farmers" because of their frustration with earlier cooperative schemes.[16]

15. E. G. Stokes to secretary of agriculture, September 13, 1920, RG 16; E. G. Moss to J. H. Warren, December 3, 1920, Tobacco Growers' Association Papers, folder 4, box 1, Southern Historical Collection no. 3322, Wilson Library, University of North Carolina, Chapel Hill (hereafter TGAP); Annual Market Statistics, Danville Tobacco Association Records.

16. Nannie May Tilley, "Agitation against the American Tobacco Company in North Carolina, 1890–1911," *North Carolina Historical Review* 24:2 (April 1947): 207–23; Report of the County Agent, 1919, Mecklenburg County, Virginia, Extension Service Annual Reports, Virginia, reel 4, Record Group 33, National Archives and Records Administration, College Park, MD (hereafter RG 33).

Despite this history, demand for cooperative solutions rose out of farmers' frustration with the 1920 harvest. Leading growers hastily arranged meetings in Wilson, Danville, and other market towns throughout the fall to discuss the problem; in December, representatives from the bright tobacco–growing states converged on Richmond to form the Tobacco Growers' Cooperative Association. Organizers hoped this new organization would overcome what they saw as the fundamental problem facing farmers: the rushed marketing of tobacco in the weeks following the harvest. They envisioned a system that would give farmers more power in selling their crops. Instead of being forced to sell to the highest bidder in a hurried and confusing auction, farmers would deliver their tobacco to the Tri-State, receive an advance on their crop, let the cooperative sell the leaves for more money, and wait for the balance of the money due them. The scheme assumed the cooperative would control enough tobacco to dictate the prices manufacturers would pay, which, of course, it never did.[17]

The low prices of 1920 created bitterness across the Bright Tobacco Belt, but turning growers' anger into support for the cooperative proved challenging. The Tri-State's charter required that 50 percent of the growers agree to market their tobacco through their warehouses for it to be binding, so organizers, aided by extension service agents on both the local and the state levels, immediately began canvassing growers for signatures. Early results were promising. Within a year, sixty-four thousand farmers from Virginia and the Carolinas had agreed to market their tobacco through the cooperative. In addition, organizers succeeded in recruiting the support of a number of business and political leaders, including *Raleigh News and Observer* editor Josephus Daniels and Virginia senator Claude Swanson, who signed up his own tobacco crop in 1921.[18]

It is impossible to paint a complete picture of the cooperative's membership, but some general patterns can be discerned from the

17. For a good account of the history of the Tri-State, see Tilley, *Bright-Tobacco Industry*, 449–86.
18. For Swanson's support, see Swanson to M. O. Wilson, November 26, 1921, Claude A. Swanson Papers 907-a, box 8, Special Collections, Alderman Library, University of Virginia, Charlottesville.

existing evidence. The cooperative was most effective in convincing small to medium independent farmers to join. These growers, unlike sharecroppers or renters, owned their land and could decide how they would market their crops. The 1920 price crash affected these farmers as much or more than any other group, in part because the low prices threatened to erode the gains they had made during the war years. The cooperative had less success convincing large planters— those who had large landholdings and grew tobacco using hired laborers, sharecroppers, or both—to join. These planters often had financial stakes in the warehouses supported by the auction system, and they did not take kindly to the cooperative's promises to "make the grass grow in the streets of Wilson" and other warehouse towns. These planters regularly barred their renters and sharecroppers from joining the cooperative despite court judgments defending their right to sell their shares however they pleased. Virginian E. A. Jackson, for example, reported that his landlord forbade him "to deliver any... tobacco to the 'Co-ops' until he was paid." Jackson rebuffed his landlord and sold to the Tri-State, but others had little choice but to deliver their crops as directed by their landlords or other creditors.[19]

The Tri-State was unique in that it reached out to both black and white tobacco farmers. African American farm families grew about half the tobacco in the Bright Tobacco Belt, and organizers understood that excluding African Americans would be simply counterproductive. Though it is impossible to determine the extent of black membership in the cooperative, it is clear that organizers' attempts to sign up black farmers were successful to some degree. "Both White and Negro Farmers in this County are successfully demonstrating that Tobacco can be marketed cooperatively," one extension service agent reported in 1922. Despite the cooperative's openness to black farmers, most met in segregated locals, and no black members rose to any sort of leadership in the organization. Nevertheless, its openness sets the cooperative apart as one of the few biracial rural reform

19. Anthony Badger, *Prosperity Road: The New Deal, Tobacco, and North Carolina* (Chapel Hill: University of North Carolina Press, 1980), 24; *Tri-State Tobacco Grower,* November 1924.

organizations between the demise of the Populists in the 1890s and the rise of groups like the Southern Tenant Farmers' Union or the Sharecroppers Union in the 1930s.[20]

The cooperative had a relatively strong, centralized bureaucracy, but building support among average tobacco farmers nevertheless required hard work on the local level, holding meetings, arranging speakers, and passing out literature. Grower anger was fairly easy to come by; harnessing it was another matter entirely. To gain support, organizers turned largely to traditional methods of publicity, giving the enrollment campaign the appearance of a religious revival or political rally. "They had big all-day meetings with picnic dinners and barbeque suppers and brunswick stews all over that neighborhood," a witness to one of these campaigns remembered. "We used to go to all of them and listen to the speeches. I don't remember what that man's name was that came to our neighborhood, but he was a natural-born orator. The farmers just stood there with their mouths open to listen to him. It sounded like a good revival sermon before he got through and it went home the same way."[21]

The Tri-State also benefited from the Cooperative Extension Service's willingness to provide the services of its county agents to the organization. Created by the 1914 Smith-Lever Act, the extension service employed county agents to educate farmers about the latest agricultural innovations. The extension service also supported home demonstration agents who worked to foster the development of modern domestic techniques among the nation's farm women. By 1920, both county agents and home demonstration agents had tried to make inroads in communities throughout the Bright Tobacco Belt. Defining their work broadly, the extension service directors of Virginia and the Carolinas jumped at the opportunity to help farmers while expanding the extension service's influence. They quickly dispatched their county agents and home demonstration workers to sign up farmers. The work generally followed the gendered division of labor consti-

20. Negro extension agent's report, 1922, Alamance County, NC, Extension Service Annual Reports, RG 33.
21. Federal Writers Project, "Gamblers All," 432.

tuted in the organization of the extension service; county agents largely worked to sign up male farmers, while home demonstration agents approached women for support. These agents worked long hours convincing farmers and their families of the benefits of selling their tobacco cooperatively, and their labor clearly helped the fledgling organization get off the ground. "I . . . put my shoulder to the wheel," one agent reported in 1922, "and went to work with the farmer, doing what he asked, going where he requested, driving night and day, getting up meetings, making talks, familiarizing myself with cooperative marketing; and preaching cooperation, organization and loyalty."[22]

The Tri-State also found support from the region's leading agricultural journalist, Clarence Poe, who lent his editorial page to the cooperative's cause. As editor of the *Progressive Farmer*, Poe had been trying for years to convince farmers to organize when the market bottomed out in 1920. In the Tri-State he saw the salvation of the region's tobacco farmers and entreated them to support the organization. Although he usually aimed his appeals at farmers' pocketbooks, Poe was not above employing the traditional southern rhetoric that conflated liberty and white manhood. "Even the ignorant Negroes in olden days did not accept slavery without protest, and thousands of them fought and struggled and died to escape," he reminded his readers in 1921. "Surely our sturdy Anglo-Saxon Southern white farmers are not now going to be content with industrial slavery." Employing racialized and gendered rhetoric, Poe hoped to rally farmers by reaffirming the Anglo-Saxon vigor of those willing to renounce the auction system while questioning the manliness of those who refused to leave the warehousemen behind. At the same time, he hoped to rouse their anger at having "to acknowledge somebody else as 'master' in fixing a price on the product of [their] own labor."[23]

The Tri-State's leaders sometimes used similar rhetoric to appeal to white male tobacco farmers. In early 1922, for example, the editor of the *Tri-State Tobacco Grower* attempted to link the cooperative's

22. Extension agent's report, 1922, Lunenburg County, VA, Extension Service Annual Reports, RG 33.
23. Poe, *Progressive Farmer*, February 26, 1921.

cause to the post–Civil War South's most potent symbol of white manhood: the Confederate soldier. "When our leaders who served under the Stars and Bars are with us still, pointing the way in the advance of 70,000 Southern fighters for economic freedom," he wrote in a preface to a letter from General James Macgill, commander of the Second Brigade of Virginia Confederate Veterans, "all is well." However, the cooperative's need and desire to attract black farmers curtailed appeals limited to white farmers. Instead, the cooperative's leaders employed broader gendered republican rhetoric that contrasted the manliness of society's "producers" with its "parasites." Praising reports that President Warren Harding supported farmers' cooperative efforts, the *Tri-State Tobacco Grower* reported, "Every real Big Man in the United States is in favor of cooperative marketing. Only 'pinhookers' and men who make money out of the 'auction' system are against it." Years later, as the cooperative fought off attacks from without and within, its leaders again turned to this language by issuing "A Call to Southern Manhood" that questioned farmers' manliness for not standing up to the "powerful forces" arrayed against them. "Farmers of the Carolinas and Virginia," pleaded director J. Y. Joyner, "if ye be men, join me in whatever voluntary sacrifice and service may be necessary in this crisis to win the victory."[24]

Such language was hardly accidental. The 1920 harvest created a crisis of confidence for male farmers. As historian Ted Ownby has argued, "The idea that a man's job was to gain a living from the soil" was one of "two central features of male culture" in the rural South. When prices plummeted, many male farmers took it personally and interpreted their inability to make a living as a personal failure. In the Bright Tobacco Belt, tradition exacerbated the problem. As with any number of agricultural products, a number of cultural markers denoting success surrounded bright tobacco. The quality of a farmer's crop, for example, largely defined his status among the greater community. A farmer who produced fine yellow leaves that brought in

24. "Our Leaders Still with Us," *Tri-State Tobacco Grower,* January 1922; "All the Big Men," *Tri-State Tobacco Grower,* June 1922; "A Call to Southern Manhood," *Tri-State Tobacco Grower,* August 1925.

high prices was seen as a good farmer who managed his crop well, whereas a farmer known for bringing dark, mottled, or "trashy" tobacco to market was often derided as ignorant or undisciplined. Given the linkage of price and quality, farmers often saw low prices as a personal failing. While the 1920 bust energized many to attack the auction system, it demoralized others. The Tri-State employed such rhetoric to rile up these farmers enough to join the cause.[25]

Poe and the other leaders of the Tri-State knew, however, that grower anger would go only so far. Smooth-talking warehousemen and tobacco buyers could quickly stamp out a farmer's cooperationist fervor with promises of higher prices and paeans to individualism and the blessings of the free market system. "Does somebody try to fool you by talking about the farmer's 'signing away his independence' by agreeing to market his crops in cooperation with his brother farmers?" Poe asked rhetorically, acknowledging the pressure warehousemen and tobacco buyers would place on farmers.[26] Aware that earlier attempts at cooperation had failed because organizers had been unable to get farmers to hold up under such pressure, the Tri-State's leaders attempted to build support for the organization in the home and turned to farm women for help.

Poe assumed that women's concerns lay closest to the domestic sphere, and he pointed to the blurry line that separated the home economy from the tobacco auction market to remind farm women that low prices impinged on their attempts to provide for their families' physical, intellectual, and spiritual welfare. "When the farmer fails to get a decent price for his products," he wrote, "he takes it out of his standards of living. He must do so. He has to get along without the improvements he and his wife desire in the way of a better home, lights, paint, waterworks, together with better school advantages for the children."[27] Poe hoped to spur women to action by reminding them of the burdens low prices placed on them and their families.

25. Ownby, *Subduing Satan: Religion, Recreation, and Manhood in the Rural South, 1865–1920* (Chapel Hill: University of North Carolina Press, 1990), 92.

26. Poe, *Progressive Farmer*, February 26, 1921.

27. Poe, *Progressive Farmer*, January 29, 1921.

The language of Poe's appeal to women was not entirely new or unique. The rural progressivism popular in the early twentieth century linked rural uplift with the domestic sphere and portrayed women's involvement as critical to solving the problems facing rural people. In reaching out to farm women, the leaders of the Tri-State, as well as many of its female supporters, regularly returned to such language. They hoped to engage women's interest by reminding them of the market's impact on their homes, their families, and their ability to improve their standard of living. In June 1922, the *Tri-State Tobacco Grower* ran an article that highlighted the impact of low prices on farm families' ability to keep their children on the farm. "Tobacco growers have had few chances in the last fifty years to sell at a profit and in fifty years a million boys have left the farms of Virginia and the Carolinas. We have the system, but not the boys to blame." The solution the writer offered, of course, was cooperation. "With cooperative marketing you will have a chance every year to merchandise your crops, instead of dumping them, and the prices will be stabilized, and country life [will] become worth living."[28] Though gender neutral, such articles likely were aimed at farm women concerned about the migration of their children away from the countryside.

One of the first direct appeals to farm women appeared in July 1922, when a North Carolina farm woman pleaded with her fellow farm women to support the cooperative. In her letter to the editor of the *Tri-State Tobacco Grower,* Mrs. Ed Carraway couched her support for the cooperative in domestic terms, describing the impact of the auction system on her family's ability to sell their crops for remunerative prices. Despite the fact that they owned their land, lived economically, and "worked in the crop rain or shine, early and late," she and her husband had "no fund to carry our children to a higher education." The market schedule, she argued, made selling disadvantageous for farmers and even threatened the moral fiber of the family. "Farmers not having the money to go to a hotel or nice boarding house were forced to eat in cheap places and camp in the camp rooms of a warehouse with hundreds of other men," she explained. "Now,

28. "A Million Have Gone," *Tri-State Tobacco Grower,* June 1922.

under such circumstances, do you think your boy could go to these crowded markets eight times a year and come back home the boy he was before he left? All this besides the uncertainty of prices on the market." The cooperative, she continued, was the only solution to the problem, as it would make the selling process less time consuming. "As I understand it, a load of tobacco will be unloaded, graded, a bill of sale given with check and receipted at once, and thereby save time."[29] Time saved and idle hands kept from the devil, a farm mother's dream.

In 1923, attracting women to support the cooperative became an official goal of the Tri-State's leadership when it became apparent that support for the organization was beginning to wane among male farmers. Recognizing the need to encourage and organize women's participation in the cooperative, they introduced two forums for channeling women's energies. First came the introduction of a "Farm Women's Page" to the *Tri-State Tobacco Grower*. Edited by Mrs. F. C. Beverly, the page provided female readers a regular mixture of cooperationist entreaties, recipes, and domestic tips. In July 1924, the organization went further and secured the services of Elizabeth Kelly, former president of the North Carolina Teachers Association, "to aid in directing work among country women and their families for cooperative marketing and community improvement."[30] These women used different implements—one, the pen; the other, the automobile and the local meeting—but both helped build support for the cooperative among the farm women of Virginia and the Carolinas.

Mrs. F. C. Beverly was active in the rural reform movements that swept the countryside in the early twentieth century. She founded the Whitmell Country Life School both to improve country children's educational opportunities and to teach the benefits of modern agricultural techniques. In her contributions to the "Farm Women's Page," she regularly tried to build support among farm women by linking domestic concerns to the problems of the auction system. In a fictional piece, for example, "Farmer John" answered a northern traveler's query about his wife's interest in the success of the cooperative by recounting

29. Carraway, letter to the editor, *Tri-State Tobacco Grower*, July 1922.
30. "Farm Women's Page," *Tri-State Tobacco Grower*, August 1923.

the disappointments of the auction system. "Many's the time I've come back home to Sarah with tears in my eyes—and 'chicken feed' in my pocket," he explained to the tourist.

> Once in '98, I think it was, when two or three of the children had begun to take some notice of Santa Claus—I went to town with a big load of tobacco and a list of toys and goodies that Sarah had her heart set on havin' for the children's Christmas— but when I drove back home the next day—Santa Claus had been to a funeral, and he didn't hear none of the singin'—I didn't even have nuf shoes and stockings to go 'round, and Sarah had to make that full-sleeve jacket her pa'd give her before we was married do her another winter. You know I told you that woman had grit—well, *then* she had need for it, for the children was cryin' for candy and I had 'bout give up hope—but she came to the rescue of me and the children, in spite of her havin' to give up more than the rest of us, for she needed clothes and shoes to go to the Meetin' House, she needed a new cook stove bad, and 'twas nearly a quarter of a mile to the spring—let alone the carpet and table lamp she'd planned on puttin' in the parlor.[31]

Though many farm women likely needed no reminder of their plight, such a story sought to build support for the cooperative by making them see the auction system as the cause of their misery.

As she did in this story, Mrs. Beverly regularly couched appeals for support of the Tri-State in terms that placed women's labors at the center of the solution to the problem of rural decline. "Do the women of the South have any influence, or should they stand off and say, 'The man's job is to market the crop'?" she queried in a 1923 article. "I contend that any problem affecting the economic and social betterment of the country is a joint problem, and requires the best thought of men and women in its salvation." She encouraged farm women to think more broadly and "see cooperative marketing as a problem in citizen-making," not simply as a narrow agricultural issue.

31. William L. Bowers, *The Country Life Movement in America, 1900–1920* (Port Washington, NY: Kennikat Press, 1974), 79–82; Beverly, "How She Gained the Coop. Spirit," *Tri-State Tobacco Grower,* October 1923.

The movement, she suggested, was not just about low prices, but about "everything that tends to uplift society." She further asserted that women could help by learning about cooperative marketing and teaching its value to their family, friends, and neighbors: "We should study, then write about them, talk them, live them." In a later article, she again told women their support was invaluable, not only to the success of the cooperative but also to the entire reform agenda. "Shall this be left to the men alone?" she asked. "No, women are now citizens, and we shall share equally the failures and successes of our State and nation." Farm women needed to help, she argued, but in ways that complemented the work of male farmers. "There is a responsibility on women that cannot be delegated to father, husband, or son. They have their own responsibilities and we must shoulder the woman's part and do it in a womanly way. It is not womanly to stand off and complain of bad roads, poor schools, dead churches, corrupt politics. The blame is on us for such conditions, and it is certainly womanly to put our shoulder to the wheel and work with the men for betterment of these conditions."[32]

Other female writers similarly appealed to farm women in the pages of the *Tri-State Tobacco Grower*. Like Beverly, these writers often assumed that women had a special duty to buttress male farmers' support of the cooperative. Florence Hamer Stubbs, for example, reminded women that their support was needed in getting the cooperative off the ground. "The *success* or *failure* of the farm man in this great effort depends to a great extent on the active interest and cooperation of us farm women," she pleaded.

> We must make the adjustment with them, we must make it possible and easy for them to make the adjustment, though it may mean some temporary sacrifices. We must help them over disappointments or grievances that may unintentionally and unavoidably come in the first year or two of the gigantic business undertaking. We must help them to see clearly, to act wisely, to

32. Beverly, "The Farm Woman Will Cooperate," *Tri-State Tobacco Grower,* September 1923; Beverly, "Community Organization," *Tri-State Tobacco Grower,* April 1924.

keep the faith! It is our adjustment, our success or failure along
with them. We cannot escape the responsibility but we may lose
our biggest opportunity.

A similar letter from "A Virginia Woman" couched women's obligations to encourage the organization's male members in religious terms.
"I beg you strong members to 'bear ye one another's burdens.' Comfort your brothers that are weak, educate them, show them the error
of their way, and bring them back into the fold before they have done
something which they will always regret."[33]

Since the Tri-State counted only male growers as members, it is
impossible to measure farm women's responses to such appeals, but it
is clear that many gave their energies in support of the cooperative.
Reports sent to the *Tri-State Tobacco Grower* indicate that the promise of cooperation sparked the interest of women across Virginia and
the Carolinas. These women organized meetings for the locals; served
as secretaries in the meetings; wrote letters, poems, and songs supportive of the cooperative; and did hundreds of other tasks to build
the membership and keep it faithful. In many cases, they formed
the backbone of the organization as the cooperative's work faced
increased challenges.

While Beverly encouraged farm women in the pages of the *Tri-State
Tobacco Grower*, Elizabeth Kelly traveled around the region teaching
women how to make themselves active in the local meetings. She
encouraged them to begin auxiliaries and to involve the entire family
in the organization. The program of one local's meeting reprinted in
the *Tri-State Tobacco Grower* records that the meeting consisted of a
"Local Program" aimed at the local's male members, an "Auxiliary
Program" for women that included a time period for instruction in
meat curing, an "Agricultural Club Program" for children that followed
the 4-H Club's format, and a "Social Program" that brought all of the
groups together following their respective business meetings. A report
about another local stated that its weekly meeting "was well attended

33. Stubbs, "Help Men 'Keep the Faith,'" *Tri-State Tobacco Grower*, August
1923; "A Virginia Woman," letter to the editor, *Tri-State Tobacco Grower*, October 1923.

by both men and women" who all listened to the home demonstration agent's presentation on the benefits of egg production.[34]

Not only did women attend meetings, but some, with Kelly's encouragement, also developed meeting programs. Maude Barnard Browne submitted a meeting program to the *Tri-State Tobacco Grower* that included time for community singing, a Bible lesson, and several poetry readings in addition to discussion of regular business. The meeting's theme of "Love of Fellow-Men," utilized a common appeal used by leaders of the cooperative hoping to remind flagging members of their obligation to honor their contracts. A Warren County, North Carolina, farm woman echoed this sentiment in a song titled "Come to the Co-op Meeting." Set to the tune of the traditional hymn "There's a Church in the Wildwood," the song encouraged farmers to remain loyal to the Tri-State by hearkening to the promise of cooperation:

> If the farmers would all pull together
> There would be no more mortgage on the mule;
> They would be as rich as city people
> And could send their girls and boys off to school.[35]

Through their contributions, women broadened the cooperative's vision by reminding members that their support of the Tri-State was about more than getting a few more pennies per pound for their tobacco.

Women's participation, however, extended beyond creating programs and writing songs. A number of women held local posts, a move supported by the leaders of the cooperative. "One of the best locals we have has a woman for secretary," the editor of the *Tri-State Tobacco Grower* reported in 1924. "She helps the chairman plan an interesting program for every meeting and members of this local do not break their contracts because they know what it is all about and have their eyes fixed on the goal." Mrs. A. W. Ferabee of Davie

34. "Local Program," *Tri-State Tobacco Grower*, December 1923; "Live Wire Local Points the Way," *Tri-State Tobacco Grower*, February 1924.
35. Browne, "Program for T.G.C.A.," *Tri-State Tobacco Grower*, September 1924; Mrs. Mulchi, "Come to the Co-op Meeting," TGAP, folder 67, box 5.

County, North Carolina, similarly served as her local's secretary and regularly submitted reports of her local's activities for publication.[36] Women's participation through these activities gave the cooperative much of the energy and focus it needed to maintain many of its local chapters.

Despite the Tri-State's recognition of women's importance to the organization and the willingness of its leaders to include women in the organization, supporters of women's involvement in the cooperative's activities brought with them cultural assumptions about the proper channels for women's work. Although their field labor helped see the crop from seedbed to market, their home work mitigated the burden of low tobacco prices, and many actually controlled some portion of the crop, farm women were largely seen as secondary, supportive actors in the production of bright tobacco. The proper forum for women's activities, the Tri-State's leaders believed, was in auxiliary organizations that would support the activities of the locals. "The women should form organizations, or have auxiliaries to the locals, in order that they may assist in this movement," Mrs. F. C. Beverly wrote in 1923. The next year, in its letter to the locals, the cooperative's headquarters' staff suggested a similar channel for women's interest in the work of the organization: "We wish to urge upon our members the importance of arranging for the women of our communities to hold special meetings of their own during the men's business sessions and to aid the men, as only the ladies can in making a real success of the social programs which follow the important business of the local."[37] The leaders and supporters of the cooperative believed women's help was critical to the success of the organization but thought this help had to be channeled through outlets that did not upset assumptions about women's proper place in tobacco agriculture.

The cooperative's policy regarding the tobacco grown by the wives and children of members also reflected organizers' assumptions about

36. *Tri-State Tobacco Grower,* June 1924. For Ferabee's reports, see *Tri-State Tobacco Grower,* March and July 1923.

37. "The Farm Women Will Cooperate," *Tri-State Tobacco Grower,* September 1923; Tobacco Growers' Cooperative Association letter to locals, May 6, 1924, TGAP, folder 54, box 4.

women's proper roles. A farm woman who controlled a portion of a crop signed over to the cooperative, they believed, was obligated to sell her share at the cooperative with the rest of the crop. "There is no reason why the tobacco sold by the wives and children of our members should be sold other than through the Tobacco Growers Cooperative Association," they explained, "and each member will be expected and required to deliver the tobacco grown by his wife and children to the point which he has chosen as his delivery point." When farm women complained about the policy, Tri-State leaders offered letters like that from Virginian Lillie Smith, who gushed over the first payment she received from the Tri-State after her husband took her crop to be sold cooperatively over her protests, to defuse their anger by reminding them of the greater purpose of cooperation. "I am [a] colored woman," Smith explained, "and hope that every colored woman and man will join the association at once if they market tobacco, for we have fed Mr. Warehouseman for a long time, and his auction gang."[38]

Overall, cultural assumptions about the proper roles for women in the cooperative appear to have had minimal impact on women's participation. Recognizing the organization's potential to improve their material conditions, farm women infused the Tri-State's mission with a missionary fervor for uplifting the status of rural people. The labor these women expended in bringing in their tobacco gave them a vested interest in the price their families received for their crops, but their concern for the success of the organization extended beyond the hope for a few more dollars at harvest. They linked the Tri-State's mission to the broader push for rural reform, making it a vehicle for not only higher prices but also broader uplift. Many of the male leaders also spoke of the cooperative's mission in such terms, but it is clear that farm women demanded that the organization follow through on its rhetoric.

It is easy, however, to overstate the amount of support the Tri-State Cooperative received. In reality, most tobacco farm families

38. *Tri-State Tobacco Grower*, August 1922; Smith, *Tri-State Tobacco Grower*, August 1923.

never supported the cooperative or at least did not remain faithful to it. A 1925 estimate of the total tobacco marketed through the cooperative showed it handled about 16.5 percent of crops, a far cry from the broad-based support organizers had hoped to build across the Bright Tobacco Belt.[39] In earlier years support had been greater, but frustration with a payout system that never paid farmers all the money due them, concerted campaigns by warehouse owners to discredit the cooperative's leaders, rumors of poor accounting and corruption, and the outright intimidation of some members all helped to erode support for the organization over time.

The challenges the Tri-State faced in keeping male farmers loyal to their contracts made it only more difficult to interest the mass of farm women in the cooperative's work. Although the inclusion of women's activities in the pages of the *Tri-State Tobacco Grower* indicates that many farm women were active in the Tri-State, it also suggests that the cooperative's leaders believed that the organization needed to reach more women. "Take your wife to your local meeting," the editor encouraged male farmers in 1924. "She should be more interested in co-operative marketing than you are because the success of our association means a better life for her and the children."[40] The promise of cooperation had obviously reached some, but not all, farm women.

Even more disconcerting to the cooperative's leaders than apathetic farm women, however, was the prospect that some women willingly undermined the cooperative's goals. Some, like South Carolinian Amy Harris, were frustrated with rules that limited their ability to market their share of the crop. "I'm a poor girl and am 21 years old," she wrote to the cooperative, "and my father is a member of the Tobacco Association. I want to know if I can sell mine on the outside. I want all of my money at the time.... I think being I am 21 years old I ought to have the right to sell my tobacco."[41] Her appeal received the custom-

39. President's Report, 1925, Danville Tobacco Association Records, reel 2.
40. *Tri-State Tobacco Grower,* June 1924.
41. Harris, letter to T. B. Young, *Tri-State Tobacco Grower,* September 1923.

ary response that selling through the cooperative would benefit her more in the long run.

Other farm women, meanwhile, helped their husbands to sell their tobacco fraudulently outside the cooperative. Despite laws that made it illegal for a farmer to knowingly sell his tobacco under another's name, dozens of cases of farmers selling their tobacco in their wives' names arose as farmers who had signed up their crops grew frustrated with the cooperative's system of paying for the tobacco over time. It is not entirely clear that farm women always supported the fraudulent sales—if a farmer wanted to do this, there was little a wife could do to prevent him—but the complaints of some of the cooperative's members indicate that quite a few of them believed that many of these women were responsible for undermining the Tri-State. "There are women, too numerous to mention," one Virginia farm woman complained in 1925, "who are claiming that they own the team and everything (or allowing the men to say they do, which amounts to the same thing) in order to put the tobacco on the auction floor, and there are others who 'claim' to be hiring men of the family to make tobacco for them." It is impossible to know the extent to which these farm women debilitated the cooperative by allowing their husbands to sell tobacco in their names; nevertheless, their lack of support for the cooperative was seen as unladylike, un-Christian, and counter to women's "natural" interests in the improvement of their home and families. "I'll say you are no Christians who will do such things," the Virginia writer concluded, "or will even allow them to be done by members of your family without doing all in your power to prevent it."[42]

Conclusion

An organization devoted to reshaping the economics of tobacco marketing is in many ways an odd place to look to understand women's

42. Mrs. W. E. Blankenship, letter to the editor, *Tri-State Tobacco Grower*, August 1925.

contributions to tobacco agriculture. Yet the history of the Tri-State Tobacco Growers' Cooperative reveals that women were central to the bright tobacco economy that dominated the South's eastern seaboard in the early twentieth century. Farm women's labor was crucial to the production of the crop; at the same time, dealing with the poverty of low prices fell largely on their shoulders. The Tri-State's organizers and supporters understood this, and they regularly reached out to farm women to enlist their support. They did so in terms that highlighted farm women's domestic concerns: the challenges of providing for their families, the welfare of the children, and their fears of falling behind their urban sisters. Hundreds of women responded to the cooperative's call to arms and helped to shape its rhetoric and its mission. No longer just a marketing organization, the Tri-State became a missionary vehicle for providing rural reform.

Not all, or even most, farm women responded to the Tri-State's call for reform, however. These women demonstrate that farm women's experiences and expectations were varied. Though denigrated as not being "true women" by some in the cooperative, noncooperating women nevertheless were as integrally tied to tobacco agriculture. They believed, however, that the ready cash offered on the auction floors best met their interests. As the Tri-State fell on hard times and fell behind on its payments to farmers, such sentiment grew as farm women recognized their families needed money in hand more than promises of a better future.

The Tri-State Tobacco Growers' Cooperative would have failed with or without the support of farm women; it simply had too many external enemies and too little internal support to overturn the auction system. Its demise, however, might have come more quickly without the dedicated work of hundreds of farm women throughout Virginia and the Carolinas. Farm women's work on the farm did not end with the Tri-State's failure, of course, and neither did their work in the community.

ANN E. McCLEARY

"Seizing the Opportunity"

Home Demonstration Curb Markets in Virginia

Early on a spring morning in April 1930, on the Saturday before Easter, approximately fifty women gathered on a vacant lot next to the firehouse in downtown Staunton, Virginia, the prosperous county seat of Augusta County, in the heart of the Shenandoah Valley of Virginia. All of the women came into the city from the countryside; some lived on farms and others in the small villages and towns that dotted the rural landscape. These were middle-aged, married women, who each brought along her husband or a daughter or two to help her. For many, their trip to the county seat was not a common occurrence; they could count the number of times they went to town every year on one hand. Work and family demanded their attention and time on the farm, and even had they wanted to go to town more often, few could drive their family cars, if they had one. An aura of excitement prevailed as each woman set up her own card table along the sidewalk and carefully arranged a selection of food she brought from home. Some displayed butter or eggs fresh from the farm, some their favorite home-baked cakes or pies, the ones that their family and friends raved about and that they served on holidays and special occasions. As they hurried to finish their displays, with the smells of fresh bread and cakes permeating the air, the women exchanged news and shared their anxieties about how the morning would go. The noise of clucking chickens resounded amid the lively

97

chatter of the women's voices, as Regina Hutchens carried in several wooden crates of live chickens and placed them by her mother's table.[1]

Town residents began to drift over to the vacant lot, even before the farm women were ready, eyeing the home-grown and home-prepared goods carefully packaged and marked with the producer's name and proudly exhibited on their tables. By the time the market opened at eight, a large crowd had gathered and cars lined the entire block. Five hundred town residents walked along the sidewalk, stopping at the individual tables to view the goods and to praise the farm women on their work and selecting items to purchase for their own families' tables. Within an hour, the farm women sold everything they brought, earning almost $150 in total sales, an impressive amount of money during the Depression years when dollars were hard to come by. Although disappointed to turn away customers, the women were pleased and quite surprised at the success they experienced on the first day of their new market. As they packed up their tables and headed back to their country homes, they must have realized that their new curb market would prove to be a tremendous success.[2]

The fifty or so women who came to Staunton on that April Saturday in 1930 and the others who would soon join them on the market participated in the county home demonstration program, which organized the curb market. Over the previous two or three decades, these women had witnessed dramatic changes in rural life and agricultural practices that affected their economic status on the farm and social standing in the community. The growth in men's commodity production overshadowed women's subsistence production, making

1. Virginia Cooperative Extension Service, *Extension Division News* 12:9 (July 1930): 2; Annual Report, Home Demonstration Work, Augusta County, VA, 1930, included in U.S. Department of Agriculture, Extension Service Annual Reports, Record Group 33, National Archives and Records Administration, College Park, MD; Hutchens Kesterson, interview by McCleary, March 10, 1993, Spottswood, VA, Augusta County Historical Society Archives, Staunton, VA (hereafter ACHSA). Although all agents—from county agents to state specialists—were required to file annual reports, the footnotes for "Annual Report" refer to Augusta County home demonstration agent annual reports unless otherwise noted.

2. Annual Report, 1930; *Extension Division News* 12:9 (July 1930): 2.

the cash their husbands and fathers earned the primary focus of the farm. Farm women had little power over these earnings, but they valued their contributions to the farm through butter and eggs sales and they had been able to maintain some control over their butter and egg income. By the early twentieth century, changes in agricultural practices and improved transportation, including the railroad and the automobile, had begun to transform even the production and marketing of their poultry and dairy products. Farm women also lost access to the use of their income, as marketing shifted from country stores to distant markets in which their husbands engaged. By participating in the curb market, Augusta County women hoped to regain some measure of economic control over their lives, allowing them to expand their production, to shift the marketing of their home-produced goods back into their own hands, and to gain a cash income over which they could have greater control.

Equally important was their desire to gain respect in their families and communities as partners and producers on the modern farm. The curb markets the women created in Augusta County reflected their yearning for the more recognized productive role that they once had on the farm. In their club projects, Augusta County members eagerly embraced the idea of home production, whether increasing their production of vegetables for sale or "improving" a room through their own labor. Drawing on modern technology and new business practices, the curb market reflects a blend of the modern idea of the farm woman as businessperson intertwined with a traditional perspective of the farm woman as producer. Besides becoming local celebrities, praised for their devotion to traditional rural values of hard work and dedication to the family farm, Augusta County club women who sold on the curb market earned the economic resources to secure their middle-class status in the rapidly changing world of the rural South between the two world wars.[3]

3. This essay comes from a larger study that attempts to look at the home demonstration program from the ground up in a community-based approach; see McCleary, "Shaping a New Role for the Rural Woman: Home Demonstration Work in Augusta County, Virginia, 1917–1940" (PhD diss., Brown University, 1996).

Participating in a curb market was a new experience for these Augusta County farm women, but such markets were not unfamiliar to rural people. Public markets, where farm families could sell their goods, date back to the colonial period, when cities like Staunton built market houses designed for this purpose. Throughout the nineteenth century, many communities across the country boasted some sort of farm market. The idea of a curb market developed and operated solely by women—like the Staunton market—did not became popular until the early twentieth century with the creation of the U.S. Department of Agriculture's (USDA) home demonstration program. The home economists who implemented this program advocated remunerative work for rural women, arguing that they needed to become more involved in commodity work to ensure equality on the modern farm. To this end, home demonstration agents devised and promoted a variety of strategies to develop and expand farm women's income-producing activities.[4]

The USDA's Agricultural Extension program reflected the broader ideas of uplift and reform that characterized the Progressive Era. Reformers defined rural life as a "problem" in modern America, and President Theodore Roosevelt established the Commission on Country Life in 1908 to find a solution. The result was a government program—the Cooperative Extension Service—established in 1914 by the Smith-Lever Act. This program supplied matching funds for each state land-grant college to establish clubs and educational programs for rural men, women, and children through which they could teach modern practices in farming and homemaking. While male agents stressed farm practices, female agents organized home demonstration clubs for women and 4-H Clubs for girls to "demonstrate" the new home economics lessons. Although scholars have criticized the extension program for its manipulative nature and self-serving goals, the program could not have achieved the success it did if no rural

4. Grace Townley, *Program for Home Demonstration Clubs,* Bulletin no. 57 (Blacksburg: Virginia Agricultural Extension, January 1920); *Extension Division News* 16:4 (February 1934): 1; Ella Agnew, "Home Demonstration Work," in *Three Years of Extension Work in Agriculture and Home Economics in Virginia,* edited by Jesse Jones (Blacksburg: Virginia Extension Service, May 1919), 56.

people participated or joined the clubs. Club membership in Augusta County never exceeded 10 percent of the white rural women in the 1920s and 1930s, but those mostly middle-class and ambitious women and girls who did enroll believed that the program fitted their needs and that it could help them achieve their personal goals.

Augusta County had long been recognized for its successful, progressive farms. Scotch-Irish and German settlers poured into the Shenandoah Valley from Pennsylvania in the mid-eighteenth century, as proprietors of large land grants recruited farm families to take up these fertile new lands at inexpensive prices. By the early nineteenth century, Augusta County farmers prospered by cultivating wheat as a cash crop, but they supplemented it with mixed-agricultural practices to create a balanced operation. The large brick and frame houses built in the nineteenth century testify to the valley's economic prosperity, producing a large percentage of middle-class farm families who owned their farms. By the 1920s, Augusta County had become one of the leading agricultural counties in Virginia and its annual county fair one of the largest in the state. As one observer noted in 1928:

> In any description of these people, one always finds them depicted as thrifty, progressive, and far-seeing. This is especially true from an agricultural standpoint, for the farmers who come from the famous thrifty Scotch-Irish or Dutch stock have learned to make the best of their soil and have tilled the soil along the most progressive and modern lines, with the result that . . . they have made our section one of the richest and most steadily prosperous parts of the country.[5]

Home demonstration work gained a strong foothold in Augusta County because its message appealed to many of its white, middle-class rural women. Raised in progressive farm households and steeped in the values of hard work that had long gained them respectability

5. Clay Catlett and Elliot G. Fishburne, *An Economic and Social Survey of Augusta County*, University of Virginia Record Extension Services 12, no. 7 (Charlottesville: University of Virginia, January 1928), 119; Robert Mitchell, *Commercialism and Frontier* (Charlottesville: University Press of Virginia, 1977), 183.

even among their urban peers, these women saw the home demonstration program as an opportunity to improve their status in the community. Like other rural women across the country, those in Augusta County found themselves in uncertain times in the 1920s and 1930s. Was their hard work still valued and appreciated? Did their familiar role as farm women still earn them the same respect? Though attracted to the new consumer culture of the period, their shrinking farm incomes during the 1920s did not enable them to acquire the same conveniences as their city friends, from running water and electricity to new furnishings for their living rooms. How might they find a way to engage in the new "culture of abundance"? Through home demonstration work, some of the more ambitious middle-class farm women and girls found an opportunity to mediate between these two worlds and to create a new vision for the modern farm women that embraced elements of both roles. The curb market became one of the central vehicles through which they would claim this middle road.

❧

Participants in the curb market recount different stories for its origins than Augusta County's home demonstration agent in 1930. Agent Ruth Jamison claims credit in an oral history interview for suggesting a curb market. The Depression hit Augusta County, she recalled, and the families with whom she worked struggled to make ends meet. "They were pretty bad off," Jamison remembered. "I had a council, the leading women from different communities would come in and plan the programs, and one woman said, 'The sheriff is taking our farms away from us because we can't pay our taxes. . . . We can live because we have enough food, but we can't pay our taxes.'" In response, Jamison suggested that they create a curb market, claiming this was an idea that "she had picked up in a magazine or something; there were markets various places." She believed that the market would be successful because Augusta County women made "the best food I ever ate," especially their cakes, bread, and pies. "So I said, now will you come in and help us to start this curb market? I told them what I had seen that they had made, and now I want you to bring that and bring all your surplus. . . . If you don't want to come to the curb market, that's alright, but I want you to help me start it."[6]

Reflecting back on the forty-year history of club work in Augusta County in 1958, several of the longtime club members wrote a play for their celebration, and the curb market figured prominently in the story. Noting that their "good reputation made a market for rural members," the play describes the beginning of the curb market:

> It must have been by the late twenties that our much loved Mrs. Coiner had heard of a country woman who brought her home-made butter to town and could not sell it. From this event Mrs. Coiner began thinking and soon afterwards read of such an organization in other parts of the country. She contacted our Home Demonstration agent—then Miss Ruth Jamison. They together studied, worked and toiled over their plot until they decided to go to the mayor of Staunton for assistance.

This description is significant for two reasons. First, the club women considered the curb market *their* idea. As farm women from more progressive farm families, they had likely read about such markets in the agricultural press, since they were more likely than other farm families to receive agricultural magazines in their households. As club members, they received the *Extension Division News,* published by Virginia's Cooperative Extension Office, a publication that promoted women's remunerative work and bragged about other such markets in the state. Second, the curb market offered an opportunity for club members to take charge of the inequities that they experienced in the marketing system available to them.[7]

Though Jamison wished to claim credit for the market years later,

6. Jamison, interview by McCleary, January 23, 1981, Blacksburg, VA, ACHSA.

7. Untitled script for play to celebrate forty years of home demonstration work, manuscript preserved in Middlebrook Home Demonstration Club scrapbook in possession of author; "Homemakers to Tell 40 Year HD Clubs' History, November 12," undated newspaper article in Middlebrook scrapbook; Annual Report, 1930.

her 1930 annual report reveals that the club women's account of its establishment is more accurate. In that report, Jamison wrote that the idea of the curb market came from an advisory committee meeting that included both her and one woman from each of the clubs, noting, "Early in the spring, the Advisory Board stated that the thing most needed in this county was a curb market on which the women could dispose of surplus products which the town merchants would not buy from them." Not only did they come up with the idea, but they also lobbied hard to get what they wanted. The club women proceeded carefully with their plans, devising strategies by which they could gain support from the city council to provide the resources they needed. They appointed a committee to present their idea to the council, and these committee members met with each council member individually to gain their support in advance of the city council meeting.[8]

Significantly, one of the concerns that sparked the club women to organize the market was the issue of marketing *butter*, one of women's traditional home products. For these women, butter symbolized the transformation that had occurred in the production and marketing of their household goods during the early years of the twentieth century and demonstrated the extent to which they had begun to lose control over their traditional sources of income. Practitioners of commercial agriculture depreciated women's work as a "sideline to the primary farm operation" and women's income as "pin money" or "egg money." Although men did not calculate the value of women's subsistence work in the same way as commodity production, women still considered their work important to the farm economy. In times of financial crisis on the farm, it was often the money earned through women's labor that kept the farm insulated from debt.[9]

Augusta County women participated actively in both dairy and poultry production and sales in the late nineteenth and early twentieth centuries. Butter, a principal local and export trade item in the

8. Annual Report, 1930.
9. Nancy Grey Osterud, *Bonds of Community: The Lives of Farm Women in Nineteenth-Century New York* (Ithaca, NY: Cornell University Press, 1991), 209, 146–47; Edward L. Ayers, *The Promise of the New South* (New York: Oxford University Press, 1992), 205.

Shenandoah Valley in the colonial period, remained a major market commodity in the late nineteenth century. By 1860, 98 percent of Augusta County farms had milk cows, averaging 4.2 cows per farm and three hundred pounds of butter per year. More than half of county farms produced enough butter to sell. Although dairy work was a shared activity on the farm, with men providing the food and shelter for the cows and cleaning the stable, women controlled milking the cows and producing butter or cheese. They might assign some of the dairying tasks to hired hands or children, but they usually performed the more skilled jobs, such as churning butter. In contrast to dairy work, women took on the primary responsibility for the family's poultry operation, from feeding the chickens to gathering eggs, often supervising children or hired hands in this work. Women used butter and eggs to trade at the country store for items they did not produce, such as cotton, buttons, thread, candlewick, or soda. Whereas a portion of butter sales typically contributed to the general farm operation, women often considered the "egg money" their own, and they had greater control over its use. Augusta County women took great pride in their products and their profits. As Ora Thompson Lotts remembered, "That's what we lived off of."[10]

Even before the advent of the curb market, farm women sold other products besides butter and eggs, marketing any surplus goods after meeting family needs. An account book kept by Fannie Wampler, who lived with another unmarried sister and her brother's family on the family farm, reveals the wide array of items farm women might sell. Her 1919 account lists sales predominantly of chicks and butter

10. Mitchell, *Commercialism and Frontier*, 183; Nancy Sorrells, *Dairying on the American Farm* (Staunton, VA: Museum of American Frontier Culture, 1993), 2–5; Amos Long, *The Pennsylvania German Family Farm* (Breinigsville, PA: Pennsylvania German Society, 1971), 115, 419–23; Joan Jensen, *Loosening the Bonds: Mid-Atlantic Farm Women, 1750–1850* (New Haven, CT: Yale University Press, 1986), 93; Osterud, *Bonds of Community*, 211; Parnassus General Store Account Book, January 1860–1861, 22, Virginia State Archives, Richmond; Ayers, *Promise of the New South*, 90; Nancy Sorrells and Linda Petzke, *The General Store* (Staunton, VA: Museum of American Frontier Culture, April 30, 1990); Lotts, interview by McCleary, March 10, 1993, Spottswood, VA, ACHSA.

but also of walnuts, apples, bacon, potatoes, onions, onion sets, one calf, and eight lambs and ewes. In 1920, she lists total sales of $375 in eggs, $101 in hens and chicks, $78 in butter and cream, and $737 in "other products," for a yearly income of $1,192. Her income, though considerable, was seasonal: for example, butter sales began May 11 and extended through November, with only one entry for December and one for January, and sales of produce occurred while the items were in season.[11]

Wampler's account illustrates women's continued dependence on poultry and dairy products into the twentieth century, but it also exposes significant changes occurring in the marketing of women's goods. The railroad and automobile opened up a wider network of competitive markets, pulling trade away from the country store. Wampler could participate in these new markets because she had a car and could travel to the burgeoning railroad towns like Weyers Cave, only ten miles from her farm. Established in the 1870s along the Norfolk and Western Railroad, Weyers Cave exemplifies the regional trading centers that emerged and attracted business away from the country stores in the early twentieth century. Weyers Cave had three or four country stores at any one time, accepting butter, eggs, poultry, bacon, dried apples, and walnut kernels, many of the same items Wampler sold, at competitive prices. By the 1910s and 1920s, specialized agricultural enterprises like creameries, poultry plants, and canneries opened, offering opportunities for farm families to sell other types of agricultural products. Weyers Cave Creamery bought cream instead of butter, sending trucks "over a wide area" to collect from farms, while the Wrenn Brothers started a poultry business that purchased eggs and poultry.[12]

Wampler now had a choice as to where she could sell her goods and what she could sell, whether butter or cream, and she could select the business that offered her the best price rather than simply depending on the country store. Her account book also reveals that these

11. Wampler, Account Book, 1919–1920, Wampler Family Papers, in possession of Wampler family, Mount Solon, VA.
12. Harold E. Skelton, *Weyers Cave's First Century* (Broadway, VA: Branner Printing Services, 1974), 12, 28–29, 35, 42.

businesses paid cash rather than offering credit. A nascent business-woman, Wampler kept close monthly tallies not only of her profits but also of her expenses. Although she was able to increase her pro-ceeds by traveling to more distant markets like Weyers Cave, she also incurred more expenses; her account book includes a list of car repairs, totaling $259, for 1920. Just as the automobile helped to bring busi-ness to these larger towns in the county, it was only a matter of time before that business would move into even larger markets. By the 1930s, Augusta County farm families began to shift their trade farther away to the larger county seat of Staunton.[13]

Whereas Wampler profited from these new opportunities to expand her business, in part because she had a car but also because she was single and could make her own business decisions, most women lost control over the process. By the 1930s, the marketing of home goods involved more time, travel, and business expertise to maximize profits, and fathers and husbands, in their minds more knowledgeable and experienced, assumed this additional responsibility. Frieda Kiracofe Miller recalled that her mother traded eggs at the country store near her house in the 1920s, because it was within walking distance, but her father marketed her mother's other goods at more distant mar-kets, such as the surplus produce that he took to the new cannery in Bridgewater. When a creamery opened in Mount Solon and her fam-ily began to sell cream rather than butter, her father transported the cream. Regina Hutchens Kesterson's father took their family's cream and butter to Staunton and the turkeys and chickens to the railroad town of Stuarts Draft, because her mother, who birthed seven chil-dren in ten years, was too busy at home to go with him. Even when husbands developed weekly trade routes in the county seat of Staunton, they seldom took their wives with them. Virginia Stickley Berry's father "went to town once a week in the spring wagon," where he had regular customers for butter, eggs, strawberries, and garden produce, but his wife accompanied him only occasionally to get goods and clothes for the family. Although Augusta County women had never had complete control over the profits from selling their butter, eggs,

13. Wampler, Account Book.

produce, or other home-grown or home-produced foods, what lever-age they had once enjoyed was quickly evaporating by the time of the Great Depression.[14]

✙

Home demonstration agents recognized the precarious situation in which farm women found themselves in the early years of the twen-tieth century. The idea that rural women and girls were entitled to accumulate and control their own income—and that they should have access to activities that would help them make money—underscored many of the projects promoted by extension home economists as well as some contemporary rural reformers. At the 1909 Virginia Rural Life Conference, Superintendent of Public Instruction J. D. Eggleston proposed how the newly established extension program could help women: "Women's industries should be recognized, whereby through central agencies the women of the various communities may be able to sell at a reasonable profit needlework, baskets, chickens, eggs, canned fruits, preserves, and other things which women know so well how to make, but which cannot be disposed of except through some central agency. If organized in the right way, these various industries will suc-ceed."[15] Because the extension service considered women's work as separate from men's, it was easier for extension home economists to declare that the income women made was their money, no doubt rec-ognizing that this had not always been the case in farm households.

Home demonstration agents encouraged club women and girls to utilize their traditional household industries to produce a surplus that could be sold for income. Club programs emphasized using modern technology and scientific methods to improve the quality and quan-

14. Frieda Kiracofe Miller, interview by McCleary, March 10, 1993, Bridge-water, VA, ACHSA; Kesterson interview; Berry, interview by Ann McCleary, July 13, 1993, Spring Hill, VA, ACHSA; Lucille Berry Masincupp, interview by McCleary, June 16, 1994, Spring Hill, VA, ACHSA; Lotts interview.

15. F. E. Ward, *The Farm Woman's Problems,* Circular 148 (Washington, DC: USDA Agricultural Extension Department, 1920), 11; Eggleston, "The Possi-bilities of Extension Work in Virginia," in *Addresses Delivered at the University of Virginia Summer School in Connection with the Conference for the Study of the Problems of Rural Life* (Charlottesville: University of Virginia, 1909), 13–14.

tity of goods for sale. Home demonstration agents began by organizing tomato clubs in the 1910s to inspire teenage girls to grow, can, and market tomatoes using modern scientific and sanitary methods and equipment, but one of the primary goals was to produce an income. Virginia's first state home demonstration agent, Ella Agnew, advocated at a 1912 rural life conference that "the country girl is a vital part of the county," and it is important for her to be able to "make an independent living and still stay at home." Agnew believed that each girl could produce $27.50 on her recommended one-tenth-acre plot of tomatoes. Ultimately, agents hoped that new canning techniques and marketing programs would help rural girls and women "turn fruits and vegetables into making money."[16]

Extension agents promoted similar activities for women, urging them to increase the output of their traditional activities, from gardening, poultry, and dairy to handicrafts like lace making or embroidery. By the 1920s, the home demonstration program required that each club engage in remunerative work. To become a "standard club," at least half of its members needed to carry on at least one profit-making project. The Centerville club secretary noted in the club's 1923 record book that one of its monthly topics "will be developed as it effects efficiency, increase of income, and general well-being." The club listed a variety of moneymaking projects in its annual report two years later, noting that among its members, "eight are country housekeepers and carry on remunerative projects such as raising chickens, turkeys, and selling cream and butter."[17]

Like Fannie Wampler, Centerville club women produced both butter and cream for sale. Ironically, as creameries emerged in towns and cities in the 1920s, home demonstration agents still promoted butter

16. See B. B. Knapp and M. E. Creswell, "Effect of Home Demonstration Work on the Community and the County in the South," *USDA Yearbook* (Washington, DC: Government Printing Office, 1916); Agnew, "Girls Canning Clubs," *Alumni Bulletin* (University of Virginia) 4 (August 1912): 421–24; *Extension Division News* 3:6 (April 1921): 3.

17. *Extension Division News* 8:4 (February 1926): 8; Annual Reports of the Spring Hill Home Demonstration Club, 1925 and 1928, Augusta County Extension Office Archives, Verona, VA.

production as an avenue for income. Virginia state director Maude Wallace argued that home demonstration work should guide women in "selecting, feeding and handling the family cow; in the care and use of the milk supply; in the making of butter; and in the sale of surplus products of the cow." USDA agent Grace Frysinger described a 1922 nationwide campaign that resulted in three million pounds of butter prepared "under supervision of the home demonstration agent."[18]

Yet during these same years, agricultural extension agents advocated commercial dairy operations among farmers, a change that would result in the elimination of women's home butter production in favor of commercial dairies. Augusta County farmers, familiar with raising livestock and intrigued with progressive agricultural ideas, enthusiastically embraced dairy work. As early as 1918, county agricultural agent Percy Manley observed that "several farmers are beginning to make dairying the major industry on their farm." Recognizing the trend toward commercial dairies, home demonstration agents developed a compromise. At the same time that she promoted home butter production, USDA home economist Florence Ward wrote that it could be more effective to send the cream to market rather than to make butter in the home. She tried to put the best light on this new situation, observing that income from cream sales "is usually greater than making and selling butter." It went without saying that selling cream saved women the time required in producing butter, but it also offered them less access to the income they earned. Creameries typically sent a check to the farm each month rather than providing a credit they could use at the country store. The emergence of creameries was the first, but not the only, development that threatened women's home butter trade. By the 1930s, margarine became widely available. But home demonstration agents' continued push for home production through the 1920s and 1930s reveals that they were not

18. *Extension Division News* 3:6 (April 1921): 3; O. B. Martin and Ola Powell, "Home Demonstration Bears Fruit in the South," *USDA Yearbook* (Washington, DC: Government Printing Office, 1920), 121; Townley, *Program for Clubs;* Grace Frysinger, *Home Demonstration Work,* U.S. Department of Agriculture, Circular 314 (Washington, DC: U.S. Department of Agriculture, 1922), 37.

willing to give up butter production without resistance. As with the farm women, butter seemed to symbolize home production to the agents, even though it would have been much easier for farm women to simply sell the cream.[19]

Although they sought to preserve home butter production, extension home economists recognized that there was greater potential for women to earn money by raising poultry. Unlike dairy work, poultry had not been commercialized to any great extent by the 1920s, so it remained firmly in women's control. The swelling cities brought a growing demand for both eggs and chickens, increasing the possibilities for income. To make poultry work more profitable, home demonstration agents expected women to lead a major transformation of the home poultry operation so that they could raise larger and more productive flocks and generate more income. They encouraged club members to create a standard-bred flock that could produce better-graded eggs, to raise good brooding hens through artificial incubation, to cull the flocks and eliminate unproductive birds, and to remodel or build new poultry houses that would confine the birds so they could be fed a more nutritious feed. Though collecting the eggs did not require much time, the new poultry practices required farm women and girls to commit more energy up front to meet higher poultry expectations. As Virginia Stickley Berry, a 4-H girl at the time, recalled, "You had to work with chickens, so you had to spend time with them." Still, Augusta County women and girls embraced poultry work: they consistently appear among the leading producers in the state's "farm flock improvement" contests to "make the flock pay" in the 1920s. Augusta County club woman Mrs. W. F. Howe led poultry production in Virginia in 1923 with an average of 229 to 249 eggs for each of her sixty hens, earning her $126 that year. Helen Teass, the county agent in 1923, recalled, "In discussing extension work with a prominent farmer, the whole country seems to be going crazy over poultry raising!" Poultry became the most lucrative club project for both

19. Annual Report, agricultural agent in Augusta County, 1916, 1918; Mildred Payne, personal communication with author, January 22, 1981, Blacksburg, VA; Ward, *The Farm Woman's Problems*, 11.

women and girls in the 1920s, netting $31,674 in annual proceeds throughout Virginia by 1927.[20]

As part of home demonstration clubs' experimentation with poultry, Ruth Wampler, a farm girl from neighboring Rockingham County, successfully raised a flock of artificially brooded turkeys for her 4-H project in 1926. Wampler's successful poultry project would become one of the events that turned the tables on home poultry operations, shifting it from women's work to a commercial business managed by men. Writing two years after Wampler's project, economist Clay Catlet predicted the change that would soon come about in Augusta County and other rural regions: "Heretofore poultry has often been looked upon as a source of 'pin money' for the farmer's wife, but of recent years, a great expansion in the industry, on a commercial scale, has taken place and the huge, aggregate economic returns from this source are now being well appreciated." By the 1930s, recognizing that poultry could present a considerable income for farmers, particularly around Rockingham County where Ruth's father, Charles W. Wampler, established a thriving poultry business, agricultural extension agents began to advocate commercial poultry work. The Poultry Department at the state extension office turned its attention away from home flocks to commercial poultry operations, redirecting its advice in the *Extension Division News* poultry column from women to men. In 1930, the year that the Staunton curb market opened, both of the leading sources of income for women—butter and poultry—were increasingly becoming men's commodity production.[21]

❦

20. *Extension Division News* 3:6 (April 1921): 3; Ward, *The Farm Woman's Problems,* 11; Annual Report, 1922; Townley, *Program for Clubs;* Martin and Powell, "Home Demonstration Bears Fruit," 118; *Extension Division News* 7:2 (December 1924): 2; Frysinger, *Home Demonstration Work,* 37; Berry interview; John Hutchison, *Extension Work in Agriculture and Home Economics in Virginia, 1927,* Bulletin no. 105 (Blacksburg: Virginia Extension Service, August 1928); Long, *Family Farm,* 425–26.

21. Catlett and Fishburne, *Economic and Social Survey,* 89; Alpha Gamma Chapter of Epsilon Sigma Phi, *College of the Fields: Some Highlights of the Virginia Cooperative Extension Service, 1914–1980,* Publication 478–025 (Blacksburg: Virginia Cooperative Extension Service, 1987), 146.

Although circumstances surrounding the establishment of Augusta County's first curb market cannot be fully unraveled, the narratives provided by the agent and by the club members reveal the significant issues that triggered its establishment. Although home demonstration agents promoted markets as early as the 1910s, it was not until the club women saw the need or had the desire for such an endeavor that they would ultimately establish them. County home demonstration agent Ruth Jamison subscribed to the extension belief that rural women should be able to earn their own money. Through her training, she heard Virginia's home demonstration director, Grace Townley, and home management specialist, Mary Settle, promote "cooperative marketing" in the 1920s as a way for women to take control of the sale of their goods. The fact that Augusta County women and girls responded so enthusiastically to club programs designed to increase home production suggests that this message resonated with them as well. The farm depression of the 1920s weakened the already fragile economic situation for most farm families, and rural women were unable to afford many consumer goods even had they wanted them. But oral history interviews suggest that it was more than their desire for cash that inspired these women to engage in remunerative work. Augusta County women had earned valuable reputations as hardworking and thrifty farm women, and they valued this reputation. At a time when city women bought popular consumer goods, farm women still prided themselves on making much of what they needed, even if it was partly out of economic necessity. They considered their productive work as a significant contribution to the farm. By 1930, the frustration over the changes in women's productive roles, symbolized by butter, fueled the fire that led to the creation of the Staunton curb market.[22]

The Staunton market became an instant success, attracting new vendors and customers. According to one account, "New faces appear . . . on each market day." Some farm women joined home demonstration clubs just so they could sell on the market, sparking a boom

22. Townley, *Program for Clubs; Extension Division News* 16:4 (February 1934): 1; Agnew, "Home Demonstration Work," 56.

in club membership. Total sales increased to $135 to $140 per week by July. Although the market closed for the winter, some club women took orders and delivered goods over these months, netting more than $1,500. When the curb market reopened in the spring of 1931, it had moved to an indoor location in a vacant store on Central Avenue where it could be open year-round. During the summer, the market expanded to include Wednesday as well as Saturday sales. The popularity of the Staunton market led club women who lived in the eastern part of the county to create their own market in Waynesboro.[23]

Although Jamison initiated the curb market through her office, club women ran it with little day-to-day involvement from the agent. Jamison appointed five club women to a market committee and charged them with drawing up "articles of agreement" for participating vendors and ensuring that all participants followed these rules. Besides setting the hours and responsibilities of the market committee and the newly appointed market manager, the regulations required women to follow the prices posted on the bulletin board each day and set a minimum "rent" each vendor had to pay per day to sell on the market, fifteen cents a day at first but then dropping to ten cents by summer. Regarding what they could sell, Jamison claimed that she had to approve the products women sold, recalling, "Nobody could come and put just any old food on." If so, there is no written record of this requirement. Instead, the last market rule stated, "Each marketer must stand responsible for the quality of goods sold on this market. Every purchase must carry the name of the seller." Essentially, the market embodied a Darwinian perspective: only the best-quality goods would survive. As Jamison wrote that first year, "Since each package contained the name of the producer those selling inferior products were soon weeded out."[24]

The curb market offered an opportunity for farm women to regain control over the sale of their dairy and poultry products, but it also reversed the current trends in how they sold them. Instead of selling

23. *Extension Division News* 12:9 (July 1930): 2; Annual Reports, 1930–1932; Masincupp interview.

24. Annual Report, 1930; Jamison, interview by McCleary, October 3, 1993, Rocky Mount, VA, ACHSA.

cream, vendors found a ready market for their "country" butter among city women, encouraging farm women to *increase* their home butter production. Rather than selling live chickens to the country stores or poultry businesses, farm women found that city women wanted "dressed poultry," killed, defeathered, cleaned, and ready to cook. Dressing poultry was a time-consuming and unpleasant task that most women dreaded, but farm women found relief by delegating this work to their husbands or children. One daughter of a curb market vendor recalled that her mother gave her and her two sisters ten cents for each chicken they dressed. The only product that remained unchanged was fresh eggs, but because these were in such high demand, women sought to increase their yield.[25]

The market carried far more than the dairy and poultry products women previously traded at the country store: farm women introduced a much wider assortment of goods than they had ever sold before. Ruth Jamison praised their "unusual initiative in the products that they have sold." They continued to trade their surplus produce, like Fannie Wampler had, but now they expanded their garden output by producing a greater quantity and variety of vegetables and promoting new kinds of foods that "could not otherwise have been disposed of for cash." They supplemented the sale of cultivated vegetables with wild plants they collected, including bittersweet, sassafras roots, and watercress. Avid horticulturalists, Augusta County women also brought some of their favorite flowers, small shrubs, and perennials in the spring and summer and wreaths and Christmas trees "for the table" in December. Recalling that they made "the best food I ever ate," Jamison encouraged women to make their favorite baked goods. Many vendors produced trendy new specialties, such as potato chips, which gained popularity in the 1920s but were not mass-produced until the 1930s. Some women incorporated foods promoted by home demonstration agents, like cottage cheese advocated through extension nutrition and dairy programs. Hazel Van Lear's comment, "We

25. Annual Reports, 1930, 1934; Jamison interview, January 23, 1981; Kesterson interview; Mary McCormick, personal communication with author, July 6, 1993; *Extension Division News* 18:4 (February 1936): 4.

sold everything that we didn't need," reverberated over and over again among the participating curb market vendors, who brought everything from jelly to puppies.[26]

Cakes, pies, rolls, salt-rising bread, cream puffs, doughnuts, and other baked goods highlighted the curb markets, reinforcing what the club women considered their "good reputations" as cooks. Most club women specialized in some varieties of baked goods, some drawn from old family recipes and others from popular trends and new cookbooks. Ina Berry and her daughter Edith earned a reputation for their "delicious cakes," including their family recipes for caramel and chocolate cakes as well as the new southern cake called "Lady Baltimore," popularized by Owen Wister in his 1906 novel of the same name; its variation called the "Lord Baltimore" cake; and one known as "Brown Stone Front," a traditional Amish cake recipe that may have been popular with some of the county's Mennonite and Amish populations. Hazel Van Lear claimed an old-fashioned pound cake as her forte, while Louie Ware straddled the fence between old and new, producing both the traditional chocolate cake and the popular new chiffon cake. Lucille Berry Masincupp specialized in pies, especially chocolate, coconut, and butterscotch. Annual reports consistently boast about the sales of baked goods. In 1930, one woman reported selling forty-eight pies on one Saturday, and another claimed to have sold $475 worth of cakes in one summer. "She says she can hardly take care of any more business," wrote Jamison.[27]

Women used the smells and sights of their home-produced goods to attract city people to the market. Several brought cooked home-cured hams and cut them there for the customers. As Jamison recounts,

26. Annual Reports, 1930–1933; Van Lear, interview by McCleary, June 14, 1994, Spring Hill, VA, ACHSA; Mary Katherine Weaver, personal communication with author, January 20, 1993, Centerville, VA.

27. Annual Reports, 1930–31; *Extension Division News* 14:8 (June 1932): 5; *Extension Division News* 15:10 (August 1933): 3; *Extension Division News* 18:4 (February 1936): 4; Berry interview; Van Lear, interview by McCleary, July 13, 1993, Spring Hill, VA, ACHSA; Ware, interview by McCleary, Spring Hill, VA, July 9, 1993, ACHSA; Masincupp interview; Jamison interview, January 23, 1981.

"As soon as [the customers] would come in, they would smell the ham, and the line would line up all the way around to here to get that ham, and of course that was a smart woman to sell that." Augusta County women used fresh-cut flowers to lure customers, collecting the blossoms from redbud and dogwood trees as well as trillium and lady's slippers and producing special winter bouquets. Although flowers did not garner large incomes, they cost little to collect, and, Jamison wrote, the women "took much pleasure in their work with them." An article in the *Extension Division News* described the Staunton curb market as a "flower shop," noting that "these ingenious women have found that the flowers get the customers there."[28]

The sight of freshly cut flowers, the smells of home-cured hams, and the display of homemade cakes and pies projected an aura of nostalgia that contributed to the success of the market. In the midst of the Great Depression, Americans became more introspective, questioning the growing materialism of an industrial society. Old-fashioned items like bittersweet, watercress, "country" butter, or home-baked caramel cake appealed to city residents longing for traditional fare for their tables at a time when factory-processed food had become commonplace in the stores. As they strolled through the market, city women could choose from a wide array of home-produced items they remembered from their childhood in a modern setting. Club members also boasted that the healthiness of their foods contributed to the market's success, writing in their 1958 play that "all of our club members and market customers have school girl complexions." The curb market's popularity can be attributed to more than nostalgia, however; economic and demographic reasons contributed to its success as well. According to state agent Maude Wallace, city women were losing their hired help who assisted in food production during the Depression years. "As the city housewives had to dismiss their

28. Annual Reports, 1930, 1934, 1938; *Extension Division News* 15:3 (March 1933): 1; *Extension Division News* 16:4 (April 1934): 4; Jamison interview, January 23, 1981; Regina Hutchens Kesterson, interview by McCleary, May 27, 1994, Spottswood, VA, ACHSA; *Extension Division News* 18:4 (February 1936): 4.

cooks," she wrote, "they have come to depend on dressed fowl and other foods from the market."[29]

Although nostalgia, convenience, and economic necessity drew city customers to the market, extension home economists believed that city women would still expect new standards of food preparation, nutrition, and sanitation popularized in the early twentieth century. Agents like Jamison sought to recast the goods, the market, and the women into a modern marketplace. Describing the Staunton curb market, the *Extension Division News* boasted, "To go in and see one of these buzzing centers in action is really thrilling, all the market women with crisp white smocks and head bands, their quality standardized products wrapped in cellophane and displayed on uniform tables recently built in."[30] Because the curb market embodied many of the basic principles of home demonstration work, agents used it as a vehicle to reinforce lessons advocated in other club projects. Club women responded like most people would: they accepted the requirements if they wanted to participate but sifted through the other recommendations and chose what they liked.

The focus on "standardization" reflected extension efforts to improve the standards of food for the family and to abide by modern recommendations for a more nutritious diet. For example, agents encouraged women to increase dairy products and expand the variety of vegetables they produced in their gardens as well as to follow new practices in food preparation. Market demonstrations further pushed this point, suggesting that women produce and package goods in a uniform manner, like customers might expect at a supermarket. Market regulations required that club members package their products in "suitable bags and wrappings," made available through the market manager. Recognizing that they could not sell on the market otherwise, vendors had to follow the guidelines for standardizing and packaging goods they sold at market, even if they did not do so at home. Market requirements also dictated that women should make their

29. Warren Susman, *Culture as History: The Transformation of American Society in the Twentieth Century* (New York: Pantheon Books, 1984), 156; Annual Reports, 1940; untitled play script; *Extension Division News* 15:3 (March 1933): 1.
   30. *Extension Division News* 18:4 (February 1936): 4.

names visible, no doubt reflecting contemporary expectations that the customers wanted to know the source of the foods they purchased in the grocery store. Yet ironically, that same requirement permitted women to personalize an otherwise ubiquitous product. In spite of the increased time and anxiety over standardization, curb market vendors felt pride in the professional appearance of their home-produced goods marked clearly with their names to illustrate their personal success.[31]

Sometimes, club women resisted extension efforts to standardize their products. Jamison respected the skills of her Augusta County club members, recalling that "instead of riding down to Blacksburg and telling them to come down and teach these women how to make things, I asked all those good women who made those good things." Yet she was not at a loss for suggestions. Jamison believed that the icings women put on their cakes were too sweet, so she conducted a demonstration on a new, less-sugary recipe, called "Comfort Icing," found in the *Betty Crocker Cookbook*. Successful curb market vendors like Ina Berry dismissed the new icing recipe; she continued to use her own "white icing" recipe that had one additional cup of sugar and considerably more corn syrup than Jamison's proposal. Like Berry, club members did not immediately surrender their traditional values and ideas but, rather, selectively adopted the recommendations.[32]

Another home demonstration goal was to create a more positive and respectable look for farm women. Agents had promoted "good grooming" through clothing contests in the 1910s and 1920s, recommending appropriate styles for clothing, hair, and accessories. Because the curb market brought farm women into direct contact with city women, the issue of respectability gained even more urgency among home demonstration agents, who argued that farm women needed to improve their dress, appearance, and posture so that city women would respect them enough to patronize their booths. The Staunton

31. Annual Report, 1930.
32. *Extension Division News* 18:9 (July 1936): 4; Annual Reports, 1932–1941; Grace Frysinger, *Home Demonstration Work*, USDA Miscellaneous Publication no. 178 (Washington, DC: Government Printing Office, 1933), 3; Masincupp interview.

market required that every curb market vendor wear a white dress, fashioned in a conservative design, and a white headband, which standardized their hairstyles. Likely, few farm women had a white dress; this would be the most impractical color for any work on the farm. Nor would white be a sensible color to wear as they were unloading produce and carrying it into the market. Yet the color white symbolized new ideas of home economics, particularly sanitation, and agents considered this ideal important for the modern market. Photographs of the Staunton market in 1941 reveal that all vendors wore similarly styled white dresses, which they likely produced at home, since extension agents still actively encouraged club women to sew their own clothes. Like their products, the market standardized the vendors' appearance.[33]

Club programs went beyond changing women's appearances to trying to influence the way in which farm women behaved in a public setting. Believing that rural women lacked social skills, which further isolated them on the farm, agents introduced demonstrations for club meetings on how "to meet the public easily and naturally" and to "help create a better understanding between farm and village people." In this regard, extension agents clearly underestimated their club members, who were already well-respected, active leaders in their communities. As middle-class women on successful farms, these club members participated actively in community groups like school-parent associations and women's church groups and organized school lunch programs, health clinics, community-beautification campaigns, and other civic-improvement projects. They already had the abilities to interact with other members of the community, not just on the farm but in the towns as well. Club women were not shrinking violets; their decision to participate in club work reflected their yearning to expand their horizons beyond the farm.[34]

The curb market underscored another primary objective of the home demonstration program: that farm women should calculate the value

33. Annual Reports, 1932, 1941.
34. See the Annual Reports for 1930 through 1940, which report on the clothing contests and guidelines for both women and 4-H girls.

of their production to the farm economy. In all of the club projects, agents required women to keep records of all the goods they produced and to calculate their income as well as the "savings" for their household in an effort to prove the economic value of their work. Some farm women, like Fannie Wampler, already kept detailed written records of their sales, so this likely was not a new lesson. Even if they did not keep precise written records like Wampler, farm women often kept an informal tally of their sales, if only in their heads. Extension agents used the curb market to transform farm women into businesspeople, teaching demonstrations on keeping business records, understanding salesmanship, creating an effective display, and establishing an organizational framework for the market. As John Hutchinson, head of extension services in Virginia, wrote in 1935, the curb markets could teach women "the value of better business methods, how to recognize quality in foods, and how to produce these quality products."[35] Participating club women maintained accurate records of their sales, which earned them respect among their families and in their communities.

The two Augusta County markets—in Staunton and Waynesboro—not only burgeoned in the 1930s but also became the largest and most profitable in the state. Total market sales from both markets increased from almost $16,000 in 1931 to more than $56,000 by 1936. In comparison, the next leading market that year grossed only $10,000, and the next four earned from $1,000 to $4,000 in income. In 1939, the *Extension Division News* reported that the Augusta County curb market had become "an outstanding business for rural women" and "continues to play an important part in finances of Augusta County farm women."

The curb markets brought many opportunities that club women valued. First, the market allowed them to earn desperately needed cash during the Depression years. In 1934, for example, sales averaged $456 per participant, and some women grossed as much as $60

35. Hutchison, *Annual Report of Extension Work in Agriculture and Home Economics in Virginia*, Bulletin no. 137 (Blacksburg: Virginia Extension Division, March 1935), 22.

Curb Market Sales in Augusta County
COMBINED MARKETS IN STAUNTON AND WAYNESBORO

Year sales	Total market selling	Members
1931	$15,804.99	60
1932	$30,592.58	108
1933	$39,441.61	122
1934	$50,641.20	111
1935	$53,963.44	108
1936	$56,872.10	97
1937	$56,021.28	87
1938	$31,100.11	77
1939	$51,421.53	62
1940	$46,614.23	60[36]

or $100 on a busy day, especially right before a holiday like Christmas or Easter. At a time when the Virginia farm family's annual income averaged only $605, club women could almost double the family's proceeds. Ambitious farm women, willing to commit a large amount of time to the market, could produce even larger profits. Josephine Wine led the market sales in 1934 with $1,550 from fresh vegetables, potato chips, bread, and baked products. Two years later, the market's most successful vendor, Nettie Shull, grossed $2,104 that year and sometimes as much as $100 a day through her "outstanding potato chip business," in addition to her specialties of old-fashioned fried apple pies, potato salad, and dressed poultry. The number of clubs and total club membership boomed during the early thirties because of the market, as women joined clubs or started new clubs in order to participate in the market. Two home demonstration clubs organized in 1930 and 1931 specifically so that the members could sell at the curb market, including Beverley Manor Club, just outside Staunton.

36. *Extension Division News* 18:4 (February 1936): 4; *Extension Division News* 22:9 (July 1940): 6; Annual Reports, 1930–1940.

Membership in this club increased to forty members in 1931 and ninety-four members the following year, with many of the women joining because they wanted to sell at the curb market.[37]

The curb market also altered women's access to the income produced through their work. Jamison recalled that before the curb market, the husband would "put [the money] in his pocket. That's what he did. She didn't give it to him. If the husband had a chance to put it in his pocket, he did." At the curb market, the club woman personally collected the money for her goods, some of which she would reinvest into her "business" by buying equipment for the home or supplies for the next market. Subscribing to Jamison's belief that women "ought to keep" the money they made, Lucille Berry Masincupp recalled, "Yes, I considered it *my money*."[38]

Curb market women proudly used their money at their discretion, as testimonials by these women reveal. Some chose to use their cash incomes to support the farm during the difficult years of the Depression. Their profits paid taxes and mortgages, provided wages to farmhands, and purchased farm stock and even tractors. For some women, their curb market work supplied most of the family's cash income during the 1930s. As one daughter recalled, the cash her mother earned was not "extra money, but money to keep us going."[39] These uses reflect their long-standing belief that they were partners on the farm and contributors to the farm economy.

Farm women also used their income for their own priorities. Some purchased new consumer goods, like clothing, that they no longer had time to or chose not to make at home. Others used the money to send their children, particularly sons, to college. Curb market women continued the tradition of bartering to obtain services they wanted, using their curb market products to trade for doctors' services, music

37. Annual Reports, 1934, 1936; *Extension Division News* 18:4 (February 1936): 4; *Extension Division News* 21:6 (April 1939): 3; *Extension Division News* 17:4 (March 1935): 2; *Extension Division News* 23:3 (January 1941): 5; McCleary, "Shaping a New Role," 79.

38. Jamison interview, October 3, 1993; Masincupp interview.

39. McCormick personal communication.

lessons, or beauty parlor appointments. Curb market vendors boasted most about the home improvements that they made with their market income, allowing them to participate more actively in the extension-sponsored contests popular in Augusta County as well as nationally throughout the 1930s. Women justified their decisions to add running water or electricity, to purchase new technology like refrigerators or stoves, and to build brooder houses because these improvements allowed them to expand their "business" and become more efficient in their work. A report of Augusta County's 1932 kitchen-improvement contest bragged that "nearly all of the improvements were paid for by money earned on the market." Some of these improvements went beyond their needs for their market businesses as they painted the exterior and interior and remodeled their bedrooms, living rooms, dining rooms, and hallways.[40]

Their store-bought clothes, new refrigerators, painted homes, college-educated children, and beauty parlor coifs helped elevate the status of these curb market vendors not just in their rural villages and towns but in the city and broader county community as well. Through their market work, club women participated more actively in the new consumer world and endeavored to fulfill some of the material expectations in the contemporary ideal of middle-class womanhood. At the same time, they gained local and sometimes statewide attention for their work ethic and their success as homemakers. Their names gained notoriety in the community. As Ruth Jamison recalled, "After they started in [selling at the curb market], they got such a reputation you couldn't get them off [from selling at the market]." In an extension-sponsored essay contest called "What Home Demonstration Work Means to My Community," curb market vendor Mrs. A. M. Berry wrote, "Many women say that our curb market has meant more to them than any other phase of club work.... In fact, I doubt

40. Annual Reports, 1932, 1934, 1935, 1939; *Extension Division News* 14:3 (January 1932): 4; Van Lear interview, July 13, 1993; Masincupp interview; *Extension Division News* 18:4 (February 1936): 4; Edna Hulvey Garber, interview by McCleary, July 15, 1993, Mount Sidney, VA, ACHSA; *Extension Division News* 15:5 (March 1933): 1; Kesterson interview, May 27, 1994.

if some of us could have carried on during the depression if it had not been for this boost to our funds and morale. We met so many fine people and made many friends among the buyers and sellers."[41]

As Berry observed, beyond their new celebrity status, market women also relished the opportunities for fellowship outside the home, one of the key factors that initially attracted certain farm women to home demonstration work. The market provided an opportunity for them to come to the city more often, weekly or sometimes even biweekly; make new friends; and create new networks in the community. Jamison wrote in her 1930 annual report that "seven women have not missed a day. They have made friends and have regular customers which they would miss them if they stayed away." One vendor stated that not only has the market proved profitable but both country and town women have made friends, creating a "comradery" between rural and town women. "I liked the social part," recalled Lucille Berry Masincupp. "I had a ball while I was there."[42]

The market turned the tables on women's access to cash and travel, and it also reversed the roles of farmer and farm woman in regard to preparing and marketing home produce. Because the curb market work contributed significantly to the overall farm income, farmers found themselves taking time from their work to assist their wives both in producing goods and in transporting them to market. As Masincupp recalls, "It was good money, and the men worked around it." On Fridays, while women prepared goods for the Saturday market, husbands and children dressed chickens, butchered meat, cracked nuts, and helped out in any way they could, as women had assisted men in the fields when their labor was needed. Although she could drive, Hazel Van Lear recalled that she needed her husband's help to set up for the market. "He drove and went with me most of the time," Van Lear said. "I went a few times by myself, but it was hard for one person to go because of unloading all that stuff on your table and

41. Jamison interview, January 23, 1981; Berry, "What Home Demonstration Work Means to My Community," Augusta County Extension Office files, Verona, VA.
42. Annual Reports, 1930, 1932, 1934; Masincupp interview.

getting ready, and then at the same time customers would be coming
to buy, and you just almost had to have two people to go."[43] While
the wives tended their busy booths, their husbands gathered near the
market to visit, much as their wives had done when they accompanied their husbands to town, and men returned to help pack up when
the market closed. For women who could not drive, their husband's
willingness to take them to market would determine whether they
could participate.

The preparations leading up to the market demanded additional
time in home production over and above women's usual work on the
farm and in the home. Market preparations, just for the Saturday
sales, lasted throughout the week. Most women needed help from
their families—their children, husbands, or other close family members—to prepare for the market. Some jobs, such as making butter,
stretched out all week. Other work, like dressing poultry and making
cakes, could be done only the day before. Women often offered daughters a share of the profits in return for their help and encouraged
them to produce their own specialties for sale. When they did not
have family members to help, some women hired girls to assist them,
paying them by the task or the day.[44]

The most time-consuming work occurred on the two days before
the market. Van Lear's description of the process reveals both the
value of her husband's assistance and the anxiety she felt about producing quality products on a tight schedule. "I usually started on
Thursday, churned, got the butter all ready, and put it in the refrigerator," she remembered. "Then I made my pound cakes on Thursday,
because it didn't hurt them to stand like it does the layer cakes. . . . If
we had vegetables or things like that to get ready, we'd do that sometimes, things that it didn't hurt. You know, everything had to go
there in perfect condition, definitely." On Fridays, Van Lear began
her preparations as soon as she finished breakfast, usually around

43. Masincupp interview; Van Lear interview, July 13, 1993.
44. Van Lear interview, July 13, 1993; Masincupp interview; Kesterson
interview, May 27, 1994; Garber interview; McCormick interview.

seven o'clock in the morning. She baked and iced the layer cakes, dressed the chickens, baked the bread, and made the cottage cheese "and half a dozen other things." After preparing the food, she began to pack up her goods. "You had to wrap all your cakes and your baked stuff, and put your ice on the chickens." She tried to finish by eleven at night, but "by the time you took a bath and got yourself decent to go to the curb market the next morning, it was even later. You didn't figure on getting much sleep on Friday night," she recalled. Preparations continued on Saturday morning: "I usually mixed the cottage cheese at mornings, put pure cream in it. . . . Well, I washed up things if I had time, but if I didn't, they stayed there until I got back on Saturday evenings. We tried to get to Staunton at seven o'clock, but we didn't always make it."[45]

Exhausted from the physical stress of market preparations, especially on Friday and Saturday, and the worries about getting everything completed on time, Van Lear would return home on Saturday, perhaps facing a kitchen full of dishes she needed to wash. By Monday morning, she would begin her preparations anew. Although the curb market offered tremendous opportunity for interested rural women, they had to squeeze their market preparations into already busy schedules. Praising the success of the home demonstration markets, USDA specialist Grace Frysinger wrote, "It is important to remember that these women do so not by laying aside the normally long hours of daily housework which every farm homemaker experiences, but in addition to those duties which she performs before and after market hours."[46]

What Van Lear does not mention in her weekly account of market arrangements is the work that she had to do on a weekly and seasonal basis to sustain her business, from planting the garden to incubating chicks. Even presumably "raw" products—such as eggs or green beans—involved a significant commitment of time and energy before

45. Van Lear interview, July 13, 1993.
46. Ibid.; Frysinger, *The Farm Woman and the Agricultural Situation* (Washington, DC: USDA Extension Service, Office of Cooperative Extension Work, 1934), 5.

they were picked or collected for market. To increase egg production, extension agents encouraged women to follow the multitude of new expectations for poultry production. To augment vegetable yields, women increased the sizes of their gardens, improved the soil, and spent more time cultivating their crops. The dairy and poultry products women sold—butter and dressed chickens—required more labor than the cream or live chickens that they had been selling. Even preparing for the market and spending most of Saturday in town took time away from other tasks at home. One wonders how farm women like Van Lear had time to add pies, cakes, and other baked goods as well as other new items like potato chips to their repertoire of weekly tasks, especially considering the time that these products entailed in the kitchen. Through their work, they added value to almost every product they sold. Farm women provided the labor to either produce the goods (like eggs) or to transform the raw goods into market commodities (like butter or angel food cake). In essence, club women did the work that city women did not want to do, be it dressing their chickens, baking their pies, or even frying potato chips, meeting the city woman's demand for convenience at the expense of the farm woman's time.

Something had to give for the curb market vendor: if she were to increase time in food production and marketing, she needed to free up time elsewhere. In response to the demands of the curb market, Ruth Jamison and her successors introduced two new program areas: efficiency and consumerism. Jamison noted that Augusta County club women selected "home management" as a major in 1932 because "women have many meetings, the market, and outside activities which caused them to want to learn to conserve time and energy in doing the everyday task." Although efficiency and "saving" time had been a goal of home demonstration work from its inception, the majority of the programs in the 1910s and 1920s required club members to spend more time to produce the new kinds of goods that they wanted but could not afford and to realize the increased expectations that extension agents promoted for the work they already did. Without a cash income over which they had control in the 1910s and 1920s, farm women could not take advantage of the modern household technology that promised to help city women alleviate household "drudgery" and make their work more efficient. By the 1930s, agents began to promote shortcuts that they hoped would still keep the extension quality standards but save time in tasks like cooking, such as "quick meals for busy days," "wholesome one-dish meals with simple desserts," and "planning community meals for efficiency."[47]

More significant, the cash that the farm women earned allowed them to purchase goods and services that they previously had to produce themselves or do without. In the early years of the twentieth century, farm women wanted to buy new consumer goods, and they did to the extent possible, but their small cash incomes and limited farm profits prevented them from participating more actively. Virginia's home management specialist, Mary Settle, recalled years later, "After all, you can't buy if you don't have anything to buy with." Instead, they took pride in refinishing an antique chair to resemble a colonial revival one in the store or sewed a stylish dress similar to one they might find in town. The curb market allowed them to enter the new world of consumerism, not just by making what they wanted but by buying it with their own money. As anthropologist Jane Adams observed in rural southern Illinois at that time, women's access to cash income did not necessarily mean less work, but it did bring more control over the money.[48]

The extension emphasis on home production exemplified in the curb market resulted in a growth in consumerism among farm women in the 1930s and 1940s. Adopting "Better Buymanship" as their major program in 1939, Augusta County club members attended demonstrations on selecting and purchasing clothing, furniture, and labor-saving conveniences and read articles by Mary Settle such as "Stop! Look! And Read the Label!" or "When a Woman Goes Shopping." Articles on consumerism began to replace those on "live-at-home"

47. Annual Reports, 1932, 1939.
48. Settle, interview by McCleary, January 24, 1981, Blacksburg, VA, ACHSA; Adams, *The Transformation of Rural Life: Southern Illinois, 1890–1990* (Chapel Hill: University of North Carolina, 1994), 106–7.

campaigns in the *Extension Division News,* as extension agents once again believed that club women needed their expert advice to succeed. Women produced for the market in part so they could consume.[49]

❦

In April 1940, the Staunton curb market celebrated its tenth anniversary. The appearance of the market had changed dramatically, from card tables lining the sidewalk in front of a vacant downtown lot to a large indoor facility that had been "freshly-painted" to celebrate its anniversary. A carefully planned arrangement of matching tables, with "all new showcases for meat and poultry" and lined with hanging scales to weigh the foods, replaced the haphazard assortment of tables that women bought at its opening ten years earlier, creating the ambiance of the produce or meat counters of a modern grocery store. Colorful arrangements of flowers brought in for the occasion decorated every table, softening the modern, sanitary tone established by the new paint, the glass showcases, and the women's crisp white dresses. The raffle of a homemade cake helped to create the mood of an old-fashioned country fair. The market manager coordinated the day's activities from her desk and recorded the daily prices for butter, eggs, broilers, and vegetables on a blackboard, which hung next to the Health Department permit, ensuring that the market met current standards of sanitation and quality. The city customers, dressed in brightly colored clothes in contrast with the uniform look of the market vendors, headed first to purchase their poultry, eggs, and baked products, the most popular items at the market. As the county agent wrote, "The town women feel that they can get better dressed poultry and fresh eggs, and better quality baked products for the money they spend than they can get elsewhere or by doing their own baking."[50]

49. *Extension Division News* 16:10 (September 1934): 6; *Extension Division News* 17:4 (March 1935): 2; Minutes of the Augusta County Advisory Board Meeting, September 12, 1938, typescript, Augusta County Extension Office, Verona, VA.

50. *Extension Division News* 22:9 (July 1940): 6; photographs of the Staunton Curb market in 1940 included in box 233, U.S. Department of Agriculture, Extension Service Annual Reports, Record Group 33, Still Picture Division,

In their white uniforms, surrounded by colorful and attractive displays of their home-produced goods, Augusta County club members portrayed a new ideal of the rural woman promoted by the extension service. The modern farm women had become the business partner of her husband, demonstrating that her productive work played an important economic role in the farm economy. No longer "backwards" or "ignorant," she embraced modern home economics standards in her work and exhibited a new confidence and pride in her skills as producer and business person. Clearly, some Augusta County women aspired to and embraced this new vision. Although only about 4 percent of white rural women in the county participated in the market at its height in the early 1930s, these women found that their involvement helped them to negotiate a new role and increased status for themselves in a changing rural world. The curb market celebrated their traditional rural values—especially their strong work ethic and their commitment to the family farm—but also created an opportunity to seek a new, acceptable, and satisfying role that allowed access to an expanding world off the farm and in the consumer world. As their farms continued to lead the state in farm income and farm value and as commodity work moved increasingly into their husbands' hands, Augusta County farm women did not want to be left behind. Through their market, club women constructed a strong visual statement to both city and country women that rural women played an important role in the modern world.[51]

As a business, the curb market offered flexibility similar to that women enjoyed on the farm. Women had the authority to choose what they wanted to sell, which icing they preferred on their cake, and how much and how often they wanted to engage in the market. They could participate in the market to suit their own needs; some sold regularly throughout the year, while others floated in and out of the market depending on personal circumstances. Lucille Berry Masincupp found that the market offered more flexibility than her teaching

---

National Archives and Records Administration, College Park, MD; Annual Report, 1940.

51. Annual Report, 1940; McCleary, "Shaping a New Role," chap. 2.

job. Some women became so successful that they left the curb market to establish their own businesses as early as 1931. Now they could sell what they wanted on their own terms and schedule. One woman packed lunches of ham biscuits, tarts, cake, and fruit for sale to the newspaper office, two stores, and several banks. 4-H Club member Edith Berry secured orders from a girls' boarding school to furnish all their cakes. Edith's mother, Ina Berry, quit going to the curb market because she "didn't have to go": she had enough orders from customers who came to her house at Spring Hill for dressed chickens or cakes, saving her the time and hassles of traveling to town. The curb market offered these women an entry into the working world off the farm. Without transportation or specialized training and education, many of these farm women would have been unable to obtain a good-paying job in the city even if they had wanted one.[52]

An article in the Staunton newspaper in 1934 titled "The Women of Augusta County" boasted about the "excellent work" accomplished by country women and questioned whether city women "have anything comparable to occupy much of their thoughts and time." After Ruth Jamison's talk about home demonstration work to the Staunton Rotary Club, the author observed:

> Those who have read in the Leader paper the full account rendered by Miss Ruth Jamison . . . must have been amazed at the comprehensive character of this work and the thorough skill in doing it shown by the women of the county. It would be difficult to point to the constructive work done by the men of the county to rival this. Miss Ruth Jamison does not say this but it is a fact that the women of the county have come to the rescue of the men, and have saved them many outlays and many hard experiences in a financial way. We would not be surprised if the facts would show they have been the senior members of the firms operating many farms. No doubt whatever the men feel very grateful to the good women for seizing the opportunity in

52. Annual Reports, 1930, 1931; Masincupp interview; *Extension Division News* 12 (July 1930): 3.

such a crisis to do capital constructive work so far reaching in its full effects.[53]

His statement "seizing the opportunity" could be taken both literally and figuratively. Though this reporter claimed that the farm women were "seizing the opportunity" in the immediate economic crisis of the Depression, the curb market meant more to Augusta County women than simply coming "to the rescue of their husbands." Instead, they hoped that their work in the curb market would help them create a more permanent role as respected business partners on the farm. Yet in spite of the pleas from extension home economists that women's work was comparable to that of their husbands, male extension agents continued to refer to its value as supplemental, even when rural women garnered a significant cash income that could double the farm income. In much the same way that the extension service divided men's work from women's work on the farm, so too did the curb market separate women's commodity production from that of their husbands. Though each now managed his or her operation, a woman could not be considered an equal partner on the farm because her sphere remained unequal.

In retrospect, the curb market, although very successful for Augusta County women, did not realize its full potential in the long run. After the Depression and wartime crises subsided, agricultural extension agents expected women to return to their homes and focus more on children and family than producing a cash income. Its greatly reduced descendent, which survived with two or three vendors into the 1960s, appeared more as a quaint relic of the past than as the integral operation it once was. With more employment opportunities available to them after World War II, few women chose the curb market. After listening to Hazel Van Lear's weekly preparation schedule, another former curb market vendor, Phyllis Wampler, remarked, "They wouldn't work that hard any more, would they?" Van Lear replied,

53. The newspaper quotation comes from an article Ruth Jamison attached to her 1934 Annual Report.

"No, I don't think they would."[54] The younger women who might have participated, including those who helped their mothers as children, realized how much this "job" required in terms of time and energy. Rural youth coming of age in the Depression had more mobility and education than their mothers, so they could choose among a wider variety of better-paying positions off the farm than those available to their mothers' generation. Few chose to follow in their mothers' footsteps.

Home demonstration efforts to carve out a productive role for farm women in the early twentieth century ultimately proved unsuccessful. By the 1950s, farm women had little opportunity to earn a separate income on the farm from their husbands and to gain the power and respect that this income would bring. But by legitimating the value of women's paid work, the curb market opened the doors to future generations of rural women to move into paying jobs off the farm. While some women and girls certainly welcomed these expanded opportunities, others may well have missed the bonds of mutuality that had connected them to the farm enterprise and the value and respect they received for their work.

54. Wampler, interview by McCleary, Spring Hill, VA, July 14, 1994, ACHSA; Van Lear interview, June 14, 1994.

LYNNE RIEFF

Revitalizing Southern Homes

Rural Women, the Professionalization of Home Demonstration Work, and the Limits of Reform, 1917–1945

It is important that home demonstration work sell itself to the people on the basis of dollars and cents.

—HELEN JOHNSTON, Alabama home demonstration agent,
to H. R. Bailey, October 16, 1930

You can readily see what a great help [home demonstration work] is to me. The actual living expenses of my little family have been lessened by half.

—VIRGINIA H. HOLSTON to Ruth Kernodle, home demonstration
agent, Hale County, Alabama, November 2, 1926

In 1921 Della Helton of Madison County, Alabama, faced a daunting future. As a teenager whose mother had died, Helton assumed responsibility for her siblings and for managing her household. The family was poor. She could neither read nor write and questioned her ability to provide for her family and to perform the homemaking tasks that could keep her family together. Helton then met local home demonstration agent Evelyn Peyton, who helped her, and the teenager joined a home demonstration club. Peyton taught Helton to garden,

135

preserve food, and sew. Helton planted a garden and began canning vegetables, borrowing the canning equipment from the agent. The teenager chopped cotton in neighbors' fields to earn money to buy sugar and jars. At the end of the season, Helton had canned enough food to supply her family's needs and had additional goods that she sold to neighbors, earning two hundred dollars.[1]

Virginia H. Holston of Hale County, Alabama, provides a similar but less dramatic example of home demonstration work. At the local agents' urging, Holston cultivated a garden, canned fruits and vegetables, and raised chickens. The supply of eggs and canned food and meat reduced her family's grocery expenses and gave her a surplus to sell for additional income.[2]

In their work with these women, home demonstration agents promoted self-sufficiency in conjunction with lessons about performing household tasks. That promotion was a part of a larger campaign that the Home Demonstration Division (HDD) of the Cooperative Extension Service (CES) promoted between 1917 and 1945. This campaign, called the "live-at-home" program, was the major focus of home demonstration work across the country from World War I until the end of World War II. Designed to provide visibility and to highlight the economic value of home demonstration work, the live-at-home program became a public relations success in increasing public awareness of home demonstration work, and individuals such as Helton and Holston benefited. An examination of the live-at-home program in the Deep South states of Alabama, Georgia, Florida, Mississippi, and Louisiana reveals, however, a disparity between the training home demonstration agents received and the nature of the tasks they faced. The difficulties that agents experienced in reconciling their training in home economics with the needs and expectations

1. Peyton, "Annual Narrative Report of Home Demonstration Agent, Madison County, Alabama, 1923," Alabama Cooperative Extension Service Papers, Record Group 71, box 120, Auburn University Archives, Auburn, AL (hereafter ACES).
2. Ruth Kernodle, "Annual Narrative Report of Home Demonstration Agent, Hale County, Alabama, 1926," box 123, ACES.

of their rural constituents resulted in a home demonstration program that had limited appeal to rural women.

Home demonstration work among black and white rural women stemmed from several reform movements gaining momentum in the late nineteenth and early twentieth centuries. The vocational or industrial education movement advocated that educational institutions supplement their academic curricula with vocational courses that taught people skills and prepared them for work in business and industry. The core principle of the vocational educational movement was that everyone—regardless of the individual's station in life—could benefit from an education. Vocational education students could intelligently choose their occupations, the quality of the workforce would improve, and prejudice against the working would be negated. Black educator Booker T. Washington recognized advantages of vocational education and became one of the movement's staunchest proponents. To Washington, vocational or industrial education represented the democratization of education in the United States. No longer would schools and colleges exclusively be the domain of elites preparing to enter the professions. Of greater importance to Washington was that vocational education represented a realistic goal that a large number of African Americans, many of them former slaves, could attain and use to become economically independent. Economic independence, Washington believed, would eventually lead to African American political and social gains. Vocational education, therefore, also represented the potential for American society to be democratized with more opportunities available for a better-educated population.[3]

Closely tied with the vocational education movement was the new discipline of home economics. Supporters and teachers, first called domestic scientists and later home economists, forcefully argued that vocational education courses should address women's needs. As male vocational educators analyzed various industrial jobs and recognized

3. Laurence A. Cremin, *The Transformation of the School, 1876–1957* (New York: Alfred A. Knopf, 1962), 118; Louis Harlan, *Booker T. Washington: The Making of a Black Leader, 1856–1901* (New York: Oxford University Press, 1972), 74, 81, 277.

that skills could be taught in a series of progressive steps, Ellen Richards, professor of chemistry at the Massachusetts Institute of Technology, argued that the same could be done for various household tasks. Richards's idea was twofold: women could be taught both proficiency and efficiency in performing household duties. Domestic science or home economics would offer all women better ways to manage their households and family income, improve their standards of living, and reduce time spent performing domestic tasks. The ultimate goal that Richards and other early home economists envisioned was that households would be scientifically managed, the nation's standard of living would improve, and women would be free to leave the domestic sphere and use their knowledge to accomplish social reforms or "municipal housekeeping."[4]

Middle-class women acting through women's clubs engaged in reforms and were among the first to recognize the value of home economics. Historically, women's associations, particularly church groups, had been active in reform activities. After the Civil War, though, a non-church-related women's club movement for white and black women began in the Northeast and spread throughout urban America. Middle-class women who had the time and interest formed literary clubs that they believed would contribute to members' edification. Soon club members realized additional benefits. Unlike in churches and most organizations, women were leaders in these clubs. They held offices, spoke publicly, and presented programs. The experience was exhilarating and empowering—not just individually but also for the group—and a spirit of sisterhood emerged. A reforming spirit in the late nineteenth century that grew into the Progressive reform movement transformed these literary circles into active women's clubs that supported child-labor reform, temperance, and slum clearance, issues categorized as natural extensions of women's interests as wives and mothers.[5]

4. Caroline Hunt, *The Life of Ellen Richards, 1842–1911* (Washington, DC: American Home Economics Association, 1958), 100–101.
5. Karen Blair, *The Clubwoman as Feminist: True Womanhood Redefined, 1868–1914* (New York: Holmes and Meier, 1980), 98, 102, 105–6, 117–18.

Conditions in the countryside focused Progressive reformers' attention on the plight of rural America. The Country Life Commission's 1909 report, prepared under the auspices of the Theodore Roosevelt presidency, confirmed that problems abounded. Nowhere were rural problems more pronounced than in the South. Illiteracy was high, as were infant and maternal mortality rates, while living standards and crop prices remained low. Tenancy and sharecropping increased as farm families' debts mounted.[6]

Farm organizations such as the Grange and Farmers' Alliance during the populist era sought speakers who could answer questions and help rural families resolve their problems. During the 1890s, Booker T. Washington began holding annual Farmers Conferences at Tuskegee Institute that other black and white institutions with agricultural interests emulated. An annual conference or periodic organizational meeting was insufficient in addressing rural people's multitude of needs, however. Tuskegee Institute responded by sponsoring a "Movable School of Agriculture" in 1906 that allowed an agricultural teacher to visit the homes of rural black families.[7]

Seaman A. Knapp, a former professor of agriculture at Iowa State University who was employed by the Department of Agriculture, developed a similar concept. Knapp focused on the principle of the demonstration. He believed that rural people, suspicious of "book learning," would resist new scientific agricultural techniques unless shown the benefits. Under Knapp's direction, the Department of Agriculture in 1904 employed white agricultural agents to teach and to work directly with farmers. Knapp realized, though, that teaching farmers scientific agriculture would not stop the perpetuation of poor

6. Clayton Ellsworth, "Theodore Roosevelt's Country Life Commission," *Agricultural History* 34 (October 1960): 163–68; William L. Bowers, "Country-Life Reform, 1900–1920: A Neglected Aspect of Progressive Era History," *Agricultural History* 45 (July 1971): 219.

7. Earl W. Crosby, "The Roots of Black Agricultural Extension Work," *Historian* 39 (February 1977): 29–31, 236–38; Allen W. Jones, "The Role of Tuskegee Institute in the Education of Black Farmers," *Journal of Negro History* 60 (April 1975): 254–56, 262–63; Felix James, "The Tuskegee Institute Moveable School, 1906–1923," *Agricultural History* 45 (July 1971): 202–3.

farming practices from one generation to the next nor would it address the myriad of other problems related to homes and the rural standard of living. Until living conditions improved, advances made among farmers would have limited significance. Knapp decided to expand demonstration work to include the organization of boys' corn clubs and girls' canning and tomato clubs. Between 1906 and 1912, boys' and girls' clubs were organized in Mississippi, Louisiana, Alabama, Florida, and Georgia. Gradually, girls' club agents, many of whom were teachers employed for two or three months during the summer, included rural women in club activities. For example, agents used canning demonstrations to explain sanitation and sterilization. Other ideas and suggestions followed that led agents to teach mothers and daughters canning, cooking, sewing, and other ways to improve their households. "Home demonstration" described the work agents engaged in as they counseled rural women and girls, and constituents used that description in their references to women agents.

The work of Seaman Knapp, farmers' institutes and conferences, and movable schools represented collective but uncoordinated efforts to uplift and to revitalize rural America. A corps of demonstration agents, Knapp argued, composed of male farm agents and female home demonstration agents, employed full-time, could address two problems. First, they could prove to rural people that new techniques worked, and second, agents could provide the needed link between educational institutions and the rural population. Demonstration agents could instigate and coordinate reforms that rural America needed.[8]

8. Roy V. Scott, *The Reluctant Farmer: The Rise of Agricultural Extension to 1914* (Urbana: University of Illinois Press, 1970), 208–13; Silver Anniversary, Cooperative Demonstration Work, 1903–1928, *Proceedings of the Anniversary Meeting Held at Houston, Texas, February 5–7, 1929* (College Station: Extension Service of the Agricultural and Mechanical College of Texas, 1929), 75, 98, 105, 107, 126, file "Farm Extension Work," box 24; Thomas Monroe Campbell Papers, Tuskegee University Archives, Tuskegee, AL (hereafter TMC Papers); Grace E. Frysinger, *Home Demonstration Work, 1922*, U.S. Department of Agriculture, Circular 314 (Washington, DC: U.S. Department of Agriculture, 1924), 1.

With rural reformers' support, Congress passed the Smith-Lever Act in 1914 that established the CES as an agency in the Department of Agriculture. Each state in turn established a state extension service headquartered at the state land-grant college and supported with federal, state, and local funds. From the beginning, racial segregation permeated extension work as dual systems were created in southern states to work with blacks and whites. Black extension services were located at black land-grant schools or prominent black institutions such as Tuskegee Institute in Alabama. Support for black extension work was limited. Federal and state funds were channeled through and dispersed by white extension administrators at white land-grant institutions. Consequently, funding for black extension work suffered. With few exceptions, black personnel took directions from whites.[9]

Sexism was also evident in the CES. State bureaucracies were divided into agricultural, home demonstration, and youth divisions with subject-matter specialists employed as advisers. Local agricultural and home demonstration agents were appointed to live and work among rural people in the counties. Because farming was vital to rural economies and southern patriarchal society viewed men as the family breadwinners, extension officials gave farmers' problems top priority. Extension employment practices and financial support favored agricultural agents. White farm agents were employed in greater numbers, had larger budgets, and received higher salaries than white home demonstration or black agents. Black agents' appointment was limited to counties with large African American populations. The prevalence of racism and sexism meant that there were

9. Alfred Charles True, *A History of Extension Work in the United States, 1785–1923* (New York: Arno Press and the New York Times, 1969), 100–115; *U.S. Statutes at Large* 38 (1913–1915), 372–75; W. B. Mercier, *Status and Results of Extension Work in the Southern States, 1903–1921,* U.S. Department of Agriculture, Circular 248 (Washington, DC: U.S. Department of Agriculture, 1922), 15; Wayne D. Rasmussen, *Taking the University to the People: Seventy-five Years of Cooperative Extension* (Ames: Iowa State University Press, 1989), 51; Earl W. Crosby, "Building the Country Home: The Black County Agent System, 1906–1940" (PhD diss., Miami University, 1977), 57, 68–70.

fewer black home demonstration agents and that they received the least financial support.[10]

Limited support for women agents hindered their work, but those receiving appointments began the overwhelming task of addressing problems that existed in rural homes. Here, too, home demonstration agents encountered difficulties. Both men and women challenged the significance of home agents' work. County officials resisted home agents' appointment to their counties because, unlike crop yields, their value was not measured in dollars and cents. Compounding the problem were attitudes about housework. From childhood, people heard deprecations of "women's work" that led many to believe that domestic responsibilities were so simple and routine that women should know "instinctively how to care for family and home." One Mississippi woman claimed that she had "married six husbands and buried them without studying domestic science." Others thought agents presumptuous in giving advice, while some rural people distrusted agents because they were government employees.[11]

Home demonstration agents recognized that they needed women's trust before they could address problems. Some rural women were familiar with Knapp's demonstration work or with the work of "Jeanes teachers." Knapp had broadened his work in 1910 to include women and girls. The Anna T. Jeanes Foundation sponsored "Jeanes teachers" in black schools, recruiting rural schoolteachers to teach women and girls to garden and to can vegetables. In addition to supervising local black teachers, Jeanes teachers worked directly with black children and their parents. These black and white teachers organized tomato and canning clubs among school-age girls and their mothers, but this type of work was seasonal and unsystematic. Teachers' pri-

10. Rieff, "'Rousing the People of the Land': Home Demonstration Work in the Deep South, 1914–1950" (PhD diss., Auburn University, 1995), 65.

11. "Fifty Years of Home Demonstration, 1914–1964," file "Correspondence," Mississippi Cooperative Extension Service Collection, Mississippi State University Archives, Mitchell Memorial Library, Mississippi State University, Starkville (hereafter MCES); Susie V. Powell, "Biennial Report of Mississippi Home Demonstration Work, 1919–1920," file "Biennial Reports," MCES; Della B. Alley Luter, "Horse and Buggy Days," file "General History," MCES.

mary responsibility was instruction in academic subjects, with gardening and canning as sidelines. There was little follow-up, and most teachers learned gardening and canning skills from attending one or two short courses at agricultural colleges.[12]

Home demonstration agents used the familiarity that women and girls had with demonstration work to meet people, then worked to gain other women's interest. Women who had participated in earlier demonstration work were contacted first; in counties where demonstration work previously had not been conducted, agents identified women who had reputations as good homemakers. Frequently, agents visited rural churches to meet people, then returned to a community to visit women individually. After meeting several women, agents proposed organizing home demonstration clubs. If women were receptive, a club was organized and usually met monthly in members' homes.[13]

Agents recognized that their success depended upon several factors. In encouraging women to participate, agents found sensitivity and tact effective approaches, but also decided that an economic argument was persuasive. Practical demonstrations were needed. Women's work in the twentieth-century South remained labor intensive. Domestic responsibilities included gardening, harvesting and preparing vegetables for meals, cooking, carrying water and wood, washing clothes, ironing, cleaning, sewing, gathering eggs, milking cows, churning butter, and

12. Silver Anniversary, *Proceedings of the Anniversary Meeting*, 75, 98, 105, 107, 126; "Jeanes Fund Report of President, Annual Meeting, January 24, 1914," file "Anna T. Jeanes Foundation for Rural Schools," box 7, W. T. B. Williams Collection, Tuskegee University Archives, Tuskegee, AL.

13. "Louisiana Home Demonstration Work," in Ellen LeNoir, "Annual Narrative Reports of Home Demonstration Work in Louisiana, 1929," vol. 606, Louisiana State University Collection, Agricultural Extension Service Papers, Louisiana and Lower Mississippi Valley Collections, Louisiana State University Libraries, Baton Rouge (hereafter LCES); Katherine Lanier, "Annual Narrative Report of Savannah District, Georgia, 1926," U.S. Department of Agriculture, Records of the Federal Extension Service, Record Group 33, Annual Reports of Extension Service Field Representatives, National Archives of the United States, Georgia, T-855, roll 22 (hereafter NARS T-855, "roll" abbreviated as "r."); "Proceedings of the Conference on Negro Extension Work, State A&M College, Orangeburg, South Carolina, January 26–28, 1927," file "Agents' Conference, 1927," box 4, TMC Papers.

caring for family members as well as chopping and picking cotton. Women performed those responsibilities with varied proficiency. Some families did not garden or raise chickens and cows because of initial expenses or because landlords prohibited any activity unrelated to cotton cultivation. In other cases, rural families did not recognize the nutritional value·of a balanced diet. To overcome these barriers and to persuade women of the importance of domestic work, agents began to "sell" home demonstration work, initiating a campaign to show rural women and their families the financial benefits of domestic work.[14]

Other individuals also needed to be sold on home demonstration work. Landlords needed to be persuaded that productivity would improve if tenants lived in a healthier environment. Agents and extension officials also recognized that if home demonstration work could be assigned a monetary value, county officials would contribute more local funds. With that financial increase, more local home agents could be appointed and home demonstration work would spread.[15]

The two projects used most frequently to initiate home demonstration work were gardening and food preservation. As agents met constituents and surveyed rural conditions, they frequently found that many families lacked an adequate food supply. Obtaining seed from whatever source they could, agents taught rural women to cultivate year-round gardens. Because many people were familiar with only a few types of vegetables, agents introduced carrots, beets, spinach, broccoli, mustard, rutabagas, kale, and cabbage. They also helped women identify vegetables that could withstand fall and winter temperatures. For those families whose landlords refused permission to plant gardens, agents demonstrated how to identify and cook edible wild greens such as dandelions, poke salad, peppergrass, and sheep sorrel.[16]

14. Rieff, "'Rousing the People of the Land,'" 69–71.
15. Thomas M. Campbell, "A Supplement to the Annual Report of the Agricultural Extension Service as Performed by Negroes, December 31, 1919," file "Annual Reports, 1919–1920," box 1, TMC Papers.
16. L. R. Daly, "Supplement to the Annual Report of the Agricultural Extension Work among Negroes in Alabama, December 31, 1931, Macon County, Alabama," box 356, ACES.

The CES provided agents with canning equipment that was carried to club meetings. Equipment included a hot water canner and small furnace, hot iron sealer, capping iron, and tins. During the 1920s, agents began using steam pressure cookers and glass jars. Agents encouraged women to can vegetables, fruits, and meats and to establish pantries so that their families would have a nutritional year-round food supply. CES horticulturalists promoted the cultivation of fruit orchards, but for families without orchards, agents instructed women in gathering and canning wild fruits such as plums, scuppernongs, figs, blackberries, and mayhaws. Other methods of food preservation taught included pickling, brining, drying fruits and vegetables, and curing meat.[17]

Some families sold excess canned goods or used preserved food for barter. Mrs. J. E. S. Rudd of Clay County, Alabama, described how girls' club members used money earned from selling canned tomatoes to buy schoolbooks and clothes and to pay other school expenses. The money enabled one child to have her teeth cleaned and filled. Dorothy McLendon Anderson recalled that during her childhood years on a farm in Terrell County, Georgia, her family used cured meat to pay bills. She claimed that her mother gardened and canned and pickled fruits and vegetables during the summer; then her parents butchered hogs and cured the meat during the winter months. Family debts such as doctor bills were repaid with cured hams and sausage. Her mother learned food preservation from the home demonstration agent and CES pamphlets.[18]

As agents worked with rural people like the McLendon family, they kept copious notes of their activities and contacts with women

17. G. C. Starcher, *Four Vegetables for Canning*, Alabama Polytechnic Institute, Circular 8 (Auburn, AL: Alabama Polytechnic Institute, April 1917); Pearl Jones, *Home Canning of Fruits and Vegetables*, Alabama Polytechnic Institute, Circular 85 (Auburn, AL: Alabama Polytechnic Institute, June 1925); Pearl Jones Haak, *Food Preservation*, Alabama Polytechnic Institute, Circular 112 (Auburn, AL: Alabama Polytechnic Institute, February 1929).

18. Rudd, "Annual Report of Home Demonstration Work, Clay County, Alabama, 1924," box 122, ACES; Anderson, interview by Rieff, December 9, 1993, Doerun, GA; Waldo S. Rice, *The Farm Pork Supply*, Bulletin 448 (Athens: Georgia Agricultural Extension Service, 1938).

and girls, partially because they attempted to quantify results of their work in dollars and cents. In her 1914 annual report, Alabama state home agent Madge Reese cited the work of Hester Sartain and Kathleen Hubbard from Walker and Marshall Counties. Sartain had canned 2,667 cans of fruits and vegetables with Hubbard canning 1,557. Reese claimed that Sartain's net profit was $146.20 while Hubbard made $124.33.[19] All local agents included these kinds of statistics in reports that state agents cited. As home demonstration work was established, agents and administrators knew that they continually needed to justify their existence to constituents, bureaucrats, and legislators.

America's entry into World War I gave the work of the CES heightened focus and provided constituents and public officials with an opportunity to examine the efficacy of extension programs. Administrators and agents recognized the challenge of mobilizing rural people. To assist their efforts, Congress increased federal extension appropriations that allowed states to employ additional personnel. Alabama's county home demonstration force grew to sixty-five white and nine black agents, Florida's force to forty-five and eighteen, Georgia's eighty-seven and twenty-nine, Louisiana's sixty-three and eight, and Mississippi's to seventy-six and twenty-seven. Black and white urban home agents were also employed in a number of Deep South cities. The opportunities and challenges created by World War I revealed the complexities of reforming rural life.[20]

19. Reese, "Home Demonstration Agent's Report of 1914, Report of Canning Clubs of Alabama, December 1913 to December 1914," box 107, ACES.
20. Mary Feminear, *Report of Home Demonstration Work in Alabama,* Alabama Polytechnic Institute, Circular 27 (Auburn, AL: Alabama Polytechnic Institute, February 1918), 9–12; Sarah W. Partridge, "Annual Narrative Report of State Home Demonstration Agent, Florida, 1919," NARS, Florida, T-854, r. 2 (hereafter NARS T-854); "Statistical Information from the State of Georgia, February 1920 Regarding Home Demonstration Work for 1919," NARS T-855, r. 3; Susie V. Powell, "Report of Home Demonstration Work in Mississippi, 1918," NARS, Mississippi, T-869, r. 3 (hereafter NARS T-869); "Girls' Canning Club and Home Demonstration Work in Louisiana, 1918," NARS, Louisiana, T-863, r. 3 (hereafter NARS T-863); W. B. Mercier, *Extension Work among Negroes, 1920,* U.S. Department of Agriculture, Circular 190 (Washington, DC: Government Printing Office, 1921), 7–8.

Concerned that agricultural agents not overshadow their agents, home demonstration supervisors maintained that rural women could play a significant role in aiding the war effort. The campaign the HDD undertook was to cooperate with the federal Food Administration in encouraging farm families to increase food production. State supervisors of home demonstration work served as home economics directors for the Food Administration, enlisting the help of nutrition, food preservation, and horticultural specialists in planning home demonstration activities. They designed a "live-at-home" program that became home agents' chief means of assisting the Food Administration.[21]

The live-at-home program expanded and sharpened the focus of home demonstration work. Gardening and food preservation projects continued, but the emphasis and urgency with which agents approached those and similar projects were different. Their object became persuading and teaching rural families self-sufficiency. That objective served three purposes: first, rural families participated in the war effort by growing more food and conserving; second, the live-at-home program gave home demonstration agents visibility and heightened the public's awareness of their work and other extension programs; and third, the live-at-home program enabled agents to prove to the public and elected officials that their work with rural women and girls had economic value. For example, Alabama agent Mary Feminear claimed that during 1918, home agents reached and influenced 115,384 people, and the "combined economic value of all club products [was] $1,057,266.68."[22]

Agents vigorously opened their campaign with the slogan Food Will Win the War. Families were encouraged to plant "victory gardens" while reducing their meat, wheat, sugar, and fat consumption. "Meatless Mondays" and "Wheatless Wednesdays" became popular ways of participating in conservation projects and ensuring adequate supplies for the armed forces. Agents demonstrated various means of

21. True, *History of Extension Work*, 145–46; Danny Blair Moore, "'Window to the World': Educating Rural Women in Mississippi, 1911–1965" (PhD diss., Mississippi State University, 1991), 123.
22. Feminear, *Report of Home Demonstration Work*, 6.

"wartime cookery," such as explaining how to mix corn, rye, barley, or rice to lessen the amount of wheat flour in baking bread, replacing sugar with honey, and using dried peas and beans in place of meat. They conducted canning demonstrations to ensure that families preserved garden products. When glass and tin became scarce for jars and containers, agents taught women to dry, pickle, and brine fruits and vegetables and to cure meat.[23]

Utilizing conservation and preservation techniques, some rural women raised a surplus of food and decided, with home agents' encouragement, to earn extra income selling their products. The concept of selling directly to the public, eliminating the merchant, appealed to people of both races. Although individuals had peddled products in the past, agents suggested the organization of "curb markets" where vendors sold weekly or monthly at a particular site. As the name implies, people sold goods from the backs of wagons along streets or in vacant lots. As the concept gained popularity, home and farm agents worked with city councils to purchase tables and to lease shelters for the markets.

Although the war did not begin curb markets, it expanded them. Louisiana and Mississippi had curb markets in New Orleans, Shreveport, Monroe, and Jackson as early as 1916. Markets in Florida and Georgia followed. An Alabama agricultural agent who visited a market in Rome, Georgia, introduced the concept to his state in 1922. By 1927 eighteen markets were open in Alabama with sales totaling over $300,000.[24]

Some agents' visibility, coupled with their message of self-sufficiency, found a receptive audience among rural women and girls

23. Powell, "Report of Home Demonstration Work"; P. H. Rolfs, "Cooperative Extension Work in Agriculture and Home Economics in Florida, 1917," NARS T-854, r. 1; Mary Creswell, "Annual Narrative Report of Home Demonstration Work in Georgia, December 28, 1918," NARS T-855, r. 3; Feminear, *Report of Home Demonstration Work,* 10–13.

24. "Girls' Canning and Home Demonstration Work in Louisiana, 1916," in "Director's Annual Report of Agricultural Extension Work in Louisiana, 1916," NARS T-863, r. 1; Powell, "Report of Home Demonstration Work"; Mary Creswell, "Annual Narrative Report of Home Demonstration Work in Georgia, 1920," NARS T-855, r. 4; Sarah Partridge, "Annual Narrative Report

and increased club membership. In Mississippi, 5,529 white women were members of home demonstration clubs in 1916, and during the first year of black home demonstration work in 1917, 432 women joined clubs. By 1918, white membership totaled 16,554 and black 10,310. In Georgia, 5,400 white women were members of clubs by 1917; by 1920, more than 17,000 had joined. In 1917, Florida had 23 black clubs; in 1920, more than 3,500 black women were members of 101 clubs.[25]

The end of World War I brought changes to the United States and to the CES. Curtailment of federal appropriations, collapse of agricultural prices after 1919, and reduction of state and county revenues that came with the Great Depression threatened home demonstration work. During the 1920s and 1930s agents faced terminations or salary reductions. Congress responded with two appropriations bills—the Capper-Ketcham Act (1928) and the Bankhead-Jones Act (1935)—that provided additional federal funds to support extension work. For home agents, though, the Depression made it incumbent upon them to demonstrate the economic value of their work. They continued the live-at-home program with renewed zeal.[26]

An adequate food supply, nutrition, and health remained primary concerns for agents as poverty and tenancy increased and conditions in the countryside deteriorated. Agents assisted public health officials in organizing rural health tours and "Better Baby Clinics" to identify children and adults who suffered from malnutrition and other health problems. Emphasis on gardening and food preservation continued. Agents worked with the Red Cross, Reconstruction Finance

of Cooperative Extension Work in Agriculture and Home Economics in Florida, February 3, 1922," NARS T-854, r. 6; Helen Johnston, "Annual Narrative Report of State Home Demonstration Agent, Alabama, 1927," box 131, ACES.

25. Powell, "Report of Home Demonstration Work"; "Georgia Annual Report of Project 4, Home Demonstration Work, 1921," NARS T-855, r. 6; "Report of General Activities for 1920 with Financial Statement for Fiscal Year Ending June 30, 1920," Florida Cooperative Extension Service Papers, Series 21, University of Florida Archives, George A. Smathers Library, Gainesville (hereafter FCES).

26. *U.S. Statutes at Large*, vol. 45 (1927–1928), 711–12, and vol. 49 (1935–1936), 436–39; Rieff, "'Rousing the People of the Land,'" 115–16, 148.

Corporation (RFC), Federal Emergency Relief Administration (FERA), and state and county welfare agencies to obtain seed and fertilizer for families listed on relief rolls. Agents oversaw the cultivation of individual and community gardens and established community canning centers. An agent from Marion County, Florida, reported that a three-acre community garden supplied four hundred families with vegetables and that volunteers canned vegetable soup that was distributed to local schools.[27]

The RFC and later the FERA provided tin cans and glass jars for relief families to use in storing fruits and vegetables. Agents bore the primary responsibility of supervising community canning centers. They located facilities and solicited contributions from county commissioners, boards of revenue, civic organizations, and individuals to purchase steam pressure cookers and sealers for public use. As many as fifteen to twenty canning centers operated in counties during the summer months, which were the peak of vegetable and fruit harvest. Any individual could use the canning centers, but only those families that the RFC or FERA certified as "needy" were provided containers. Cecile Hester of Lauderdale County, Alabama, gave canning demonstrations to more than three hundred women who were not members of home demonstration clubs. Pearl Rowe in Walker County, Alabama, told of families donating fruits, vegetables, and meat to centers so that families without gardens or meat supplies could have provisions. The district home agent for northwestern Florida reported that dur-

27. J. A. Kitchens, "Annual Narrative Report of Farm Demonstration Work among Negroes in Alabama, December 31, 1932," box 356, ACES; Lucile Braswell, "Annual Narrative Report of Home Demonstration Agent, Conecuh County, Alabama," box 159, ACES; Hazel Bratley, "1935 Annual Narrative Report of Nutrition Work in Louisiana," NARS T-863, r. 39; Mary L. Collings, "Annual Report of Home Demonstration Work in DeSoto Parish, Louisiana, 1933," NARS T-863, r. 35; Mary Gautreaux, "Annual Narrative Report of Louisiana State University Agricultural Extension Work, Iberia Parish, Louisiana, 1933," NARS T-863, r. 35; Bertha Lee Ferguson, "Annual Narrative Report of Specialist in Home Gardening and Canning for the State of Louisiana, December 1, 1932 to July 1, 1933," NARS T-863, r. 34; Flavia Gleason, "Home Demonstration Work in Florida, 1933," NARS T-854, r. 23.

ing 1933, families within her district canned more than 180,000 containers of food. Ellen LeNoir, state home demonstration agent for Louisiana, claimed that in 1934 relief families in her state canned more than 4 million quarts of food, whereas the Georgia nutrition specialist reported in 1935 that more than 1 million containers of food were canned in community canning centers.[28]

In their canning work, agents focused on helping the needy; that assistance was appreciated. Agent Ruby Lee Hudson of Marengo County, Alabama, commented: "The citizens of our community are poor and are in need. Most of us are thankful for any help received but it seems that this work has been more beneficial than anything given to us. The people learned to do something that could be repeated year after year. The pantry shelves are filled for winter use."[29]

Agents promoted self-sufficiency in other areas of domestic life. They taught women to renovate clothes, use discarded material in making new garments, and look for unusual sources of material such as feed and flour sacks. Home demonstration clubs held contests specifically for dresses made from feed or flour sacks. Mattie Mae English of Caddo Parish, Louisiana, told that one club woman related that her daughter quit school because she was embarrassed by her clothing. After the pair attended a sack dress contest, the mother proclaimed that her daughter "ain't a bit ashamed to wear sack dresses now and me and her together has made four." Mrs. W. L. McCoy of Henry County, Alabama, "made use every opportunity" by making a collar and cuffs for a winter coat from two opossums that her sons had killed. Completion of her coat, she said, gave her "the pleasure of knowing that [she] conceived the idea, the fur [was] real

28. Hester, "Annual Narrative Report of Home Demonstration Agent, Lauderdale County, Alabama, 1933," box 153, ACES; Rowe, "Annual Narrative Report of Home Demonstration Agent, Walker County, Alabama, 1933," box 153, ACES; "Home Demonstration Agents and Emergency Relief Work," file "Gleason, Flavia, 1934," FCES; Ferguson, "Report of Specialist in Home Gardening and Canning."

29. Hudson quoted in Lois Miller, "Annual Narrative Report of Home Demonstration Agent, Marengo County, Alabama, 1934," box 156, ACES.

and not imitation, and that it is different from any other coat in the county."[30]

Additionally, agents demonstrated how to use available materials found around homes and farms to make improvements. Cast-off lumber could be used to repair steps, porches, floorboards, windowsills, and clapboards and to build cupboards, closets, and pantries. Wooden crates could be used for tables, chairs, and hassocks. Whitewash was inexpensive to make and easily tinted with pigments found in clay. Moreover, agents suggested a variety of uses for lard cans, tin cans, and pickle and jam jars and demonstrated how to make baskets and rag rugs.[31]

Because most rural families needed additional income, agents encouraged women to sell their handicrafts and extra commodities. The Clay County Basket Association in Alabama was one of the most successful efforts in marketing handicrafts. For families whose annual income averaged less than $500, the basket cooperative contributed significantly. One woman stated that she earned $225 one year; another related that although unable to perform farmwork, she could weave baskets and used her basket money to pay taxes, make home improvements, and buy necessities for her family.[32]

Curb markets continued and expanded during the 1930s as rural women sold fresh and canned fruits, vegetables, and meat; dairy products; baked goods; and various other items that they made or produced at home. In Alabama by 1940, sales exceeded $420,000 in the

30. Lu Ann Jones, *Mama Learned Us to Work: Farm Women in the New South* (Chapel Hill: University of North Carolina Press, 2002), 173–74; English, "Narrative Report of Home Demonstration Agent, Caddo Parish, Louisiana, 1933," NARS T-863, r. 34; Mamie B. Andrews, "Annual Narrative Report of Home Demonstration Agent, Henry County, Alabama, 1929," box 136, ACES.

31. Mamie B. Thorington, "Annual Narrative Report of Home Demonstration Agent, Henry County, 1930," box 140, ACES; "State Home Demonstration Council Minutes, 1938," file "Cooperative Extension Service Homemakers' Council," MCES; Mary Jessie Stane, "State Narrative Report for Home Demonstration Department, 1926, Louisiana," NARS T-863, r. 17.

32. Mrs. J. E. S. Rudd, "Annual Narrative Report of Home Demonstration Agent, Clay County, Alabama, 1928," box 133, ACES.

thirty-two markets that served whites and the five that served African Americans. Seventeen markets operated in Mississippi during 1933, while in Florida, sales exceeded $217,000 that year. In 1935, sales in Georgia's twenty-three curb markets surpassed $600,000. The difference the live-at-home program and curb markets made in income of vendors is evident in their personal stories. Mrs. A. P. Satterfield of Etowah County, Alabama, reported that she made $1,006 in curb market sales in 1928 and $1,300 another year. Although her family lost their farm during the Depression and became tenants, Satterfield managed to pay cash rent each year from her curb market sales. B. T. Pompey, Alabama's black state home demonstration agent, referred to "the $136 one woman earned over three months [in 1930] was more than three bales of cotton brought that required six months to make [plus] time and labor."[33] Pompey's reference suggests that while the live-at-home program promoted self-sufficiency, it also encouraged some degree of economic diversification.

Agents' efforts led to membership increases in home demonstration clubs. In 1940 agents reported 41,714 white and 21,701 black club members in Alabama; 8,051 white and 1,529 black members in Florida; 29,236 white and 9,529 black members in Georgia; 17,414 white and 1,454 black members in Louisiana; and 22,616 white and 13,927 black members in Mississippi (see Figure 1). Although a majority of rural women did not join a home demonstration club, these membership numbers nevertheless suggest that a significant number chose to engage in home demonstration work. Their reason

33. Diana B. Williams, "Annual Narrative Report of Home Demonstration Agent, Etowah County, Alabama, 1928," box 133, ACES; Diana B. Williams, "Annual Narrative Report of Home Demonstration Agent, Etowah County, Alabama, 1937," box 168, ACES; Mary Agnes Gordon, "Narrative Report of Home Marketing, Mississippi, December 1, 1932, to December 1, 1933," file "Narrative Report—Home Marketing," MCES; Wilmon Newell, *1933 Report of Cooperative Extension Work in Agriculture and Home Economics, Florida,* NARS T-854, r. 23; *Georgia Farm Accomplishments Report of State Agricultural Extension Service, 1935,* NARS T-855, r. 70; Pompey, "Supplement to the Annual Narrative Report of Extension Work among Negroes in Alabama, 1930," box 356, ACES.

Figure 1
Percentage of Farm Families with Home Demonstration Club Members

ST	Year of Highest Enrollment, 1914–1950		Club Membership		Number of Farms		Percentage of Farm Families with HD Club Members	
	White	Black	White	Black	White	Black	White	Black
AL	1942	1945	47,604	32,867	158,382	73,364	30.0	44.7
FL	1950	1945	20,029	2,751	49,415	7,506	40.5[#]	36.6
GA[N]	1942	1944	43,936	11,505	156,901	59,132	28.0	19.4
LA	1950	1944[NI]	24,574	6,119[NI]	83,525	40,656	29.4[#]	15.0
MS	1944	1945	25,271	15,582	131,552	159,540	19.2	9.7

[N]Figures after 1944 were not available.
[I]Adult enrollment that included women and men.
[#]Percentages were based on 1950 census data; other percentages were based on the 1940 census.

Source: *Statistical Abstract of the United States,* 1951, table no. 675, p. 575; *Statistical Abstract of the United States, 1952,* table no. 704, p. 585. Danny Blair Moore in his dissertation, "Window to the World: Educating Rural Women in Mississippi, 1911-1965" (PhD diss., Mississippi State University, 1991), 201, maintained that white home demonstration club enrollments peaked in Mississippi in 1918 with 34,069 members. A conflicting source states that white club membership in 1918 was 16,554. Determination of the peak years of Alabama club enrollments have been revised since the publication of "Go Ahead and Do All You Can: Southern Progressives and Alabama Home Demonstration Clubs, 1914-1940," in *Hidden Histories of Women in the New South,* edited by Virginia Bernhard, Betty Brandon, Elizabeth Fox-Genovese, Theda Perdue, and Elizabeth H. Turner (Columbia: University of Missouri Press, 1994). In a footnote in that essay, the author had previously concluded that white Alabama enrollments peaked in 1948 and black enrollments in 1953.

for joining was that they saw the live-at-home program assisting rural women with keeping their families fed, clothed, and sheltered despite a paucity of resources. Home demonstration club members felt some measure of empowerment as agents showed them ways of addressing their situation instead of passively allowing circumstances to control their lives. Agents believed that as nonclub members observed club women's accomplishments that they, too, would be persuaded to join a home demonstration club.[34]

When the United States entered World War II, home demonstration agents once again advocated, as they had during World War I, that rural families demonstrate patriotism through self-sufficiency. The Food for Victory and Food for Freedom campaigns encouraged families to participate in the live-at-home program. Rural people responded enthusiastically. They planted "victory gardens"; gave special attention to conserving meat, flour, and sugar supplies; and contributed to various salvage drives. Agent Ella Mae Faircloth from Jefferson County, Florida, reported that 80 percent of home demonstration club members cultivated victory gardens during 1942. Numerous families killed hogs and then cured or canned the meat because they believed that "they [are] helping neighbors who will have to depend on getting their meat supply from the market."[35]

Agent Camilla Weems claimed that agents in Peach and Houston Counties, Georgia, persuaded approximately 1,000 nonfarm families to plant victory gardens. She also reported that African American home demonstration club women throughout Georgia canned, dried, or brined garden products; made cheese; and butchered hogs and cattle. During 1944, Weems claimed that they sold more than $18,000 worth of pork and beef, rendered 7,700 pounds of lard, and made more than 93,000 pounds of soap. All home agents increased their food preservation, preparation, and nutrition demonstrations; explained how to use ration coupons; and suggested alterative foods for rationed items. Additionally, homemakers collected fat in salvage drives because they were told the fat could be used in manufacturing explosives.[36]

34. Rieff, "'Rousing the People of the Land,'" app. D, 278.
35. Faircloth, "Agent's Monthly Report, Jefferson County, Florida, February and December 1941," Record Group 800,000, I-46, box 1, Jefferson County School Board Records, 1914–1964, Florida State Archives, Tallahassee.
36. Weems, "Annual Narrative Report of Negro Home Demonstration Work, Georgia, 1944," NARS T-855, r. 136; Lena Worley, "Annual Narrative Report, Banks County, Georgia, 1944," NARS T-855, r. 136; Elizabeth Forney, "Home Demonstration Supervisors' Joint Report, 1943, Alabama," box 209, ACES.

The effort agents invested in the live-at-home program, however, did not obscure changes apparent in rural life during World War II—growing consumerism and a decline in rural population. War industries and work in military camps attracted women and men to jobs away from the farm. Those rural women who worked outside their homes had little inclination or time to participate in the live-at-home program. Moreover, higher agricultural and livestock prices during the war increased the income of those families that remained exclusively engaged in agriculture. Agents and CES administrators were not oblivious to the changes and recognized that the home demonstration program's survival required refocusing. Ironically, as agents promoted the live-at-home program they also began teaching rural women how to shop, examine products, and compare product quality and prices. The decline in rural population meant that agents had fewer constituents, leading CES personnel to look to towns and cities for prospective members. Because urban people were consumers and higher commodity prices enabled many rural people to purchase their household needs, the live-at-home program was no longer appropriate. In 1945, the HDD retired the live-at-home program and changed its agenda to assist rural and urban constituents in becoming informed consumers.[37]

Although the live-at-home program actively engaged rural women and their families in dealing with their poverty, the program also reflected the contradictions and limitations of home demonstration and extension work in general. The zenith of the live-at-home program occurred during the 1920s and 1930s, a time when American agriculture became commercial agribusiness. Labeled "business progressivism" by historian George B. Tindall, this trend emphasized production, efficiency, and profitability. Advocates argued that if farmers increased their production, diversified their crops, and maximized their efficiency, then income would increase, the rural stan-

37. "Report of National Conference of Home Economics Extension Workers, Washington, D.C., April 25–27, 1951," file "Economic Conference, Washington, D.C., 1951," box 5, TMC Papers; Gladiola Branscome, "Narrative Report of Home Demonstration Work, 1946, Tallahatchie County, Mississippi," MCES.

dard of living would improve, and prosperity would eliminate many rural problems. Extension administrators at the state and national levels embraced so-called business progressivism and were convinced that teaching scientific agriculture and home economics would increase farm productivity and income. As historian Mary Hoffschwelle maintains, home economists believed that extension work could "rehabilitate rural life through economics, not pedagogy, simply by making the farm more profitable." For home demonstration club members, this meant assisting their husbands in making farms more productive and profitable; the live-at-home program was their means of accomplishing those objectives. Their belief was that a self-sufficient home would enable a farmer to invest more of a family's resources in farming activities. Although the live-at-home program assisted rural people in reducing expenses during lean years, it had a negligible impact on farm profitability.[38]

Moreover, as home agents professionalized their service, demonstrations became specialized and less practical. Home economics was a young discipline in the early twentieth century as extension work began. Home demonstration agents realized that they had to prove themselves to extension administrators, state and county officials, and the public in two ways. They first had to demonstrate the financial benefits of their work, and the live-at-home program enabled them to assign economic value to their work with rural women. Second, because society took homemaking for granted as work that women innately knew how to do, agents needed credibility as professionals to "distance themselves from 'amateur housewives.'" Possessing a baccalaureate degree in home economics became a prerequisite for extension employment after 1920. In Alabama, by 1930, twenty-seven of forty-three white home agents held bachelor's degrees, and all sixteen African American agents received home economics training at Tuskegee Institute. Out of a 1930 force of forty-one, Louisiana employed twenty-two white agents who held bachelor's degrees in

38. Tindall, *The Emergence of the New South, 1913–1945* (Baton Rouge: Louisiana State University Press, 1967), 224; Hoffschwelle, "The Science of Domesticity: Home Economics at George Peabody College for Teachers, 1914–1939," *Journal of Southern History* 57 (November 1991): 669.

home economics. All six black home agents received training through conferences and short courses at Southern University (formerly Southern Institute).[39]

Home economics courses at colleges and universities proliferated after 1920, becoming specialized as home economists finessed techniques and integrated technology into housekeeping. At Alabama Polytechnic Institute (later renamed Auburn University), the one-semester foods course that covered preparation, cooking, serving, hygiene, cleaning, and care of kitchen furnishings expanded to seven courses by 1925. There were three courses titled Foods that introduced students to food production, cooking, and table service. In Foods II, students studied advanced cooking and menu planning. Two courses in nutrition discussed food requirements and nutritional diseases, and a food marketing and purchasing course covered production, transportation, storage, and sale. Mississippi State College for Women in 1929 offered five separate courses simply titled Clothing and a course called Appropriate Dress. The clothing courses addressed selection, cost, principles of hand and machine sewing, design, and a study of fabrics. In Appropriate Dress, students studied "correct dress for the individual and the occasion." The University of Georgia, Florida State College for Women, and Louisiana State

39. Glenna Matthews, *Just a Housewife: The Rise and Fall of Domesticity in America* (New York: Oxford University Press, 1987), 146–47; Ellen LeNoir, "1935 Annual Report for Louisiana Home Demonstration Work," NARS T-863, r. 39; Flavia Gleason, "Narrative Report of Home Demonstration Work in Florida," Annual Reports, 1917–48, FCES; Katherine Lanier, "Annual Narrative Report of Savannah District, 1926, Georgia," NARS T-855, r. 22; Susie V. Powell, "Annual Report of Home Economics Extension Department, January 1, 1917–January 1, 1918, Mississippi," NARS T-869, r. 2; L. N. Duncan, "A Summary Report of the Alabama Extension Service for the Year Ending December 31, 1923," in Spright Dowell, "Report to Board of Trustees, 1924," box 1, folder 6, Spright Dowell Collection, Auburn University Archives, Auburn, AL; L. N. Duncan, "Director's Report for the Alabama Cooperative Extension Service, 1929," box 136, ACES; W. B. Mercier, "Administrative Work and Statistical Reports of Director of Extension Work in Louisiana, 1930," vol. 518, LCES; W. R. Perkins, "Administrative Work and Statistical Report of the Director of Extension Work in Louisiana, 1921," vol. 517, LCES.

University expanded their home economics curricula similarly during the 1920s and 1930s.[40]

The specialization that home agents learned in home economics courses influenced their attitudes and demonstrations, promoted domesticity, and trivialized their work. In their efforts, agents "rationaliz[ed] as many household processes as possible" to set standards against which housewives could measure their competency. No matter how many improvements were made in living conditions, agents suggested additional ways that rural women could improve their skills and productivity as homemakers. Project areas of the live-at-home program—food preparation, food preservation, home improvement, clothing, handicrafts, health sanitation, gardening, poultry raising, and dairying—remained unchanged from 1917 until the program's end in 1945. Home agents encouraged rural women to hone technical skills as homemakers and to work toward achieving the domestic ideal of the "perfect home." Agent Pearl LeFevre of Claiborne Parish, Louisiana, confirmed that home demonstration work "educat[ed] women to appreciate the finer things of life [and taught] better methods of doing things that have to be done in the most pleasant and profitable manner." Mildred Simon in Macon County, Alabama, presented demonstrations on selecting flatware, giving formal teas, preparing buffet suppers, knitting, crocheting, letter writing, selecting and operating electrical and nonelectrical household equipment, and decorating rooms. Barbour County, Alabama, agent Frances Crawford taught dress fitting, tailored finishing, selecting appropriate

40. Dana King Gatchell, "Home Economics and Its Growth and Development at Alabama Polytechnic Institute, 1914–1942," Records of the School of Home Economics, box 12, Auburn University Archives, Auburn, AL; Mississippi State College for Women, *45th Annual Bulletin, 1929–1930* (Columbus: Mississippi State College for Women, n.d.), 126–27; Jessie J. Mize, ed., *The History of Home Economics at the University of Georgia* (Athens, GA: Agee, 1983), 13, 134–36; Florida State College for Women, *Catalogue 1914–15* (Tallahassee: Florida State College for Women, 1915), 68–70, and *Catalogue June 1925* (Tallahassee: Florida State College for Women, 1925), 103, 108–12; *University Bulletin*, Louisiana State University and Agricultural and Mechanical College, 1929–1930, 246–50.

colors for a personal wardrobe, and dry cleaning, while Bessie Barker in Chambers County, Alabama, gave demonstrations in preparing foods for tea and afternoon parties and tea service and presented clubs with decorative ideas such as stenciling and setting up "outdoor living rooms."[41]

Agents continually pushed rural homemakers toward the elusive objective of achieving the "perfect home," declaring that they would elevate their family's standard of living and assist their husbands in making their farms productive. Mrs. Winn Martin, a member of the Foley Club in Baldwin County, Alabama, remarked that she believed her home demonstration club "[did] me and my family more real service" than the other organizations to which she belonged. "I received a real incentive to work towards that ideal home which is always dear to a woman's heart." Progress that women made toward achieving the "perfect" or "ideal" home affirmed their value as home-makers and the desirability of country living, but to others these topics seemed frivolous and made agents vulnerable to charges that they catered to the wives of prosperous landowners. Preoccupation with the nuances of homemaking was a far cry from Ellen Richards's intent of women using home economics to curtail their housework so they might participate in reforms in their communities.[42]

The live-at-home program also perpetuated individualism. Business progressivism promoted individual initiative and self-reliance in its formula of efficiency and productivity. Home demonstration agents taught rural women that improving and modernizing farm homes was an integral part of making their farms efficient, productive, and profitable. Although the program's duration corresponded to the years of an escalating migration from the countryside to towns

41. Lefevre, "Annual Report of Home Demonstration Agent, 1930, Claiborne Parish, Louisiana," NARS T-863, r. 27; Simon, "Annual Narrative Report of Home Demonstration Agent, Macon County, Alabama," 1937 and 1938, boxes 168 and 175, ACES; Crawford, "Annual Narrative Report of Home Demonstration Agent, Barbour County, Alabama, 1937," box 167, ACES; Barker, "Annual Narrative Report of Home Demonstration Agent, Chambers County, Alabama, 1937," box 167, ACES.

42. Quoted in Verna Patterson, "Annual Narrative Report of Home Demonstration Agent, Baldwin County, Alabama, 1937," box 167, ACES.

and cities, it encouraged rural people to look toward their homes and farms for prosperity rather than maintaining the viability of rural communities and building relationships among rural communities and towns. Agents periodically promoted community-beautification projects, building community houses, and annual countywide rallies and contests where home demonstration club women and girls displayed canned goods, dresses, handiwork, and other completed projects. Although these activities instilled pride in individuals and clubs, they did little to address problems rural communities experienced, such as declining population, nor did they address problems related to the share system of labor—sharecropping and tenancy—that dominated southern agriculture. Instead, they reinforced the idea that a family's well-being lay with each individual's productivity. For rural women, that meant confining their activities to their homes.

When home demonstration agents were appointed to counties, they had little guidance in "putting their work over" with rural women and often found their constituents' diverse needs overwhelming. Some agents were sensitive to the plight of the poor and willingly worked with women from both the tenant and the landowning classes. Increasingly after 1920, demonstrations emphasized new technology and household management, subjects that held limited interest to women whose families lived at a subsistence level. Agents recognized that tenant women often lacked—and could not afford—basic supplies and equipment used in demonstrations, such as cooking utensils and garden implements. One African American agent lamented, "I was convinced that we were simply revealing to the people the things they might do if they had access to the equipment such as we were carrying[;] the lessons taught for the most part would be remembered more or less as a dream after [we] departed the community."[43]

Despair, apathy, and tenants' short tenure on farms posed additional problems. "[We] ain't got nothin and don't want nothin; [we] just want to be left alone" were common retorts. Frustrated Turner

43. Mary Segers, "Annual Report of Home Demonstration Work, Escambia County, 1926," box 127, ACES; Hoffschwelle, "Science of Domesticity," 668; Harry Sims to Thomas M. Campbell, December 12, 1922, file "Harry Sims," box 6, TMC Papers.

County, Georgia, agent May Betts observed that "the greatest draw-back to our work on this project [gardening] is tenantry [*sic*]." When she asked tenants to plant a fall garden, she stated that their reply was, "What's the use to plant a garden for the chickens and stock to eat up? Or why plant fruit and flowers when we will not be here next year?" An African American agent working with Tuskegee's Movable School of Agriculture found that tenants "[do] not feel that [they] should spend money for demonstrative materials that [they] cannot take with them if they move." Agent Zelma Jackson in Chambers County, Alabama, commented that she had one club whose members primarily were "renters." When "renting time" came, the majority of the women moved, and the club folded. The remaining members decided to join other clubs.[44]

Some tenant women saw home demonstration club meetings as social gatherings that they did not have the time or inclination to attend. Husbands sometimes reinforced their wives' hesitancy to participate. Claiming that "women's place [was] in the home and not in any kind of club," they objected to meetings or activities that took wives away from the farm. Another issue that kept tenant women from joining clubs was that club meetings were held in members' homes. Many tenant women were ashamed of the condition of their homes and were uncomfortable entertaining. An agent in Shelby County, Alabama, related that "three of six houses had toilets and only two had more than three rooms. Pigpens and cow pens were located fewer than thirty feet from the houses."[45]

44. Betts, "Annual Narrative Report of Home Demonstration Agent, Turner County, 1926," T-855, r. 25; "Annual Report of Movable School Work, State of Alabama for the Year Ending November 30, 1940," box 42, TMC Papers; Jackson, "Annual Report of Home Demonstration Work, Chambers County, 1924," box 122, ACES.

45. L. E. Fry, "A Preliminary Statement on Rural Housing," March 1938, file "Reports," box 3, TMC Papers; Regina Matlock, "Annual Report of Home Demonstration Work, Perry County, 1926," box 123, ACES; Mabel Feagin, "Annual Report of Home Demonstration Work, Bullock County, 1929," box 135, ACES; Powell, "Annual Report, January 1, 1917–January 1, 1918, Mississippi"; Wayne Flynt, *Poor but Proud: Alabama's Poor Whites* (Tuscaloosa: University of Alabama Press, 1989), 88.

Agents recognized that their acceptance in a county depended upon their involving the wives of both landowners and tenants. Sometimes wives of landowners hesitated to join home demonstration clubs because they did not see how the live-at-home program could benefit them. Mattie Mae English, a Caddo Parish, Louisiana, agent, was told that home demonstration work was for the "tenant class of people." When the Depression came, though, calls came "from big plantation people to assist with beef canning, pork curing, canning of vegetables, and growing of gardens." Wives of landowners in Sumter County, Alabama, told agent Clara Hall that they did not want to be identified with the "hardworking Farm Women." As was the case with English, Hall persuaded them that home demonstration work could benefit them as well. Other agents preferred to work only with the wives of landowners and disregarded tenants, finding it easier and more appealing to present specialized demonstrations to clubs of more affluent women rather than to show poor women how to cull chickens, build a sanitary privy, or plant a vegetable garden. Consequently, some agents were more successful than others in involving rural women from various socioeconomic levels in the live-at-home program and other home demonstration work.[46]

Home demonstration agents, both white and black, invested time and energy in organizing home demonstration clubs among landowners' wives and secured landowners' permission before working with tenants. Although agents' effort could have been utilized more effectively elsewhere, their concern for securing landowners' approval was political. The CES needed the support and cooperation of local elites, state legislators, congressmen, and senators to maintain extension funding. An agent who crossed a local politician or landowner was subject to transfer or dismissal.[47]

46. English, "Narrative Report of Home Demonstration Work, Caddo Parish, Louisiana, 1940," T-863, r. 54; Hall, "Substitute Agent's Report, Status of Work," included in "Annual Report of Home Demonstration Work, Sumter County, 1930," box 140, ACES.

47. Maxwell, interview by Rieff, Talladega, AL, August 28, 1990, tape in Rieff's possession; Thomas M. Campbell, "Annual Report of Negro Extension Work Containing Narrative Statistics for the States of Georgia, Florida, Alabama,

Although black home agents encountered many problems related to racial and sexual discrimination, they did not have to deal with the diverse socioeconomic spectrum that confronted white agents. J. C. Ford, who was the black state agricultural agent in Alabama, in 1941, contrasted the number of black farm operators in Alabama who were landowners (21.4 percent) with the number of white farm operators who owned their farms (50.1 percent). He concluded that "the economic standards of all farmers in Alabama is very low, [but] the standards of living for Negro farmers are substantially lower than those for white farmers. This has to be kept in mind when preparing an extension program for Negro[s]. Negro agents find it necessary to devote much time to food, health, sanitation, and little economies."[48]

For those tenants who joined home demonstration clubs and participated, the live-at-home program offered a superficial response to their problems. Agents treated symptoms that rural people experienced. In their work, they stayed within the perimeters that southern society set; they did not perceive it in their individual interest or in the interest of the CES to challenge established customs, traditions, or systems of labor. Geneva County, Alabama, agent Carrie Threaton observed that tenants "never take much interest in schools, churches, up-building the land, or in constructive citizenship. To reduce tenancy would be a great benefit to Alabama." Her view, and that of other home demonstration agents, was "if they can do anything toward correcting the problems at home, then they will be helping solve those southern problems that concern the nation." While home demonstration work (and extension work in general) represented rural reform from federal and state governments down through society, agents viewed success reflected in the individual improvements that rural people made.[49]

Mississippi, Louisiana, Oklahoma, and Texas—1925," file "1925 Reports," box 1, TMC Papers; "Professional Ethics in Extension Work and County Personnel Relationships," box 8, TMC Papers.

48. Ford, "Annual Report of the Coordinator of Negro Work, Alabama Extension Service, 1941," box 356, ACES.

49. Threaton, "Annual Report of Home Demonstration Work, Geneva County, 1939," box 180, ACES; Grace Carlson, "Annual Report of Home Demonstration Work, Escambia County, 1939," box 180, ACES.

In evaluating home demonstration agents' use of the live-at-home program, important factors to remember are the agents' limitations and the restrictions under which agents worked. Although most agents had rural backgrounds and some had lived under the share system, they worked for the CES primarily to help rural people and to support themselves. They did not see it as their place to challenge existing customs but focused their attention and energy toward alleviating the worst of circumstances that they observed. The suspicions and reluctance that rural people had toward outsiders attempting to change rural life posed challenges and frustrations for agents. Through the program, agents drew public attention to home demonstration work and assigned it economic value. A large number of rural women in the Deep South found the program and agents' demonstrations applicable in their lives, while others remained aloof and criticized agents for performing impractical and frivolous demonstrations. The specialized training that agents received in college home economics curricula had little relevance to people who had the most basic needs. In the end, the live-at-home program failed to live up to its premise—that a self-sufficient home would enable farmers to invest more family resources in farming activities and, in turn, promote farm profitability. It was not possible for the southern countryside to be revitalized through self-reliance and self-sufficiency alone. Although the live-at-home program did not alleviate the poverty of rural women, it did ease their burdens.

LOIS E. MYERS

"You Got Us All a-Pullin' Together"

Southern Methodist Deaconesses in the
Rural South, 1922–1940

On Christmas Day 1938, near Bethel Springs, Tennessee, farming families gathered in a one-room country church and listened reverently as their neighbors recited poems, sang carols, and acted out the nativity story. Then, they watched joyfully as every child received a gift. The simple celebration was memorable for this community for whom all previous Christmases had been just another day of hard work. This year, weeks of preparation had preceded the special day, as families met at the church in the evenings to learn hymns and rehearse the pageant. Farm women, and a few men, made time in their busy days to spend at the church creating children's toys. Lacking cash to purchase playthings, they expended their imaginations instead. From muslin, cotton stuffing, yarn, and paint, they fashioned dolls; from tobacco tins and broomsticks, they formed toy trains; and from broom handles and wooden apple boxes, they made hobbyhorses.

At the center of all the activities, encouraging and organizing Bethel Springs's first Christmas party, was a newcomer in the community, Marjorie Minkler. She was a single white woman, a college graduate, sent to western Tennessee as a deaconess consecrated by the Methodist Episcopal Church, South (MECS) under the sponsorship of the Woman's Missionary Council (WMC). As was the case for most rural Southern Methodist churches, Bethel Springs was a circuit church, having a minister who traveled between several churches, vis-

166

iting each site only once a month. Without a resident leader, the people lacked direction to organize a Sunday school or vision to garner resources to improve the social and economic conditions of their community. To remedy the situation, Minkler set specific goals for her work in Bethel Springs: "to develop a spirit of co-operation, to create a community consciousness, to awaken people to problems confronting the community, and to arouse in them a determination to face these problems realistically." The Christmas party was a successful first step toward achieving the missionary's goals, as became evident following the festivities when one of the local men told her, "'I've lived in this place all my life. Allus [always] some was a-pullin' one way and some was a-pullin' another. But you got us all a-pullin' together.'"[1]

During a period of eighteen years, 1922–1940, the WMC recruited and trained forty-eight rural deaconesses and home missionaries like Marjorie Minkler for specialized work in the southern countryside. Funded at the grassroots level by local women's missionary societies, the missionaries represented a distinctive, practical response by Christian women to problems faced by twentieth-century rural southerners in the years between the two world wars. In annual reports written for the WMC and the various supporting conference mission boards, missionaries shared the challenges they faced in rural work. Largely untold outside Southern Methodist women's literature, the stories related by rural deaconesses verified the desperate conditions and broad cultural diversity of southern rural communities in the years before, during, and immediately following the Great Depression. Their stories demonstrated, too, the positive outcomes for individuals, families, churches, and communities when a few women dedicated their minds and hands to making life better in the southern countryside.

❧

1. Woman's Missionary Council, *Twenty-ninth Annual Report of the Woman's Missionary Council of the Methodist Episcopal Church, South* (Nashville: Publishing House of the Methodist Episcopal Church, South, 1939), 192 (the latter published all such annual reports); Minkler Morris, "Pullin' Together," in *Along the Way: Stories by Church and Community Workers in Kaleidoscopic Ministry,* by Church and Community Workers Organization (Nashville: Committee, 1986), 66.

The first WMC home missionary appointed to rural work was Willena Henry. The story of her entrance into missionary work provides clues for understanding the gendered context of church missions, the religious motivations behind women's dedication to missionary service, and the ways the WMC encouraged, educated, and equipped women for missionary service.

Born in Comanche, Texas, in 1881, the oldest child and only daughter of a preacher and a preacher's daughter, Willena Henry joined the Methodist church when she was nine years old. Years later she remembered, "We had a little Junior Missionary Society and my desire for missionary work was born there." Her mother died in 1892, and her father remarried two years later. Before finishing high school, she left home to become a teacher in Indian Territory. From her meager teacher's salary, she managed to send money home to help her father, stepmother, and four younger brothers. During a brief leave from teaching, Henry took a business course at Southwestern University, a Southern Methodist institution in Georgetown, Texas. She used her stenographic training in various jobs to supplement her salary upon her return to teaching in Indian Territory in the winter of 1902. She stayed active in church work and in 1905 attended a conference at Epworth-by-the-Sea, the Texas state Methodist encampment near Corpus Christi. "While there," she later testified, "I answered a call to consecrate my life for service in whatever way the Lord might lead."[2]

From 1906 to 1909, Willena Henry attended the WMC training school for women church workers at Scarritt College in Kansas City, Missouri. She financed her way through school performing housekeeping chores and answering the telephone in the dormitory. Upon graduation in 1909, she was consecrated by the church as a deaconess and appointed to assist the pastor of the Methodist church at Crossett, Arkansas, a company town completely owned by the Crossett Lumber Company. She served five years among logging camps and sawmill villages, where her ministry included placing orphans in adop-

2. Henry, "Miss Willena Henry, 1909," in *Historical Sketch of the Woman's Missionary Society, Central Texas Conference, Methodist Episcopal Church, South,* by Mrs. J. H. Stewart (Fort Worth: Conference, 1929), 48.

tive homes; organizing a night school for working men; leading Sunday school classes, youth programs, and women's missionary societies; and teaching cooking classes. Henry's 1911–1912 annual report listed 888 home visits among the lumber camp population. Her appointment to Arkansas echoed the pioneering work of her own great-grandfather John Henry, who in 1818 built the first Methodist church in Arkansas.[3]

During 1914–1915, Willena Henry returned to Oklahoma to pioneer missions work among immigrants working in coal mines around McAlester and Hartsborne. She managed a community center, directing social services for women and children and night school for men, and conducted home visits among families in the district under her charge, an area covering seven villages populated by a reported six thousand immigrants from twenty nations.[4] Poor health required her to take seven years' leave from the WMC, but even as she recuperated in Texas, she continued to work when able in Methodist settlement houses and hospitals near cotton mills in Dallas and coal mining camps at Thurber.

In 1922, when she was forty years old, Henry was ready to return to full-time home missions work. Her availability coincided with a request for a professional worker to initiate rural missions in northeast Arkansas, an appeal originating from the Jonesboro District Woman's Missionary Society (WMS) and forwarded by the North Arkansas Conference WMS to the WMC. The request and its subsequent response followed distinctly Methodist organizational relationships, termed *connectional*, wherein the local charge (a ministerial assignment to a church, a circuit comprising two or more churches, or a mission) relates to a district, a subdivision of a geographical annual

3. WMC, *First Annual Report*, 1911, 441; WMC, *Second Annual Report*, 1912, 401; WMC, *Fourth Annual Report*, 1913, 212; George Walter Balogh, "Crossett, Arkansas: The History of a Forest Industry, a Community, and Change" (master's thesis, University of Central Arkansas, 1981); James A. Anderson, *Centennial History of Arkansas Methodism* (Benton, AR: L. B. White Printing, 1935), 487.

4. Noreen Dunn Tatum, *A Crown of Service: A Story of Woman's Work in the Methodist Episcopal Church, South, from 1878–1940* (Nashville: Board of Missions, Woman's Division of Christian Service, 1960), 293.

conference, so named because it meets yearly, which in turn sends delegates to quadrennial General Conference meetings, which determines church policy. The WMC and its societies at the church, district, and annual conference levels operated under a board appointed by the MECS General Conference. The WMC met each spring to allocate resources to meet the needs expressed by the various districts and conferences. In response to the request from the Jonesboro District WMS, the WMC appointed seasoned veteran Willena Henry to the task with the understanding that the district and conference women's missionary societies would raise funds to cover her expenses. Subsequently, the WMC began designating as "rural work" not only church work in agriculture regions but also the kinds of social ministries Henry had performed in lumber and mining camps.

Arriving in Blytheville, Arkansas, in July 1922, the deaconess surveyed nearby rural communities and began work in the area of Promised Land. The following spring she reported to WMC, "We have visited the homes and the school, helped in the women's work, in the Sunday School, and in the social life of the community; conducted a Bible study hour two Sunday nights a month with an average attendance of seventy-six." She accomplished the home visits by horseback, riding, as she said, "day in and day out from home to home." Her familiarity with local families proved helpful the next winter when flu broke out across Promised Land. "I spent many days on horseback," she wrote, "with a big basket of food going from house to house where from two to nine were ill. Rain and snow made all visiting except horseback impossible, and often the horse had to wade through water and ice knee deep. In spite of the weather, I made eighty visits that month." During the following months, she spread out into other communities, organizing a Sunday school at Chiggoe Ridge and a women's community club at Big Lake, where she found "the most needy field I ever saw, nothing but water, wickedness, and booze."[5]

In 1923, the district purchased "a Ford touring car" for the rural missionary's use, allowing her to carry three girls to a summer youth

5. Ibid., 213–14.

conference in Searcy. There Henry met a Japanese Christian woman, whom she invited to speak at Promised Land. That experience, the deaconess reported, "was worth a great deal to our boys and girls, who had never seen a Japanese before, and the whole Church was benefited by her visit." Henry continued broadening the community's understanding of the world by organizing the women into a missionary society. The rural women supported her efforts, as proved in her statement to WMC: "One of the greatest joys of my work among the country people was the woman's missionary society—the faithful half dozen and the heroism of all. Willing to walk in the dust and heat or to come in a wagon, sitting on planks and driving the mules, willing to sweep the church to get money to pay on my salary—these are some of the sacrifices they made."[6]

After two years in northeastern Arkansas, Willena Henry returned to Texas, where she resumed work in the Dallas settlement house and led Bible study classes for working women. Upon leaving Arkansas, she stated, "The rural work has a bigger place in my heart than any work I ever did. But for health and home reasons I'd still be there. I didn't move because I wanted to. The rural field is the needy, fruitful field." Circumstances prevented her return to rural missions, however, for in 1925, upon the death of her stepmother, she moved to San Antonio to become the primary caregiver for her aging father.[7]

☙❧

Willena Henry's experience illustrates the impact of gender upon vocational ministry within Southern Methodism. In the opening statement to a brief autobiographical memoir composed in 1928, she confessed, "I do not like to write about myself for a person whose great grandfather was the first Methodist preacher in Southern Arkansas, and whose maternal grandfather was so good a preacher as was Rev. W. R. D. Stockton, and whose father was as great a soul winner as was Rev. H. B. Henry, certainly would have amounted to more in the Kingdom of the Lord than I have. I am ashamed that I have done so

6. WMC, *Fourteenth Annual Report*, 1924, 231.
7. Ibid.

little."[8] Her role models for vocational Christian service were men who, being men, received authority from the church to carry out their callings by preaching the Gospel and administering a church.

As a woman, Willena Henry could obey her calling only as a layperson. Denied access to careers in the clergy, Southern Methodist women found outlets for ministry through mission institutions, established, funded, and operated by women. Vocational opportunities for women became available in 1878 through the Woman's Board of Foreign Missions and in 1890 through the Woman's Board of Home Missions. In 1910, the MECS General Conference combined the two boards into one overarching organization, the Woman's Missionary Council. During its existence, the WMC repeatedly promoted the role of women in the life of the church. In 1932, the WMC expressed its case supporting professional women clergy in a formal report to MECS leaders, but the argument was largely ignored, appearing, as its authors admitted, in a time when "the tradition of a man-directed church" prevailed.[9]

Southern Methodist women adopted the universal motto of American Protestant women's missionary societies, "woman's work for woman," a theme formulated in line with the mid-nineteenth-century concept of separate spheres for men and women. Mission-minded women gave the motto a positive spin, believing "it took women to reach other women and children with the gospel." Staying within their sphere, they worked out their callings as teachers, nurses, and social workers. Women viewed their gendered ministry as an opportunity to create connections between women of diverse cultures and circumstances on the basis of their common experiences as women. They came to believe, as missions professor Dana L. Robert explained, that "conversion to Christianity would not only provide eternal salvation for women everywhere but it would help raise their self-worth and improve their social positions in oppressive, patriarchal societies." Theressa Hoover, deputy general secretary of the Women's Division, Board of Global Ministries, United Methodist Church, from 1966 to

8. Henry, "Miss Willena Henry, 1909," 48.
9. Methodist Episcopal Church, South, Woman's Missionary Council, *Report of Commission on Woman's Place of Service in the Church* (Nashville: Woman's Missionary Council, 1932), 92–93.

1990, stated in her study of gender relations in Methodist missions that the women's programs adopted as their focus "the evangelical, physical, and social needs of marginal people—especially women and children, who could not be reached by male missionaries abroad and who were ignored by church and society at home."[10]

As a Southern Methodist woman, Willena Henry, then, would express her calling to ministry through missionary service dedicated to the causes of women and children rather than in the pulpit like her forefathers. The church denied her the right to ordination, which invested ecclesiastical authority, but she could receive affirmation from the church through consecration to the lay office of deaconess. The all-male MECS General Conference approved the office of deaconess for home-mission volunteers in 1902 and placed full responsibility for selecting, training, appointing, and financing deaconesses under the women's missionary organization. Approved by European Protestant denominations for almost half a century and by the Methodist Episcopal Church fourteen years earlier, the female diaconate traced its origins to the first-century community ministry of Phoebe, as recorded in the New Testament (Rom. 16:1–2). The office of deaconess institutionalized gendered ministry, as it represented "an official recognition by the church of women's traditional societal functions as nurturers, teachers, servants, nurses of the sick and dying—caregivers for the poor, the young, and the elderly." The WMC emphasized that the deaconess was neither a preacher nor a female deacon, but her authorization and appointment by the church empowered her "to do some things she could not otherwise do." The most obvious benefit was participation in policy making through representation on the WMC deaconess board, a privilege that separated the consecrated deaconess from other female home missionaries. Her primary role was to be "a leader of women," meaning that "instead of hindering them or doing the work they should do, they learn from her how to work more

10. Robert, introduction to *Gospel Bearers, Gender Barriers: Missionary Women in the Twentieth Century,* edited by Dana L. Robert (Maryknoll, NY: Orbis Books, 2002), 7; Hoover, *With Unveiled Face: Centennial Reflections on Women and Men in the Community of the Church* (New York: Women's Division, General Board of Global Ministries, United Methodist Church, 1983), 13.

effectively, and are led out into lines of service they had not entered until she, as a skilled worker, pioneered the way." After empowering local women to assume responsibility for their own programs, the deaconess moved on to another site.[11]

Only single women or widows, unencumbered by dependents, qualified because the deaconess devoted her entire time to God's service. Her commitment, however, was not for life; she could retire or take leaves of absence as necessary. Age requirements remained flexible, but the ideal recruit was between twenty-four and thirty-five. Policies curtailing service at age fifty proved bendable, though, as in the case of Annie Price, appointed at sixty-one to organize a kindergarten and women's English class among Hispanic people in Alpine, Texas. At first, deaconesses worked unsalaried. By 1920, however, policies allowed them an annual stipend of nine hundred dollars. The WMC provided direct support for foreign missionaries and home missionaries appointed to schools, but for rural workers, district and conference mission boards furnished the missionary's room, board, and transportation. Although deaconesses lived together in cities, in rural areas, where they often worked alone, they lived with local families.[12]

For twenty-five years, deaconesses wore a required uniform: a long black dress, large white neck bow, and black bonnet with white ties. The purpose of the uniform was to "secure economy, good taste, introduction, and protection when needed." The uniform identified the deaconess in the same way a frock coat distinguished some preachers. In 1927, long after most American women had bobbed their hair

11. Carolyn De Swarte Gifford, introduction to *The American Deaconess Movement in the Early Twentieth Century*, edited by Carolyn De Swarte Gifford (New York: Garland, 1987), 2; Mary Helm, "What a Deaconess Is, and What She Is Not," in Woman's Home Mission Society, *Sixteenth Annual Report* (Nashville: Woman's Home Mission Society, 1902), 119.

12. Tatum, *Crown of Service*, 319–31; Mary Agnes Dougherty, *My Calling to Fulfill: Deaconess in the United Methodist Tradition* (New York: Women's Division, General Board of Global Missions, United Methodist Church, 1997), 68–76; WMC, *Tenth Annual Report*, 1920, 165–68; Emory Stevens Bucke, ed., *The History of American Methodism*, vol. 3 (New York: Abingdon Press, 1964), 122; Price, "Annie E. Price, 1923," in *Historical Sketch*, by Stewart, 82; WMC, *Twenty-ninth Annual Report*, 1939, 193–94.

and shortened their hemlines, the deaconess uniform became a plain black or white dress with white tailored collar and cuffs and, more significantly, became optional. As late as 1939, to her first meeting in her first northern Alabama rural mission assignment following her consecration, deaconess Elizabeth Thompson wore "a simple black silk dress with prim white collar," but, she confessed later, underneath it all she wore "a red petticoat for courage!"[13]

Educational prerequisites for deaconesses included a high school diploma, the equivalent of two years' college-level work, and another two years' specialized training at a laity training school, like Scarritt College. Before her commissioning, a deaconess completed two years' supervised probationary service, a requirement often met through field-work placements at the training school. A solemn ceremony of consecration held each spring during the annual WMC meeting marked the beginning of a deaconess's ministry, whereupon she received a twelve-month renewable appointment to service appropriate to her training and experience. Most of the deaconesses entered urban settings, becoming teachers in vocational schools, social workers in settlement houses, directors of cooperative homes for working women, or Bible teachers and matrons in Methodist dormitories on state college campuses. Some became assistants to pastors, leading a church's educational and recreational programs. By 1939, the WMC had organized its home-mission projects within seven major categories bearing descriptive titles: City Work, Educational Institutions and Homes, Industrial Work, Negro Work, Cuban Work, Mexican Work, and Rural Work. That year, WMC deaconesses numbered 208, with 167 in active service, 29 retired, and 12 on study sabbatical. Forty home missionaries also appointed by WMC assisted with the organization's eighty-eight projects in sixteen states.[14]

ᘔ

13. Helm, "What a Deaconess Is," 119; Thompson, "Appointment—the Old Way," in *Along the Way*, by Church and Community Workers Organization, 8.

14. Methodist Episcopal Church, South, Board of Missions, *Missionary Yearbook of the Methodist Episcopal Church, South* (Nashville: Board of Missions, 1939), 38; Juanita Brown, "A Venture in Home Missions," *World Outlook* (August 1940): 17.

In addition to revealing elements of gendered ministry, Willena Henry's story also indicates the role religious training played in inspiring missionary service. Education in missions began for Methodist girls at home, as they read WMC magazine stories of heroines spreading the Gospel around the globe; at church, where missionary society women encouraged them to volunteer for Christian vocations; and at summer Bible conferences, where they met missionaries on leave face-to-face. Through sermons and church doctrine courses they learned that from its founding, Methodism sought to bring people into the Christian fold by first improving their living conditions. Convinced of individual worth and hopeful for ultimate perfection, Methodists believed that the outcome of faith in Jesus Christ was not only expectation for heavenly reward but also acceptance of personal responsibility to work for the betterment of human experience this side of heaven. For Methodist women, believing that societal conditions aided or impeded individual advancement, the hope for human progress depended upon the foundation of strong, stable, Christian homes, and to that purpose they dedicated their work.[15]

Under such influences, some women—many of them with rural backgrounds—felt called by God to dedicate their lives to vocational church service. Born in rural Coryell County, Texas, in 1877, Annie E. Price remembered fifty years later that her father, a Methodist preacher and revivalist, "was a social service worker in his day (without bearing the name); he was never too busy looking after the needs of his own family to stop and help relieve the suffering and the distress of his neighbor." Her mother also impressed Annie, who wrote, "Mother was kind and had innumerable friends. Being the mother of ten children, she naturally was absorbed largely with home interests; however, she was never too occupied to pay special attention to the person most 'down and out.' With this for background, naturally missionary work appealed to me." Years later, while teaching in public schools, Annie Price read an article in a woman's mission magazine that

15. John Patrick McDowell, *The Social Gospel in the South: The Woman's Home Mission Movement in the Methodist Episcopal Church, South, 1836–1939* (Baton Rouge: Louisiana State University Press, 1982), 50.

influenced her to dedicate her life to full-time church service with the challenging words: "Somewhere you and I ought to take hold of a cause that is great and needy, and put into it our intelligence and our love, for Christ's and for Humanity's sake."[16]

Mamie Robinson, born in 1891, in rural Bell County, Texas, attended a country school and spent two years at Baylor College for Women preparing for "what she thought was her life work, viz., to teach in the rural schools and to help needy churches." She continued her education at Sam Houston Normal College, in Huntsville, Texas, and there, during campus revival services, "the call came to give all her time and service to Him who gave His life for her."[17]

At her consecration service in 1936, Eva Crenshaw, from the village of Martin, in northeastern Georgia, testified, "After college I taught school a number of years, during the last few of which there came to me a great desire to give myself in service to my own people—rural people. When the opportunity was offered I came to Scarritt, eager and alert for anything that would prepare me to meet the needs of rural people." Furthermore, she said,

> I love the country. I love the soil, but I am not unaware of the hardships of farm life. I have had first-hand experience of them all my life. But in addition to sympathy and love and knowledge of the needs of rural people, I know I must have something else, or I will be an utter failure. I must have the spirit of Christ. I believe I am facing these problems in His spirit. Therefore, I am gladly willing to accept this challenge to service.

Crenshaw realized her calling to rural work in a career spanning thirty-four years.[18]

Upon accepting the call to career ministry, a woman faced years of

16. Price, "Annie E. Price," 82–83.
17. Robinson, "Mamie Robinson, 1923," in *Historical Sketch*, by Stewart, 83.
18. Woman's Missionary Council, *The Council Bulletin* (Nashville: Woman's Missionary Council, 1936), 25; Alice Lucy Cobb, *A Tapestry of Service: 100 Years along the Way in Church and Community Ministry* (New York: General Board of Global Missions National Church and Community Worker's Organization, 1989), 126.

preparation before realizing her goal. To help mission volunteers meet strict requirements, the WMC furnished vital applied educations. From its beginnings in 1844, the MECS had promoted women's education. In fact, 46.4 percent of the 207 MECS colleges operating from 1850 to 1933 were women's colleges. To outfit women as pious Christian wives and mothers and as exemplary leaders among other women, Methodist female academies and colleges, as well as co-educational institutions, provided for women a curriculum based upon the domestic arts, fine arts, and liberal arts. By the turn of the twentieth century, some Methodist colleges provided courses in secretarial training, as evidenced by Willena Henry's business education at Southwestern University.[19]

Missions work required acquisition of particular skills, and so the WMC developed a school specifically for female students whose goals carried "an emphasis on service rather than academic performance." Modeled on the Chicago Training School operated by the Methodist Episcopal Church, the Scarritt Bible and Training School opened in 1892 in Kansas City, Missouri, under the auspices of the MECS Woman's Board of Foreign Missions. Conference WMS groups collected special offerings to fund scholarships for mission candidates at Scarritt. After the turn of the twentieth century, with approval of the office of deaconess and the introduction of sociology into the curriculum, Scarritt turned out increasing numbers of home missionaries. In 1924, the training school relocated to Nashville, Tennessee, where it became Scarritt College for Christian Workers, a coeducational professional school for senior or graduate students committed to church service.[20]

19. Statistics from Clarence Moore Dannelly, "The Development of Collegiate Education in the Methodist Episcopal Church, South, 1846–1902" (PhD diss., Yale University, 1933), 69; Amy Thompson McCandless, *The Past in the Present: Women's Higher Education in the Twentieth-Century South* (Tuscaloosa: University of Alabama Press, 1999), 55–61.

20. Virginia Lieson Brereton, "Preparing Women for the Lord's Work," in *Women in New Worlds: Historical Perspectives on the Wesleyan Tradition*, edited by Hilah F. Thomas and Rosemary Skinner Keller (Nashville: Abingdon, 1981), 181; Tatum, *Crown of Service*, 303–17; Dougherty, *My Calling to Fulfill*, 170–80; Brereton, "Preparing Women," 178–99.

In an era when women rarely found welcome in theological seminaries, Scarritt prepared women for missionary service by providing a curriculum covering the potential tasks women might face on the mission field, from bookkeeping to performing sacred music. Method courses involved them in social science research projects, especially community surveying, and culminated in applied clinical experience. When Willena Henry initiated rural work in Arkansas by visiting local families, she put into action casework skills learned in field experience at Scarritt College. Home visitations allowed missionaries to see first-hand the conditions among which women and children lived in order to formulate plans of action for meeting their physical and spiritual needs.[21]

❦

Called, trained, and consecrated, Southern Methodist deaconesses entered rural ministry motivated and prepared. In 1922, the WMC began rural work with two missionaries assigned to projects in two states, and in 1939, the organization had available thirty-eight women for appointment to thirty-two rural communities across the South and Southwest. At the grassroots level, WMC rural projects refused to fit a single description, accommodating instead the particular needs of each location. Some women stayed one year in each place along a multichurch circuit, whereas others served entire circuits at one time. Some deaconesses remained with an annual conference doing one major job for a period of years. Others moved around from year to year, and some switched back and forth between rural and urban missions.[22]

Appointments for deaconesses often fell into the category of pastor's assistant. In rural churches, however, a pastor's work was spread over several congregations on a circuit, and the women occasionally

21. Margaret H. Hawkins, "Scarritt College Students in Community Service," *World Outlook* (July 1936): 16; Mary Agnes Dougherty, "The Social Gospel according to Phoebe: Methodist Deaconesses in the Metropolis, 1885–1918," in *Women in New Worlds,* ed. Thomas and Keller, 361–63.
22. Board of Missions, *Missionary Yearbook,* 1939, 38; Brown, "Venture in Home Missions," 17.

found themselves leading worship services and preaching in the pastor's absence. In 1931, Mae Wess Bell arrived at her assignment in Searcy District, Arkansas, in the middle of revival season and soon found herself "filling the pulpit" in the pastor's absence. Ora Hooper, in Louisiana during 1932, both "filled" the pulpit and conducted "personal evangelistic work." In 1936, Minnie Lee Eidson reported that in Smithville, Oklahoma, "more than in other years the deaconess has been called upon to substitute for the pastor in conducting church services." More often, though, the rural women missionaries shared the experience of Dora Hoover, who during 1932 to 1933 in Wheeler, Mississippi, accomplished "one more year's work for Jesus, ranging from scrubbing churches to every phase of Christian service except preaching from a text."[23]

Most rural workers found strong local mission boards willing and able to finance their work, but some had to organize from scratch the mission societies that eventually supported them. They traveled hundreds of miles a year by foot or horseback or fought muddy roads and mountain grades with automobiles furnished by local WMS women. They met rural families where they lived, including Ozark Mountain cabins, Mississippi Delta houseboats, and East Texas tenant shacks. The missionaries served congregations meeting in church buildings blessed with electric lights and comfortable pews, as well as in homes and schools. They brought people together under the shade of open-sided brush arbors, shelters with crude coverings made of tree branches or scrap lumber, or under the sky in open clearings with logs as benches. In some cases, women's missionary societies built and furnished rural community centers modeled on urban settlement houses where several deaconesses lived together and directed weekday social services for the population.[24]

Rural missionaries worked side by side with southern women of different races and multiple ethnic backgrounds. They ministered to

23. WMC, *Twenty-second Annual Report,* 1932, 348; WMC, *Twenty-third Report,* 1933, 223, 224; WMC, *Twenty-seventh Annual Report,* 1937, 285.
24. See, for instance, reports from Calvert, AL, in WMC, *Twenty-second Annual Report,* 1932, 349; and Cairo, GA, in WMC, *Twenty-fifth Annual Report,* 1935, 238.

people suffering the devastation of both floods and drought. In addition to cooperating with the Red Cross and state boards of health in confronting epidemics of influenza and arranging immunization clinics for tuberculosis, diphtheria, smallpox, and typhoid fever, they invited county nurses to rural sites to hold baby clinics and teach family health care classes. Working with county demonstration agents, they organized cooking and gardening classes and canning kitchens. Often their first contact outside the local church in a rural neighborhood was the school, and some took full-time jobs in the schools as teachers or principals in order to extend their contacts with the community beyond the church programs they also directed. Their work with young people encompassed not only Epworth League, the Methodist Sunday-evening church training program for adolescents and young adults, but also Girl Scouts, Boy Scouts, Camp Fire, 4-H, and Girl Reserves.

Noreen Dunn Tatum, author of a comprehensive WMC history, described the scope of rural deaconess activities: "Reading books for children, government pamphlets, Bibles, songbooks, story papers, recreation supplies, and first aid materials became standard equipment for her. She helped to get electric lights and adequate public transportation in her area; she used her car as an ambulance, as a Sunday school bus, and as a free taxi in emergencies." As always, her ultimate goal was evangelism. "There were times," explained Tatum, "when she was the only Christian leader to minister to the soul needs of people in a neglected and isolated area. She cheered the discouraged, lifted the fallen, nursed the sick, buried the dead, consoled the brokenhearted. In hundreds of ways she pointed men and women, young people, and children toward Christ, their hope and their salvation."[25]

In 1922, the same year Willena Henry began work in Arkansas, Bessie Brand pioneered rural missions in the North Mississippi Conference. As assistant to the pastor of the four-church Shuford Circuit, she paid regular visits to 150 families in her first year. At the start of her assignment, Brand drove the "mission Ford" supplied by the conference WMS hundreds of miles to survey ninety-three rural

25. Tatum, *Crown of Service*, 295.

churches in the region, discovering a severe lack of women's and children's programs. Four out of five churches had no Sunday school, and half had neither a missionary society nor an Epworth League. The survey results indicated a trend typical across southern rural churches, few of which supported religious instruction programs or had the benefit of lay leaders equipped to teach the Bible and church doctrine. Her observations of the circuit, with its four churches—Shuford, Lovejoy, Pisgah, and Olivet—revealed a population that was "pure Anglo-Saxons, small farmers, and most of them own their homes." Their average income was low, she reported, because of the difficulty of marketing farm products over poor roads. During 1923, Brand helped establish a community library at the Lovejoy church, and the book collection grew within two years to three hundred volumes, all donated by the conference WMS. She also arranged visits from the county demonstration agent who taught bread making and sewing, as well as ways to grow "better gardens" and create "prettier yards."[26]

Within two years, in the four churches under her care, the rural worker reported significant changes benefiting young people, including Christian education classes in the consolidated school, active Epworth Leagues, and vacation Bible schools. With her help, women in all four churches organized individual missionary auxiliaries and formed a common society for service projects, including sewing pillowcases for the Methodist hospital and selling hens to raise funds to paper the church parsonage. In July 1926, when Bessie Miller replaced Bessie Brand at Shuford Circuit, Mississippi, she found that after four years under the influence of a missionary, rural women were beginning to solve their own problems. They "visited the sick, quilted for the orphans and needy of the community, collected 'poundings' for the pastor, gathered up chickens for a church painting fund, peddled flavoring extract for some other causes, and so on," she observed.[27]

WMS groups in other states adopted the rural mission models proven effective in Arkansas and Mississippi and supported their own

26. WMC, *Thirteenth Annual Report*, 1923, 213; WMC, *Fourteenth Annual Report*, 1924, 63, 232; WMC, *Fifteenth Annual Report*, 1925, 196.
27. WMC, *Fourteenth Annual Report*, 1924, 63–64, 232; WMC, *Fifteenth Annual Report*, 1925, 196; WMC, *Sixteenth Annual Report*, 1926, 204–5.

conference deaconesses to organize mission societies in the rural churches. Bert Winter's work among rural women in the North Georgia Conference convinced her that women's mission societies benefited country women by providing "contacts with the outside world not otherwise obtainable by many of these women. It gives opportunity for social contacts, so needed in scarcely populated areas, and is a real educative force through its literature and other cultivation methods." Among the six churches in the Greenwood Springs Circuit, Aberdeen District, North Mississippi Conference, in 1929, Ethel Cunningham found women eager for organization. "All they needed was a start," she noted. The work proved so popular, she added, "Impassable roads or lack of heating facilities may cause Sunday schools to close, but they do not prevent our women from meeting in the homes for their Missionary Societies." In 1932, in southern Arkansas, women continued to be the priority as Willie May Porter ministered among oil field camps. Following a site visit there, the president of the district WMS wrote, "Her contacts with the women in their homes means much in their lives, her interest in the orphan little ones, deprived of a mother's care, the good literature she secures from the El Dorado Public Library for the isolated women to read and later discuss with them, are things no statistics can correctly estimate."[28]

In their work, rural deaconesses confronted the poverty caused by farm tenancy and the crop-lien system. In Helena District, North Arkansas Conference, in 1926, Virginia Hall took up residence in a seven-church circuit at Cherry Valley, where she saw for the first time the results of farm tenancy. "I do not like the system," Hall confessed, "but I do like the tenants, and I pray that by the end of the year we will have worked out many plans that will bring happiness into the starved lives of the women and children of this section." She went immediately to work, and after only three months, she stated,

28. WMC, *Eighteenth Annual Report*, 1928, 255; WMC, *Twentieth Annual Report*, 1930, 363; Mrs. L. K. McKinney, "Camden District Mission Work," in *Annual Session of the Little Rock Conference Woman's Missionary Society*, by Methodist Episcopal Church, South, Little Rock Conference Woman's Missionary Society (Conway, AR: Society, 1932), 52 (the latter published all such annual session reports).

"With the help of the good people of Wynne, we were able to give a box containing clothes, food, candy, fruit, and toys to fifteen families Christmas, and this was indeed a happy time." Her appeals for medical help also proved successful. "One Wynne man," she said, "has given me money enough to start a medicine fund, for many of the people are not able to buy medicine, let alone have a doctor. Arrangements have been made with our Tri-State Hospital in Memphis, to care for anyone we send for treatment or operations, and we are to have one-day clinics at two different places." The next year, she teamed with the Red Cross to distribute quinine and mosquito netting among white and black tenants. She estimated that during 1927–1928 she delivered "about two thousand articles of clothing."[29]

In 1928–1929, Bess Eaton took up the work begun by Virginia Hall among the tenant families in Helena District. Schools and churches in the area had recently consolidated, a process that, the deaconess observed, "has many advantages but leaves isolated rural communities without a logical center." Though the children "very readily come to the school," many country people did not have transportation into town for church services. Eaton recognized among the tenants "a reticence characteristic of rural people which prevents them from being totally happy even in our small town Churches." The following year, Jessie Mae Byers worked in Helena District, where she "found situations I never dreamed existed in the United States, a country so-called Christian." Tenancy caused families to move so often, she discovered, that many children never attended school, much less church. Although many tenants ignored her help, some responded to her encouragement "to clean themselves and their houses, put their children in school and begin to take an interest in the spiritual things of life."[30]

Tenants living in the southeastern corner of Rusk County, Texas, tried to make a living farming cotton during the Great Depression.

29. WMC, *Seventeenth Annual Report*, 1927, 203–4; WMC, *Eighteenth Annual Report*, 1928, 252; North Arkansas Conference WMS, *Thirteenth Annual Report*, 1927, 55–56.
30. WMC, *Nineteenth Annual Report*, 1929, 195; WMC, *Twenty-first Annual Report*, 1931, 283; Noreen Dunn, "Why I Am a Home Missionary," *Missionary Voice* (July 1930): 20.

Life afforded few pleasures until the women of the Texas Conference provided home missionary Janet C. Head to Caledonia Methodist Church. She organized multiple indoor and outdoor social and recreational activities for all ages. "These social activities are meeting a vital need of our people," explained the missionary, "for their lives were entirely lacking in any type of social activity, except dances, until we organized these groups." In an effort to engage the community to support the church, despite its poverty, the conference helped Head organize a financial budget whereby farmers donated proceeds from one acre to the church, 4-H boys and girls tithed on one-acre crops, and women contributed profits from sales of Sunday eggs. Her visits in the community within one year carried her more than twenty-five hundred miles. The deaconess also arranged health examinations for the children and led a women's 4-H Club and canning kitchen to improve family diets.[31]

Sometimes rural missionaries had to take the church to the tenants, as well as bring the tenants to church. In 1939, near Magnolia, Arkansas, Josephine Fort discovered a community of tenant farmers living three miles away from any church. "During the warm months, the worker organized a church school under a brush arbor," she reported. "There was an average attendance of 42. The pastor of the nearest church gave them two services a month, on Saturday night, with an average attendance of 60. Arrangements have been made to take them to the nearest church by school bus."[32]

Poverty also was the lot of southerners in the highlands. In 1928, when Mae Sells and Brooksie Davenport initiated work for Louisville Conference, Kentucky, among the tobacco farms in the Marrowbone Valley, they discovered an economically diverse community. They reported to the WMC, "The status of the people varies from those who are worth about $50,000 all the way down to the 'sang-diggers' who live miles back in the hills and come to the store in the fall to sell the ginseng roots they have gathered and dried." Valley schools

31. Martha Stewart, "Financing a Church on Cotton and Eggs," *Missionary Voice* (October 1931): 38; WMC, *Twentieth Annual Report*, 1930, 368–69.
32. Little Rock Conference WMS, *Annual Session*, 1940, 52.

remained unconsolidated, and five churches of three denominations provided weak ministry. In 1929, in addition to the usual missionary activities—visiting, organizing, witnessing—Mae Sells set about creating two detailed maps of the valley. One, a county map, showed sites of schools and churches, both white and black, and traced voting precincts. The second map, imposed over the first, also showed every home, business, lodge, store, and governmental office in the area. Sells drew lines on the maps from the farthest home in every direction to the main community centers, in order to indicate their "range of influence." She ordered blueprint copies of the maps for interested people, with the goal of increasing "community consciousness, pride, and accomplishment." While Mae Sells mapped Marrowbone Valley, Brooksie Davenport moved on to Monticello, Kentucky, where she found a community "thickly settled with poor people." Although 75 percent of the families owned their homes, most were "a two-room box house" perched on "three or four acres of steep, rocky land." The deaconess made about four hundred home visits in her first six months there and reported hearing repeatedly, "'We are so glad you are here. Nobody ever tried to do anything with us before. We're just Hill Billies.'"[33]

From 1926 to 1953, deaconess Bert Winter worked for the North Georgia Conference WMS, accumulating the longest tenure for a WMC rural worker with a single conference. She left a record of service encompassing all the kinds of ministry programs in which rural missionaries of the MECS and its successor, the Methodist Church, engaged, well summarized in one year's report: "teaching, guiding, planning, organizing, hunting, and training leaders, and trying to help with the problems in the homes, communities, schools, and churches, and of helping the people to know Christ." In 1938, Winter stated clearly her work's purpose: "To help people to think of the farm, not as a place just to 'make a living,' but as a place for living the abundant life, is the task to which we would give ourselves day by day." Most unusual, however, was her success in achieving cooperation between

33. WMC, *Nineteenth Annual Report,* 1929, 199; WMC, *Twentieth Annual Report,* 1930, 365, 366.

gender-separated denominational entities and between city and country church women. During the second year of her appointment, Winter's reports of neglect and need among rural churches caught the attention of the North Georgia Conference General Board of Missions, which then agreed to cooperate with the conference WMS to broaden the program for rural relief, an unprecedented and unique combined mission effort between MECS men and women. The deaconess's work came under the direction of the resulting joint committee, which authorized her to conduct a survey of the ten districts within the conference to assess the greatest needs.[34]

Results of Winter's 1928–1929 survey verified some of the most glaring problems among rural southern churches. The foremost difficulty stemmed from the fact that too many churches and too few pastors served a rapidly dwindling population. She discovered six rural circuits in which one pastor covered eight churches, fifteen circuits where a single pastor preached at six churches, and twenty-five circuits where the pastor served five different churches. For all their work, rural church pastors received poor salaries. The survey revealed that pastors at sixty-six rural circuits received annual salaries of less than one thousand dollars, a fact that prompted her to note that the rural pastor was "often so overwhelmed and depressed in his efforts to provide for his wife and children the necessities of life that his best effort is not released for the good of the people." More than half the churches she canvassed had no conference-appointed minister but only a temporary "supply or junior pastor." Winter's survey also exposed two other problems common across the rural South: "In many places only about one-third or one-half of the population belonged to any church," and "in many places about four to eight people paid all that was paid to the pastor."[35]

Over the next several years, the joint committee responded to the rural worker's findings by providing financial support for additional

34. WMC, *Twenty-fifth Annual Report*, 1935, 239, 325.
35. WMC, *Eighteenth Annual Report*, 1928, 256–57; WMC, *Nineteenth Annual Report*, 1929, 198; WMC, *Twentieth Annual Report*, 1930, 364–65; James Cannon, *History of Southern Methodist Missions* (Nashville: Cokesbury Press, 1926), 325–35.

pastors to relieve the strain on the largest circuits and by sponsoring preaching schools for rural pastors. Women from several Atlanta and Gainesville churches helped rural churches in material ways, contributing songbooks and an organ; sending food, gifts, and trees for Christmas parties; and furnishing valuable medicines. They provided subscriptions to mission literature for rural societies, and some even drove to the country to assist in vacation Bible schools. City WMS women supported college scholarships for promising but poor rural women and eased burdens on rural pastors by funding their attendance at the pastor schools and, at least twice, by furnishing them new suits.[36]

For increasing numbers of southerners, living in the country was becoming less about the family farm and increasingly about oil, gas, or mining development or commercial agriculture. Beginning in 1927, the Little Rock Conference WMS supported a deaconess to serve among the oil field camps in Camden District, Arkansas. Willie May Porter, who served there from 1928 to 1935, told the WMC after her first year, "I have been able to correct many false impressions which I had of the oil fields. Contrary to tales which I had often heard, I am just as safe from harm here as in any place I have ever been." The oil companies provided employees consolidated schools, school buses, and improved roads, yet a sense of impermanence prevailed. Families lived in tiny, hastily constructed shacks, but they could afford automobiles "nearly as large as the house." Although houses were small, the women "made bright, cheery homes." The din from crowded camps and nearby oil pumps, however, often made conversations difficult for the deaconess during home visits. Porter found the people "well nourished and well clothed, living to-day and taking little thought of to-morrow, economically or otherwise." Most people there had once belonged to a church, she discovered, but the transitory nature of their employment and lack of attention from local pastors influenced them to "take a vacation" from religion. Her job, she decided, was to get people back into church, and her method was to involve

---

36. WMC, *Nineteenth Annual Report*, 1919, 198; WMC, *Twentieth Annual Report*, 1930, 364–65; WMC, *Twenty-fourth Annual Report*, 1934, 314.

them in restoring usefulness to broken-down church buildings. Southern Arkansas, she found, provided all too much proof that the vast majority of open-country church buildings across the South were inadequate for the basic needs of worship and Bible study and lacked facilities for community activities and recreation. In one camp, the deaconess began a Sunday-school class for teenage boys, whom she led in improving the one-room "shack church" with paper and paint. The boys took great interest in the project, she reported, and even brought furnishings and decorations from home to make the church more comfortable. She also taught a twelve-year-old girl to play piano, filling one church's need for an accompanist and furnishing the girl a lifetime skill.[37]

In 1934, when the chair of the district mission board visited the area, she found Porter holding a community meeting in a formerly abandoned church, which through her efforts was now "straightened up, roof repaired, cleaned and painted on the inside with nice benches in place and a general air of being ready for services about it." On Sundays, the building filled for Bible classes and preaching services. The deaconess arranged occasional visits by town and city church members, including lay ministers who filled in the vacant weeks between the circuit preacher's presence and city pastors who held Sunday afternoon services in the country. Encouraging such city-rural cooperation was part of the work of a district deaconess, who spent time in town at churches, lodges, and women's clubs making speeches, asking for contributions, pleading for volunteers, and thanking donors. When southern Arkansas oil camps began closing, Porter took her experience in building churches to sawmill and farming communities. In 1935, at Bolding, the twentieth community in which she had worked, she reported full refurbishing of a church that was once "an abandoned boxed house without windows or doors with boards on tin buckets and fruit crates as seats" and the construction of a building for another church that began "with logs for seats under

37. WMC, *Eighteenth Annual Report*, 1928, 254; Little Rock Conference WMS, *Annual Session*, 1930, 56–57; WMC, *Nineteenth Annual Report*, 1929, 196; WMC, *Twentieth Annual Report*, 1930, 366–67; WMC, *Twenty-fourth Annual Report*, 1934, 313.

the open sky." From 1936 to 1943, Porter performed similar services among oil boom camps rising in the Marshall and Tyler districts of East Texas.[38]

Like oil boom towns, commercial farms created mission opportunities. In Orange County, Texas, Kishi Colony, established in 1907 by a native of Japan, was an eight-thousand-acre rice farm that employed Japanese, Mexican, French, and American workers. In 1923, Cleta Kennedy responded to the colony's application for assistance and established Terry Methodist Chapel among its diverse cultures. Four years later, missionary Virginia Hicks led daily vacation Bible schools there, organized recreational activities, and campaigned for improved health care and living conditions among the workers. Also that year, kindergarten teacher Maybeth Sykes held classes for twelve pupils who spoke four different languages. The sponsoring conference WMS considered the program successful when they heard that a Japanese woman from the colony had opened a Sunday school in her home upon her return to Japan and, again, in 1934, when the Terry mission became a self-supporting Methodist church.[39]

In the late 1930s, the WMC provided a rural worker to serve in Arizona, where irrigation enabled profitable cotton production. At Casa Grande, in 1938, Bertha May White discovered cotton pickers living in "pitiful" conditions: "a leaky tent, dirt floors, huts made of brush and tin cans, and shacks that hang together in some unknown fashion constitute the homes of families consisting of from four to eleven children and sometimes more. The ground, or the floor, with maybe one mattress for the entire family, is not infrequently the only

38. Mrs. L. K. McKinney, "Camden District Deaconess Work," *Arkansas Methodist* (August 9, 1934); Little Rock Conference WMS, *Annual Session*, 1934, 48, 49; WMC, *Twenty-fifth Annual Report*, 1935, 240–41; Methodist Church, Texas Conference Woman's Society of Christian Service, *History of Woman's Work: Texas Conference, Methodist Episcopal Church, South, 1928–1940, the Methodist Church, 1940–1955* (Bryan, TX: Woman's Society of Christian Service, Texas Conference, 1955), 420.

39. Hicks, "Furnishing Happiness," *Missionary Voice* (October 1927): 35; WMC, *Fourteenth Annual Report*, 1924, 57; WMC, *Seventeenth Annual Report*, 1927, 186–87; Methodist Church, Texas Conference WSCS, *History of Woman's Work*, 419.

sleeping arrangement obtainable." With donated supplies, White distributed reading materials, food, clothing, and, at least once, a mattress. The next year, her work centered in a Farm Security Administration migrant camp about seventeen miles west of Phoenix. There she organized a women's sewing group that made dresses and layettes from "thousands of yards of new material" donated by generous mission societies. Although the deaconess reported that she had "no average day," she stated, "I conduct a children's story hour, teach sewing and cooking, conduct a furniture-making class (using egg crates), captain a Girl Scout troop, dispense old clothing, shop for those who have no way to go to town, take people to and from hospitals, visit, arrange funerals, drive my car as a Sunday school 'bus,' teach Sunday school, lead the singing sometimes, and occasionally do the preaching . . . and I love it all!"[40]

Rural deaconesses furnished social services among black as well as white communities and among people of diverse ethnic origins. From 1900 to 1940, in an era when segregation was enforced by both law and violence, the WMC played revolutionary roles in addressing social needs among black southerners and raising white cooperation toward bettering race relations. From WMC leaders, Southern Methodist women heard that responsibility for improving race relations was their unique inheritance. God had raised their awareness, developed their abilities, and provided them opportunity at this juncture in history to remedy the problems created by previous generations.[41]

Furthermore, gender blended with race in compelling the WMC to help black women. According to United Methodist Church pastor and race relations scholar Alice G. Knotts, "White women could identify with African American women in the experience of womanhood

40. WMC, *Twenty-ninth Annual Report*, 1939, 187; WMC, *Thirtieth Annual Report*, 1940, 305–6.
41. McDowell, *Social Gospel*, 84–115; Jean Miller Schmidt, *Grace Sufficient: A History of Women in American Methodism, 1760–1939* (Nashville: Abingdon Press, 1999), 275–80; Alice G. Knotts, "Race Relations in the 1920s: A Challenge to Southern Methodist Women," *Methodist History* 26:4 (1988): 199–212; Alice G. Knotts, "Methodist Women and Interracial Fairness in the 1930s," *Methodist History* 27:4 (1989): 230–40; WMC, *Twenty-seventh Annual Report*, 1937, 134; WMC, *Twenty-eighth Annual Report*, 1938, 162.

in caring for home and family, and comprehending the yearning for fairness which African American women had for their children, their husbands, and themselves." Also, Knotts contends, the WMC's experience of being subject to the control of an all-male board aided their understanding of black frustration under white domination and linked them with black women in the common cause of women's rights.[42]

Beginning at its annual meeting in 1920, the WMC appointed women to the Commission on Race Relations to study means of cooperative efforts for improving life for black women and children. Two groundbreaking gatherings followed that same year, bringing white and black women leaders together to discuss their common concerns. Among the dramatic outcomes of these meetings was an explosion of educational efforts in racial consciousness among Southern Methodist women, from the denominational level on down to the local auxiliary. Through mission magazines, program materials, and state and regional gatherings, the word spread concerning "the achievements and potential of blacks, current conditions that hindered their progress, and the responsibility of whites both for current conditions and for needed improvement." By 1923, interracial cooperation committees were carrying out projects within more than four hundred white women's mission auxiliaries. In 1937, for example, a North Carolina WMS furnished parenting magazines and Sunday school literature to rural black churches and supported a health clinic for rural black children. In 1938, one South Georgia auxiliary's interracial activity carried women into the countryside, where they visited a Rosenwald school. In their report to the WMC, they said, "We furnished books, maps, pictures, kitchen equipment, and other helps. Had a county doctor talk on mosquitoes and malaria control. Met with colored mothers to speak on care of sick, control of flies, and home beautification. Discussed many problems of plantation life."[43]

In subsequent years, the WMC aided organization of women's mission societies in black Methodist rural churches and, beginning in

42. Knotts, *Fellowship of Love: Methodist Women Changing American Racial Attitudes, 1920–1928* (Nashville: Kingswood Books, 1996), 34, 36, 37.
43. Ibid., 93; Board of Missions, *Missionary Yearbook*, 342–43; WMC, *Twenty-eighth Annual Report*, 1938, 21, 147.

1924, cooperated with the Colored Methodist Episcopal Church in cosponsoring annual summer leadership schools for black women, including rural women. Hosted first by Paine College in Augusta, Georgia, and later by other black Methodist colleges across the South, and taught by WMC leaders, the schools provided advanced training for black women, particularly pastors' wives, in teaching and leading Sunday schools, youth programs, and women's missionary societies. Alice Knotts identified mutual benefits from the leadership schools at the denominational level: "When both black and white women lived and studied together for a week, it gave white leaders opportunities to hear the concerns of educated African American Christian women who were leaders in their own communities and conferences." The benefits reached the local level, too, when white societies provided scholarships to support black women's participation in the schools and invited the sponsored delegates to confer with them upon returning from the school. Knotts stated, "The process of supporting a local African American delegate to attend these schools, then studying community needs with her and her associates, and gradually working together on local projects linked women across racial lines in Christian service."[44]

Efforts to bring social services to black families and to promote interracial cooperation appeared in the annual reports of rural home missionaries. In 1930, deaconess Ora Hooper, assigned to the Louisiana Conference's rural work in Lake Charles District, reported that during the previous year she had visited and presented a talk to "federated Church societies for Negroes" and had "encouraged and strengthened" Girl Reserve work among the black societies. In 1932, in northern Georgia, Bert Winter led chapel services among schoolchildren and recalled, "Always their appreciation pays for the efforts, especially in the colored schools." The same year in southern Georgia, Bessie Miller spent part of her summer teaching in Paine College's Pastors' School. Also in 1932, in Rusk County, Texas, Martha B. Stewart organized a "union program with the Negro Epworth League

44. Tatum, *Crown of Service*, 235–36; Knotts, *Fellowship of Love*, 81; WMC, *Twenty-eighth Annual Report*, 99.

in this community, and this month (March 9–16) we held the first
Negro Daily Vacation Bible School ever held in this community." The
next year, working with rural black women, Martha Stewart organized
the community's second vacation Bible school and held weekly sewing
classes for black girls.[45]

From 1933 to 1940, in Arkansas, white missionaries not only
worked with black women in conducting vacation Bible schools but
also cooperated with them in organizing community clubs and women's
missionary societies and in securing relief programs for black families
with special needs. Whenever possible, they encouraged mutual efforts
between white and black women. In southern Arkansas, in 1938,
Josephine Fort recounted, "Some of the [white] missionary societies
plan to help the negroes have Bible Schools for their children this
summer. They have also helped the negro churches by giving literature." The next year, she expanded the work, reporting, "Around Magnolia, there is a large section of negroes. The worker, feeling the need
of improving their standard of living in some way, organized a Better
Home Club. They meet in the new Home Economics Building at
the negro school," an arrangement facilitated by the school's home
economics teacher, whom the deaconess praised as "very capable."
The black school also opened its doors on Saturdays for Josephine Fort
to conduct children's Bible classes. Thirty-five children attended, she
reported, representing families from five different black churches.[46]

In 1936–1937, in Louisiana, Shiela Nuttall led a story hour for
black children. In 1938–1939, in Virginia, Minnie Webb Forrest
reported having "had the privilege of promoting the Junior Red
Cross in the Negro schools" as well as "sponsoring a Negro Church
Vacation School," the first of its kind in the county. "It was held," she
said, "in the Negro Baptist Church and in a tobacco warehouse just
next door." The teachers, only one of whom was white, represented
both the Baptist and the Methodist churches, and "the most significant

45. WMC, *Twentieth Annual Report*, 1930, 364; WMC, *Twenty-third Annual
Report*, 1933, 222, 225, 226; WMC, *Twenty-fourth Annual Report*, 1934, 315.
46. Little Rock Conference WMS, *Annual Session*, 1933, 51; 1934, 41;
1938, 53; 1939, 53; 1940, 52.

thing," the deaconess remarked, "was every teacher held a college degree."[47]

Some home missionaries reported attempts to raise racial awareness among rural whites. In Oklahoma, in 1936–1937, Minnie Lee Eidson organized a white high school glee club that prepared "a program of appreciation for the Negro race, to be presented to the entire school." In Kentucky, in 1937–1938, Mae Sells made sure the traveling children's library established among area schools included books on "interracial understanding and friendship."[48]

Methodist women's rural work in Alabama first focused on people "of mixed, red and white races" who called themselves "Indian Cajans." In 1929 Laura Frances Murphy and Obra Rogers began work at Byrd Settlement, about forty miles north of Mobile. Populated by 275 people, Byrd Settlement consisted of "two general merchandise stores of small, one-room proportions; one cold drink stand; a shabby, unpainted one-room public school, a neat, painted parochial school owned by the Roman Catholic Church; and a rather ill kept Methodist Church." Area lumber and turpentine industries, once prosperous, no longer provided the people a living. "They find themselves unable to cope with modern life," Murphy wrote, adding that many found bootlegging their only means of support. Rogers relied on multiple skills, talents, and raw nerve to address the situation in Byrd Settlement. While serving as nurse, she also taught literacy classes, organized baseball games, and planned and executed Sunday school and Epworth League programs. Having no car, she walked four to ten miles a day for home visits, which she considered vital to her acceptance in the community. She explained, "I am trying to cultivate the women. It is with them that I come in closest contact—over a sick child, over a meal, over an expectant mother. One gets near to these women by visiting in the homes." Murphy became a public school teacher among the Indian Cajans at nearby Shady Grove Settlement,

47. WMC, *Twenty-seventh Annual Report*, 1937, 284; WMC, *Twenty-ninth Annual Report*, 1939, 193.
48. WMC, *Twenty-seventh Annual Report*, 1937, 286; WMC, *Twenty-eighth Annual Report*, 1938, 326.

where she rented a single room in a dilapidated house. She opened a Sunday school at Shady Grove but also made a five-mile trek to Byrd Settlement on Sundays to teach there. The missionary's willingness to live in their homes, walk everywhere like they did, teach their children, and listen to their needs won the people's respect.[49]

In the 1930s, the WMC established missions work in Texas among Hispanic people primarily of Mexican descent, some of whom had lived north of the Rio Grande for many generations and others who worked in the state but still considered Mexico their primary home. Mamie Robinson was a pastor's assistant in rural circuits sponsored by the Texas Mexican Methodist Conference along the state's southern border. Moving about South Texas in the company of a Hispanic pastor and his wife, camping in vacant houses or church buildings, Robinson organized vacation Bible schools during the day and assisted the pastor with evangelistic services during the evenings. She passed out tracts and Bibles and helped pave the way for the local people to organize Methodist congregations in predominantly Catholic neighborhoods, including Iglesia Metodista Mexicana at Hebronville. After four years in South Texas, Robinson went to work among Hispanic laborers in rural Central Texas, working from Austin and Georgetown north to Waco. There she discovered much poverty among the people in her charge, and the deaconess sought "an opportunity to minister to them in a spiritual way" while providing them food, clothing, and medicine. She helped people find work when they had none and encouraged children to attend school when "poverty or lack of interest on the part of their parents" had kept them away. Eventually, Robinson could claim that she had organized vacation Bible schools for Hispanic children in rural Texas communities from Laredo, on the Mexican border, to Sherman, near the Oklahoma line. Everywhere she went, she enlisted the help of local women, Anglo and Hispanic, and when no Protestant women were available, she found

49. WMC, *Twenty-first Annual Report,* 1931, 286–87; Murphy, "Among the Cajans of Alabama," *Missionary Voice* (November 1930): 18–21; Murphy, "Byrd Settlement—a New Field of Service," *Missionary Voice* (February 1931): 32–33, 36.

Catholic women willing to serve alongside her. Through such co-operative efforts, she hoped to raise "a better understanding between the races."[50]

In 1939, Katie Herndon accepted assignment to Waco, Texas, to work with rural Hispanic families, whom she located by traveling "good roads and bad, into river bottom lands and over Texas hills—into the 'byways and hedges.'" Her service included visiting in homes, where she left Spanish-language religious tracts as well as "tuberculosis prevention literature," organizing clubs in schools and churches, gathering women for "worship and discussion," and holding prayer meetings in homes.[51]

In 1931, students in training at Scarritt College began field experiences in rural work. For the most part, Kansas City and Nashville had served as the urban laboratories for Scarritt's service education, but many students devoted their summers to "vacation service" in rural areas. During 1931 and 1932, Scarritt students assisted rural missionary Willie May Porter in conducting vacation Bible schools for oil camp children in southern Arkansas. In 1936, Scarritt College committed resources to additional rural experience for its students with the creation of the Rural Training Project, a joint venture with the Tennessee Conference and the Woman's Section of the MECS Board of Missions. Sarah McCracken supervised the students' rural field work in nine locations in Middle Tennessee. Working through a single church or a circuit of several churches and in both one-room and consolidated schools, the students directed a variety of activities, including games, dramas, Girl Scout troops, Sunday schools, and community singings for children of both races. In 1937, field workers organized vacation Bible schools among black communities and raised funds to send a rural black woman to the Lane College Leadership School. With community self-sufficiency their goal, students learned "to gradually broaden the scope of activities so that the church

50. Robinson, "Five Years in the Texas Mexican Conference," *World Outlook* (June 1938): 31, 41; WMC, *Twenty-eighth Annual Report*, 1938, 329; WMC, *Twenty-ninth Annual Report*, 1939, 194–95.
51. WMC, *Thirtieth Annual Report*, 1940, 310–11.

may take an increasingly important part in a social, recreational, educational, and religious 'design for living.'"[52]

Other Southern Methodist schools also provided rural field experience for students. In 1932, students from Grenada College, in northern Mississippi, led eight vacation Bible schools under the direction of deaconess Ethel Cunningham. In 1936, Sue Bennett College in London, Kentucky, appointed Mae Sells as director for a training project that took college women into rural communities with traveling libraries and into rural churches to lead Sunday schools and organize youth groups.[53]

❦

The stories told by rural missionaries raised the awareness of WMC leaders to the dire circumstances under which southern rural families lived. At the spring 1929 annual meeting, the WMC dedicated itself to the cause of improving rural life, through

> educating ourselves and Church concerning the conditions that prevail in rural communities and the obstacles that prevent the growth of our rural churches . . . promoting home and farm ownership among all people, black and white . . . studying the means whereby the farmer may increase the economic returns of his labor and his ability to support community enterprises . . . providing for rural congregations well-trained, full-time country-minded pastors who preach a social gospel . . . providing every such Church with a parsonage . . . promoting the consolidation of rural churches.[54]

In 1930, the WMC appointed a Committee on Rural Development, which launched such a pervasive campaign through mission

---

52. Juanita Brown, "Scarritt College Students in Vacation Service," *Missionary Voice* (March 1931): 32; Little Rock Conference WMS, *Annual Session*, 1931, 71–72; WMC, *Twenty-second Annual Report*, 1932, 348; Elizabeth Watson, "Co-operating in Rural Community Service," *World Outlook* (July 1937): 20.

53. WMC, *Twenty-second Annual Report*, 1932, 352; Tatum, *Crown of Service*, 296.

54. WMC, *The Council Bulletin* (Nashville: Woman's Missionary Council, 1929), 33.

magazines that no member of a Southern Methodist WMS escaped encouragement to become personally involved in solving rural problems. Likewise, at conference WMS meetings, rural causes received attention, as in 1933 when the Little Rock Conference WMS heard a plea that the society take "a particular interest in the rural woman whose life is often lonely and circumscribed. She longs for contacts which will bring her friendly and helpful interests outside the routine of her daily life. We should have a keener consciousness and a deeper appreciation of our dependence on these rural sisters of ours and out of this should come about acquaintance, friendship, better understanding and a loyal cooperation between the women of the rural and city groups."[55]

Raised awareness among urban societies facilitated the work of deaconesses in organizing rural women into missionary societies and successfully equipping them for community service. In 1937–1938, fifteen years into the WMC rural program, the Committee on Rural Development, led by Mabel K. Howell, a sociology instructor at Scarritt College, and Dorothy Tilly, the future civil rights leader, evaluated rural church mission societies and found that half were involved in health programs and two-thirds cooperated with "sister societies" in town. Two years later, a similar survey revealed that 45 percent of rural societies conducted self-help programs, including

> securing rural libraries; promoting family gardens; securing of better housing for tenants; providing school lunches for underprivileged children and canning food in advance to make this possible; encouraging adults to attend opportunity school; cooperative study classes on rural problems; establishing curb markets; securing nine months' school term; painting school houses; providing transportation for rural school children; providing legal aid; founding rest rooms for women in nearby towns; and what is by far the greatest activity, the promotion of community health.[56]

55. Little Rock Conference WMS, *Annual Session*, 1933, 27.
56. WMC, *Twenty-sixth Annual Report*, 1936, 152–53; WMC, *Twenty-seventh Annual Report*, 1937, 144–45; WMC, *Twenty-ninth Annual Report*, 1939, 151; WMC, *Thirtieth Annual Report*, 1940, 162.

In spite of all the positive outcomes, the deaconesses' uplift efforts among southern rural communities were practically invisible outside the missionary society. Although rural people constituted two-thirds of the southern population and the MECS had an overwhelmingly rural membership, the General Conference produced only one study of rural life, the *Report of the Rural Work Commission.* Authorized in 1934 and completed in 1938, the report contained a wealth of statistics reinforcing recommendations for changes in church policy to confront deteriorating rural conditions, but it came too late to make a difference before the southern and northern branches of the Methodist Episcopal Church merged in 1940. Only two women were among the twenty people on the Rural Work Commission, and the WMC's rural missionaries received scant recognition in the report. Even within the WMC, rural work played only a minor role, accounting in 1939 for a mere 2 percent of its annual budget and 18 percent of the home-mission personnel. Although the WMC directed most of its resources toward urban problems and came late to an awareness of rural needs, the fact that Southern Methodist women took any strong, positive action toward ameliorating problems in the rural South is exceptional not only within their own denomination but also within all southern Protestant church history.[57]

❧

In 1940, the Methodist Episcopal Church, South, together with the Methodist Episcopal Church, from which Southern Methodists had separated in 1844 over sectional differences on the issue of slavery, and the Methodist Protestant Church, combined to form the Methodist Church, an antecedent denomination of today's United Methodist Church. Termed *unification* in denominational literature, the merger brought southern women into the national mainstream of Methodist work. Upon unification, the WMC and its counterparts

57. McDowell, *Social Gospel,* 49–50; Walter G. Muelder, *Methodism and Society in the Twentieth Century* (New York: Abingdon Press, 1961), 355; Methodist Episcopal Church, South, Rural Work Commission, *Report of the Rural Work Commission of the Methodist Episcopal Church, South* (Nashville: Board of Missions, 1938), 44–45; Board of Missions, *Missionary Yearbook,* 1939, 38, 76.

in the other two uniting denominations dissolved into the Woman's Division of Christian Service, and the cause of rural missions fell under the newly organized Bureau of Town and Country Work. Headquartered in New York, the bureau nevertheless expanded rural missions significantly in the South under the influence of its first three executive secretaries, all southern women with long WMC service records. The bureau executive secretary from 1946 to 1954 was Marjorie Minkler, the former rural deaconess who had once helped the Bethel Springs, Tennessee, church families pull together for their first Christmas celebration.[58]

During the years of the WMC rural work program, deaconesses often expressed exasperation with the problems confronting the rural South. As Elizabeth Thompson confessed in 1939, "The temptation sometimes comes to cry out at the lack of vision—tangible results are delayed." But, she added, "Just as often comes the realization that foundations are being laid for long years to come, and change comes slowly in rural areas. But can anything be more worthwhile and challenging than to feel people growing?" In an era of uncertainty and change for the rural South and in a day when religious ministry was limited by gender, a few determined southern women, called and trained to put faith into action, entered the countryside, looked rural people lovingly in the eye, grasped their hands, and empowered them to make things better. "Working together," explained rural deaconess Alberta Wilson, "we have learned that the trail that leads to a place of service becomes a shining path to God."[59]

58. Cobb, *Tapestry of Service*, 25.
59. WMC, *Thirtieth Annual Report*, 1940, 305; WMC, *Eighteenth Annual Report*, 1928, 255.

CONNIE PARK RICE

"Shepherdess of the Hills"

The Salvation Army Mountain Ministry of Cecil Brown

Hills that rise to thousands of feet; valleys in which corn grows ten feet high; people whose friendliness and hospitality is almost boundless; a land untouched by most of the modern vices; a distant civilization clinging to the old traditions, to the old laws that made this a great land, raising its children in the fear and love of God, learning ever anew the old-time religion; proud of its heritage without knowing that it is proud. It is a land of giants in which the Salvation Army has made a humble beginning, the foundations of a building, on the cornerstone of which is written the name of Cecil Brown, a girl whom God has used, and is using, to the end that His people may be blessed and that Jesus may be lifted up among her people.

—"Circle Corps Founded," *War Cry,* October 24, 1936

They called her "the maid of the mountains" and "shepherdess of the hills." Her name was Cecil Daisy Brown. In 1935, Brown established the first Salvation Army mission in Appalachia. The Salvation Army was known as an "urban" religion, and Brown's mission remained the only corps outside of a city for decades. Brown's history in the mountains of western North Carolina is unique and both complements and complicates the history of mountain mission work. Unlike most mountain mission workers, who were middle-class reformers from outside the region, Brown was a working-class woman born and raised in the established cultural traditions of the region, who moved outside the region, welcomed the opportunities available to her in the Salvation Army, and then returned to the mountains, bringing the traditions of the Salvation Army with her. To establish her mission, Brown blended army traditions with mountain life, creating success — and conflict.

The Salvation Army had been in the United States for more than forty years by the time Brown became a Salvationist in 1923. In the United States, as in England, the Salvation Army used the language and culture of the working class to bring people to Christ. Hymns were set to popular tunes, circus posters advertised meetings, and parades and open-air meetings drew people from the streets. Their use of working-class culture, their belief in instant conversion, and their use of female preachers challenged traditional conceptions of class and gender hierarchies. Indeed, the holiness theology of the Salvation Army encouraged women to participate in the church on an equal basis with men.[1]

Writers on the Salvation Army experience in the United States suggest that the Salvation Army had to alter itself in order to appeal to an American society that was dominated by commercial culture as well as one that was "evangelical and unabashedly nationalistic." Author Diane Winston argues that America's commercial culture played a significant role in the development of the U.S. corps, describing it as "a faith transformed through its interaction with the surrounding culture." Accordingly, the changes that occurred in the army following its arrival in the United States suggest that religion and society have an impact on each other and that both are altered by the encounter. In their studies, these authors have identified the Salvation Army as an "urban religion." Cecil Brown's experiences in North Carolina,

1. Herbert A. Wisbey Jr., *Soldiers without Swords: A History of the Salvation Army in the United States* (New York: Macmillan, 1955), 1–5.

however, reveal that it was also a rural religion and that when religion and culture collided in the mountains of Appalachia, both were indeed altered by the encounter.[2]

As the industrialization of Appalachia brought thousands of industrial workers into the mountains to work in the timber and mining industries between 1880 and 1920, the Salvation Army made an attempt to attend to the spiritual needs of those workers. As a result, not only did the Salvation Army adapt itself to America's ideology and commercial culture, but it also adapted to the geography and culture of Appalachia. To reach the working class, Salvationists, most of whom were women, were pitching tents, driving up riverbeds, and riding horses and trains into the mountains, taking God's message to the small towns and timber and coal camps of Appalachia.[3]

The army's first ventures into Appalachia took place in the northeastern areas of the region, in industrial cities that were home to steel- and glassworkers and, occasionally, timbermen. As early as March 1883, the Salvation Army opened its first West Virginia corps in the steel town of Wheeling. Despite their early ventures into West Virginia, the Salvation Army considered the South a hard field in which to establish their work. According to statements made in the *War Cry*, the official newspaper of the Salvation Army, army officials believed that the classes of people that the Salvation Army traditionally ministered to had less money in the South than in the North and, therefore, made it more difficult for the southern corps to be self-supporting. Second, southern men and women saved at the army penitent forms,

2. Pamela Jane Walker, "Pulling the Devil's Kingdom Down: Gender and Popular Culture in the Salvation Army, 1865–1895" (PhD diss., Rutgers University, 1992), 30–33; Norman Murdoch, "The Salvation Army: An Anglo-American Revivalist Social Mission" (PhD diss., University of Cincinnati, 1985), 395–400; Deborah Vansau McCauley, *Appalachian Mountain Religion: A History* (Urbana: University of Illinois Press, 1995), 342; Winston, *Red Hot and Righteous: The Urban Religion of the Salvation Army* (Cambridge, MA: Harvard University Press, 1999), 5, 252.

3. "Down in Dixie," *War Cry*, January 4, 1896; "Cotton Pickings Down in Dixie," *War Cry*, February 1, 1896; "Reminiscences," *War Cry*, June 29, 1944; District and Regional Records, Logan, West Virginia, the Salvation Army Archives and Research Center, Alexandria, VA (hereafter SAARS).

or confession sites, often turned to established churches rather than becoming soldiers in the army. Salvationists blamed this on the addiction that both sexes had to the use of tobacco and snuff, practices that were unacceptable to the holy living promoted by the Salvation Army. The army also believed that "owing to the warmth and lassitude of the climate," many were lacking "the 'push' and 'go' enterprising energy" needed to make a successful Salvationist. Many of the army's difficulties in the South can be linked to the poverty of the region, which made it difficult to support corps financially. This was particularly true in the Appalachian region, where often poverty was linked to the infamous company store. In addition, army policies clashed with southern culture. The Salvation Army shocked the South with its national campaign to reach blacks that Commissioner Frank Smith, commander of the American forces, initiated in 1885 as well as its use of women preachers who dressed in military uniforms and paraded through dirty streets. Despite the perceived difficulties, the army tried to establish corps throughout the South, including southern Appalachia.[4]

Between 1883 and 1935, the army established corps in towns and cities throughout the region, often using them as bases from which to extend their ministry into nearby coal and timber camps. Salvationists were expected to move into cities with few resources, build a corps, and, after it was self-sufficient, move on. Headquarters often transferred officers every few months, although assignments could last as little as a week. Field assignments later lasted from one to three years, and Salvationists expected numerous assignments during their careers. Living quarters, along with Salvation Army halls, were mostly rented and often consisted of a few rooms over a store or an empty train shed. Officers could not draw a salary until they paid all of the expenses, a task that was often difficult. In fact, their salary was not guaranteed, and poor sales of the *War Cry* often meant that the soldiers went without food. With military organization and dress, they

4. "Chattanooga," *War Cry,* February 15, 1896; Allan Satterlee, *Sweeping through the Land: A History of the Salvation Army in the Southern U.S.* (Atlanta: Salvation Army Supplies, 1989), 33–43.

sang hymns set to popular tunes, created Salvation Army bands, advertised commercially, and earned money from selling issues of the *War Cry* and collecting donations in tambourines at open-air (street) meetings, stores, and saloons. These early Salvationists maintained Salvation Army traditions, but they were also willing to expand beyond the urban areas into the smaller rural industrial centers in order to minister to the working class.[5]

When Cecil Brown opened the first Salvation Army mission in the mountains of North Carolina in 1935, the home-mission work of mainline denominations such as the Baptists, Methodists, and Presbyterians had been going on in the mountains for decades. Influenced by the Christian America movement (1860–1890) and revitalized by the Social Gospel movement (1890–1920), mainline churches set out to bring both religion and education to the "peculiar people" in a "peculiar land" in an effort to save the mountaineers from themselves. Viewing mountaineers as unchurched and, perhaps, lost to God, they traveled through the mountains on foot and horseback setting up churches, day schools, farm schools, Sunday schools, and orphanages. Mainline Protestants, alarmed and suspicious of the mountaineers, sent numerous missionaries to evangelize and uplift upland Christians. Although the majority of home-mission workers genuinely wanted to provide churches, schools, clinics, and social services to the region, many "never really understood, or liked, the people."[6]

Brown's mountain ministry mirrored the home-mission work of mainline denominations in many ways. Brown also traveled on foot and horseback through the mountains, establishing churches, Sunday schools, day schools, and boarding schools and providing needed services. Yet Brown's ministry was also very different. From its incep-

5. In addition to articles in the *War Cry*, the activities of Salvation Army workers in Appalachia are detailed in the Phillipson Papers, Record Group 20.41, SAARS.

6. McCauley, *Appalachian Mountain Religion*, 341–42; Henry D. Shapiro, *Appalachia on Our Mind: The Southern Mountains and Mountaineers in the American Consciousness* (Chapel Hill: University of North Carolina Press, 1978), 3–4, 267–68; Loyal Jones, *Faith and Meaning in the Southern Uplands* (Urbana: University of Illinois Press, 1999), 3–14.

tion, the Salvation Army was an urban religion, and for almost two decades, Brown's mountain corps remained the only Salvation Army corps outside of a city. Her role in mountain mission work also varied greatly from that of previous female mission workers. Unlike the outside middle-class reformers who believed their special qualities as women made them "social housekeepers," Brown was a native mountaineer from a working-class family, and she was a Salvationist, with a spiritual and administrative authority that transcended gender, class, and culture.[7]

In many ways, Brown fits the profile of other "hallelujah lassies," or Salvation Army women. Like the majority of females recruited as Salvation Army officers, Brown was a young, single woman from a working-class family. Raised on Hurricane Creek in the western mountains of North Carolina, Brown lived in a rural area with constrained choices for women. Most of the men in the region were farmers or worked in the timber industry. Limited opportunities available to women in rural areas and small towns often created a restlessness that resulted in their leaving the region, and many shared a common experience: apprehension due to industrialization and urbanization.[8]

Brown was no exception. After seven years of schooling in Hurricane and two terms of high school thirty miles from home at Clyde, North Carolina, Brown was also restless and uncertain about her future, and not without reason. Few opportunities were available to women in Haywood County, an area dominated by farming and the timber industry. Census reports reveal that in most white families with single daughters between the ages of eighteen and thirty listed, the daughter's occupation was listed as "none." Among farm families, single sons of the same age were reported as farmhands or laborers, a designation given to few female family members. Although a few

7. Walker, "Pulling the Devil's Kingdom Down," 41–42; Lillian Taiz, "Hallelujah Lasses in the Battle for Souls: Working- and Middle-Class Women in the Salvation Army in the United States, 1872–1896," *Journal of Women's History* 9 (Summer 1997): 84.

8. Lillian Taiz, "Hot Saints and Hallelujah Lasses: Class, Gender, and the Salvation Army in the United States, 1872–1914" (PhD diss., University of California at Davis, 1994), 71–73, 76.

single women obtained jobs as schoolteachers or in dry goods stores, many of those were widows. Whereas white wives rarely worked outside the home, black women, married or widowed, often worked outside the home as cooks or domestics or took in laundry. Clearly, single white females were expected to live and work at home until they married. Brown wanted more, so her parents sent her to stay with an older brother in Asheville. It was there, in October 1923, that she discovered the Salvation Army. Brown became a regular army "lassie" and an assistant to Captain Dorothy Guice, officer in charge of the Asheville Corps, in January 1924.[9]

As a child, Brown learned spiritual lessons from a circuit-riding Methodist minister who traveled throughout the mountains. After the Methodist Church closed their old circuits, the mountain inhabitants were left without a minister to attend to their needs. Uncomfortable in middle-class churches, Brown found acceptance in the army's working-class religion, and, like the women before her, she was given a spiritual authority that transcended gender boundaries as well as membership in an organization that provided opportunities for advancement based on her own accomplishments. As a Salvationist, Brown achieved holiness that separated her from the sin and behavior of her previous life as well as her home and family. Brown became a member of a sacred community devoted to God's work.[10]

After Brown attended Salvation Army Training College for nine months in Atlanta, Georgia, the army promoted her to captain. She was assigned to Reidsville, North Carolina, in 1929, followed by assignments at Statesville, Salisbury, and Goldsboro. Brown fulfilled her army assignments, but she wanted to go back to the mountains. She constantly thought of home, conscious that "back in Max Patch region the old church circuits had been discontinued. Little churches

9. Bill Sharpe, "Maid of the Mountains," *State* 21:5 (July 4, 1953), Salvation Army Southern Headquarters, Atlanta, GA (hereafter SASH); U.S. Department of Commerce, Department of the Census, *Thirteenth Census of the United States* (Washington, DC: Government Printing Office, 1912), Haywood County, North Carolina; "She Saw a Vision," *Asheville Times*, September 8, 1957; Satterlee, *Sweeping through the Land*, 138.
10. Taiz, "Hallelujah Lasses in the Battle for Souls," 90.

stood abandoned and dying on the hillsides. Far back in the coves and the gulfs of the Smokies were 'lost' families and settlements, slowly forgetting their faith." Feeling that God had called her to provide spiritual guidance to her own people, Brown expressed her concern over the lack of church services and the spiritual neglect of the mountain people to her divisional commander. She stated that for five years, she "had 'had the vision'—had felt called to do this work," and one particular quotation stood out in her mind, "The mountains are mine, saith the Lord." Years later, commenting on her desire to return to the mountains, Brown stated, "I had nothing more in mind than to hide-away from the city and carry on the old Methodist circuit rider's work that died out with the horse and buggy." Convinced there was a spiritual need in the mountains, the Salvation Army assigned Cecil Brown to Waynesville, North Carolina, in January 1935. The army gave her three to four months to establish a mission in the mountain areas, and on October 1, 1936, the Waynesville Circle Mountain Corps officially opened.[11]

On her first Sunday in Waynesville, having no church of her own, Brown and two of her sisters set out for the old country church at Fines Creek. When the three girls walked in, dressed in the blue uniforms and the coal-scuttle bonnets of the Salvation Army, the music and singing stopped and the people stared. Brown wasted no time reestablishing the old Methodist circuit. To reach the people, she walked on foot through the coves and hollows of the Great Smoky Mountains. There were no roads, except for one rough road that led to the community of Hurricane. Long distances separated the mountain communities; sometimes she walked seven or eight miles before reaching another house. Brown knew the people and she knew the culture. More important, they knew her. The *War Cry*, reporting on the opening of Brown's mountain corps, stated, "People here can point to the place where she was born, a mountain farm. They watched her grow up. They prayed for her when she came to the

11. Sharpe, "Maid of the Mountains," 2; "She Saw a Vision"; Brown, "Mountain Life" (February 1956), Cecil Brown file, SASH (hereafter CBF); memorandum from Alfred Tyler, divisional commander, to the field secretary, October 7, 1936, Waynesville, NC, file, SASH (hereafter WNC).

Training College, and a great wave of joy swept the mountainside when she came back to work among her own people." She lived among them, often helping with the housework. Staying in the homes not only helped her to get closer to the families but also gave her the opportunity to explain her work since some of the people were skeptical of women preachers. Brown's biggest opponent was Walter Rathbone, an older member of the Shelton Laurel community who opposed the establishment of a Salvation Army Corps because he did not like "women preachers."[12]

Brown soon won their hearts. She conducted her first religious service in the hayloft of a barn at Little Creek. Officially, the army's mountain mission work began in the Redmond schoolhouse at Shelton Laurel, a community twenty-two miles from Waynesville. In less than three months, Brown established company meetings (Sunday schools) at Shelton Laurel, Big Bend, and Hurricane. Services often were held in the one-room schoolhouses located near the communities. Most had leaky roofs and no windows; at Hurricane, there was no roof. Sometimes Brown spent the night in the schools, sleeping on the benches, often locking the doors because bootleggers occasionally slept in the schoolhouses too. The services grew, and before long there was a "three-piece band consisting of a cornet, an accordion, and the inevitable Salvation Army bass drum."[13]

In 1937, the army sent another officer, Lt. Thelma Colton, to assist Brown and provided funding for the construction of a building in Maple Springs Gap near Max Patch Mountain. Eventually, Brown and her female assistants established nine mountain missions throughout Haywood County and Madison County, North Carolina. The Salvation Army citadel at Maple Springs had an auditorium that seated two hundred people along with classroom space and living quarters for the workers. It became the center of the mountain circuit, with the officers visiting the outlying centers on Sunday morn-

12. Wesley Bourterse, "Chapter III: Hill Side Harvest Fields," CBF; "Salvation Army Circle Corps Launched in Pisgah Park Mountain Region," *War Cry,* October 17, 1936; Cecil Brown and Thelma Colton, "Trophies of Grace Abound in the Maple Springs Corps," *War Cry,* September 19, 1942.
13. "Maj. Brown, 51, Dies; SA Mountain Worker," undated clipping, CBF.

ings and then returning to the citadel in the afternoon to hold preaching and Sunday school services. Included in the Mountain Mission District were Shelton Laurel, Bonnie Hill, Little Creek, Miller's Gap, Big Bend, White Oak, Spring Creek, and Cold Springs Lumber Camp. Mountaineers, including Brown's parents, Joseph and Maggie Rogers Brown, and her three brothers, Fletcher, John, and Sam, donated the land, supplied the lumber, and furnished the labor for many of the missions. Brown had to walk or ride horseback eighteen miles to get to Big Bend, a community of approximately 50 people. In an area plagued by feuds and shootings, most of the people at Big Bend could remember only one religious service ever being held in the community.[14]

A local sawmill owner donated the lumber for the building at Hurricane where more than 150 people attended company meetings and as many as 400 showed up for outdoor meetings. At the Cold Springs Lumber Camp, Harry Lee Liner, the superintendent of the Gordon Lumber Company, invited Brown and Colton into the camp to preach, although he did not attend the services himself. The lumber company had a government contract to thin out several million acres of national forest, and more than 600 men, women, and children lived in the camp. To meet the needs of the workers and their families, the company built a school and a church for the Salvation Army in the community. In addition to the missions, in 1938, Walter Rathbone, who had initially opposed Brown's ministry, donated the land and logs for a log cabin for Brown to live in at Shelton Laurel.[15]

That same year, Commissioner W. A. McIntyre from the Central District gave Captain Brown $150 to buy a horse for her mountain mission work. "Dixie Lee" aided Brown in her work and became almost as well known as Brown, appearing in numerous pictures in the *War Cry*. In addition to preaching, Brown and Colton tended to

14. Ibid.; Merle J. Hamilton, "Shepherdess of the Hills," *War Cry*, September 5, 1936; Brown and Colton, "Trophies of Grace," 7; "The Salvation Army Mountain Mission Appeal," June 26–30, 1939, CBF; "Mountain Leader Gets New Home," CBF.
15. "Mountain Leader Gets New Home"; Brown and Colton, "Trophies of Grace."

the sick, conducted funerals, and sometimes served as undertakers. The Salvationists also opened a day school at Miller's Gap when seventeen children who lived beyond Max Patch Mountain were unable to reach any school. A boarding school for girls enabled girls who lived in remote areas to attend school. Teaching first grade through high school, the school offered both religious and vocational training, and many of the students became Salvationists. Along with the citadel at Maple Springs, the Salvationists established a community center and farm where they raised cows and pigs and grew grain for the livestock and fruit and vegetables for themselves. They also established numerous church groups including Home Leagues, Corp Cadets, and Young People's Legions. In addition to her regular duties, at Christmastime Brown also served as "Lady Santa Claus," organizing Christmas parties in each of the communities and bringing gifts to all the children.[16]

In her mountain ministry, Brown adapted traditional Salvation Army methods to fit the geographical and cultural environment. Although Brown and her assistants occasionally held meetings on the street corners in nearby towns, their outdoor meetings and revivals held throughout the mountains of North Carolina, Tennessee, and Georgia were literally "open air." Traditionally, Salvationists used their tambourines to collect money on the streets and at meetings, but in the mountains "tambourine collections" were door-to-door. At special meetings, revivals, and singing conventions, money was collected traditionally—in a large coffeepot that officials from the Haywood Ramp Convention provided.[17]

From the beginning, music was an important part of the religious services. On the first Sunday in August 1936, Brown held the first annual singing convention, and more than 250 people attended. The convention began when the U.S. Forest Service asked families to move away from the Pisgah National Forest Reserve. The sings brought former neighbors together again. Over the years, mountain commu-

16. Brown and Colton, "Trophies of Grace"; McIntyre to E. I. Pugmire, October 3, 1938, WNC; Hamilton, "Shepherdess of the Hills."
17. "Salvation Army to Hold Annual Singing Sunday," *Waynesville Mountaineer*, July 31, 1952; "Maj. Brown, 51, Dies."

nities, lumber workers, farmers, and members of the Cherokee Indian Reservation attended the meetings. Salvation Army officers, particularly from the Southern District, also visited and participated in events held in the Mountain Mission District. The songs they sang at the mountain mission were not Salvation Army hymns set to popular tunes, however. In the mountains, the Salvation Army won the hearts of the natives with renditions of "The Old Time Religion" and "The Cabin on the Hill." They sang only the old songs, ones that the people remembered from their childhood—"mountain ballads that had re-echoed over the familiar hillside for over a decade." Shaped notes were used for the music and stringed instruments such as guitars and mandolins accompanied the singers rather than the traditional Salvation Army brass band. Cherokee groups sang hymns in their native tongue. An article in the *War Cry* reported that their mountain gospel music "was proof that William Booth was right when he said that the Salvation Army should 'get into the skin' of whatever country in which they happen to be working." Whereas staff bands traditionally played at Salvation Army meetings as the crowd assembled, in the mountains it was the choir that gathered the people together. The number of people attending the annual singing conventions increased every year, and by 1951 more than 2,250 people from eleven states attended the all-day sing.[18]

In 1944, the army awarded Brown the army's highest honor, the Order of the Founder, for her extraordinary mountain ministry. The *War Cry* and newspapers throughout the region called her the "shepherdess of the hills" or the "maid of the mountains," labels that invoked gendered images of both innocence and whiteness. The *War Cry* claimed that the story of the "mountain girl who, converted and trained as a Salvation Army officer, and then returned to native hills to carry the Gospel to her own people" mirrored a Harold Bell Wright

18. "Maple Springs, Carolina Mt. Corps, Enjoys an All Day Sing," *War Cry,* September 4, 1948; "Salvation Army Circle Corps Launched in Pisgah Park Mountain Region," CBF; Tom Higgins, "Maple Springs Gap Home," *Canton Enterprise,* August 1, 1957, 2; Ivy H. Waterworth, "Mountain Music Resounds at Maple Springs in Twelfth Singing Convention," *War Cry,* September 3, 1949.

or a John Fox Jr. novel. The *War Cry* emphasized the romanticism of the story and, by doing so, often invoked the negative stereotypes of mountaineers created by the local color writers. Brown was not happy with the stereotypes. Following a Salvation Army Convention held in Gatlinburg, Tennessee, in February 1956, Brown wrote in her newsletter, *Mountain Life,* that she was indignant when guest speakers from New York or "someplace below-the-ridge" stood and spoke "about those 'depressed' people in the southern mountains." In the newsletter, she stated, "Why bless your heart, the fellow that is doing the talking is the only one who knows that we are depressed. Nobody in these parts have felt depressed." Clearly, Brown had a strong regional identity, and she resented the image of mountain culture that her fellow officers often presented.[19]

Without a doubt, this image of innocence and whiteness appealed to southern readers to whom the army looked for support. The southern ideal of womanhood still lingered, and, despite a genuine effort of the Salvation Army to minister to blacks, the southern corps struggled with the race issue in the South. Jim Crow, whether de jure or de facto, made organizing difficult. Despite Frank Smith's early campaign to break down the wall separating blacks and whites and equally minister to both, his idealism was not realized. Like other religions, as the army became more popular and acceptable to the general public, or mainstream, the more it conformed to surrounding society and culture. Although the corps had been nonconformist in the past, the pervasive public sentiment that culminated in *Plessy v. Ferguson* in 1896 meant that less emphasis would be placed on the participation and equality of blacks in the southern corps. Blacks publicly responded to an article published in a daily Washington, D.C., newspaper in 1911 that stated, "The Salvation Army may yield to the demand of its members from the South and draw the color line and separate the races in the meetings." In an article written to Commander Evangeline Booth and the Salvation Army and published in numerous black

19. "Major Cecil Brown Designated First District Officer of Mountain Missions," *War Cry,* November 9, 1946; Hamilton, "Shepherdess of the Hills"; Brown, "Mountain Life," (n.d.), CBF.

newspapers, African American minister J. Milton Waldron chastised the army, stating that "it is impossible to see how it can refuse to receive into its ranks on terms of equality men and women who have accepted Jesus Christ simply because they are of a darker hue" and that blacks would have the extra burden of "fighting the prejudices and hypocrisy of any Christian organization (so called) which shall follow the behests of those who hate men because of race, color or previous condition of servitude." In the 1920s, Salvation Army Corps in the South also reacted in a variety of ways to the increasing presence of the Ku Klux Klan (KKK). Although most Salvationists fought with the KKK or ignored it, in Nashville, Tennessee, members of the KKK often appeared at open-air meetings and dropped twenty- or fifty-dollar bills into the tambourine. In Lynchburg, Virginia, the KKK had permission to use the corps for meetings.[20]

Though the images of innocence and whiteness may have contributed to Brown's success, the publicity given to Brown may also have contributed to the criticism of Mountain Mission District within the Salvation Army's Southern Territory. Some of her fellow officers called the Mountain Mission work a "farce." Others resented her receiving the Order of the Founder. They believed that she was doing what all Salvationists were expected to do and that, in many ways and contrary to Brown's descriptions of the hardships she faced, it was easier for her because she was "living with her own family and using them as workers and working among her own kin people and among the natives where she had been raised."[21]

Anyone experienced in mountain mission work knew, however, the struggles and sacrifices needed to make it work and that it was "easier to start a mission work than it was to keep it going." Looking back on her years in the mountains, Brown stated,

20. Norma T. Roberts, *The Black Salvationists* (Nyack, NY: Salvation Army Eastern Territory, 1997), 30–31; J. Milton Waldron, "A Ringing Letter to Commander Evangeline Booth and the Salvation Army," *Pioneer Press*, March 11, 1911; Satterlee, *Sweeping through the Land*, 92–94.

21. James P. Henry, "Inter-Office Communication" Confidential Report from Henry to Salvation Army leaders in the Southern Territory, September 13, 1957, 2, WNC.

Had I known what my hands would have done during twenty-two years of hard work I may have been frightened, but twenty-two years ago I wasn't afraid of anything. So I set to work—I haven't let one blade of grass grow under my feet and today I am happy to look over the ground I covered and thank the Heavenly Father for His promise to me; as I stood on top of the Mountain here and looked over these vast Mountain ranges I had His promise, "The Mountains shall be Thine."

When medical problems forced Brown to retire in June 1956, she wrote, "Away back yonder months ago, when I made up my mind I was going to retire and use a little sense and take the doctor's orders, I said there would be no silly sentimental tears shed regarding my giving up my life's work and the home that had cost so much—tears, pain, agony, and my health." Yet the finality, along with the sadness that accompanied it, was not lost on Brown. In describing her preparations for retirement, Brown, with a slightly ironic note, wrote, "I had prepared what I thought was a good farewell sermon to preach in all the Centers as I went around for my last service, but when it came time to start my rounds I found out that my Bible with my farewell sermon had been packed in one of the boxes labeled 'junk.' That sermon will never be used." To celebrate Brown's retirement, the annual singing convention at the Mountain Mission at Max Patch was changed from the first Sunday in August to June 10.[22]

The Salvation Army transferred Capt. and Mrs. James P. Henry, commanders of the Salvation Army post in Asheville, to the Mountain District. The transition did not go smoothly. Henry reported that when he carried a trunk into the Maple Springs Headquarters on June 12, 1956, Brown screamed at him, saying that she had not cleared out and that she thought that the Salvation Army Territorial and Divisional Headquarters had not given her a fair amount of time to move her belongings. In the same confidential report to the South-

22. R. P. Smith, *Experiences in Mountain Mission Work* (Richmond, VA: Presbyterian Committee of Publication, 1931), 67; Brown, "Mountain Life" (February 1956), CBF; Brown, "Mountain Life" (n.d.), CBF; "Max Patch Sing Planned June 10 to Coincide with Major Brown's Retirement," undated clipping, CBF.

ern Territory Headquarters, Henry stated that after taking command, "we found very few soldiers and none in uniform with the exception of the immediate staff." Henry reported that "in times past," the mission at Timber Ridge "had a lot of Methodists, and when we came, not even one Salvationist."[23]

Henry also claimed that antagonism existed between Brown and some of the officers assigned to mountain work. According to him, officers were "sent out" because they were not liked or because they did not comply with Brown's demands and that lieutenants "have told time and time again that they were treated like servants and hired hands rather than Salvation Army officers." The stories existed earlier. In 1949, Field Secretary Lt. Col. Charles Dodd asked Brig. Ruth Gibbs to check on the status of officers assigned to the Waynesville Corps because he heard that there were heavy losses there. Gibbs replied that none of the officers removed from the officers' role were from the Waynesville Corps and that there were no heavy losses. However, she also stated in the memorandum, "It is my understanding that Lts. Morton and Faddon were not very happy there and were glad when they were farewelled. We have always had 'rumors of unhappiness' among the assistants but the records do not reveal any serious difficulty. I believe the 'mountain girls' fit into Waynesville far better and are more acceptable to Major Brown."[24]

Disputes also emerged between Brown and Henry over army property. When Brown first retired, she was still living in a house behind the citadel at Maple Springs. Her personal belongings packed in a nearby garage, Brown planned on taking an extended trip though the Northwest and Canada. One morning Henry went to the small store and post office known as the trading post, only to find the office locked. Brown left the keys in the Salvation Army mailbox at Waynesville along with a briefing on the district and a personal note for Henry. In the note, Brown stated that the garage above the citadel was her personal garage and contained personal items and that when

23. Henry, "Inter-Office Communication," 5.
24. Ibid., 2; memorandum from Dodd to Gibbs, May 3, 1949, WNC; memorandum to Dodd from Gibbs, May 4, 1949, WNC.

she returned and had time to clean, she would turn it over to the army. Brown also claimed that the mailbox located at the trading post was her personal mailbox until she returned from her trip and moved to the family farm at Hurricane. Henry obviously did not view either one as Brown's "personal" property since both were on Salvation Army land, especially the mailbox that was in the form of a large rock pillar and embedded in the concrete of the trading post porch. Months later, when Brown arrived home from her trip, a dispute arose over the Hurricane View Cemetery. Brown claimed that although the cemetery was on government land that the army leased, it was a "family cemetery" and asked that family members be contacted before any spaces were allotted. Henry insisted that the graveyard belonged to the Salvation Army.[25]

Brown continued to live at Maple Springs and next door to Henry, creating more friction between the two. Henry wrote to the Southern Territory leaders that one year and three months after her retirement, Brown was still living next door and had not cleaned out the garage. He reported, "She has repeatedly stated that she was going to make trouble for us and when we had the above disagreement over the cemetery, she told me, personally, that she hated the Salvation Army, that she regretted the day that she joined and that she wished to God that she had burned every building to the ground before she left."[26]

Religion, work, and home were irrevocably intertwined in Brown's mind. In order to establish a successful mountain mission, Brown blended Salvation Army traditions with mountain culture to create a mission that was uniquely hers, one that she dominated. Officers who questioned or were unused to Brown's methods, including Sr. Capt. and Mrs. James Henry, were viewed as "outsiders" who threatened the status quo with a return to strict army discipline. Perhaps she sensed in them the same condescension for mountain people that she found in the annual meetings in Gatlinburg. One thing is clear. At the time of her conflict with Henry, Brown identified more with

25. Henry, "Inter-Office Communication," 3–4.
26. Ibid.

mountain culture than with the Salvation Army community. On her retirement trip out West, she attended the services of a different denomination every Sunday. When Brown arrived in Calgary, Canada, the Salvation Army Citadel announced that the territorial commander of Canada, Commissioner Booth, would be doing the weekend services. There were more than one hundred Salvationists in full uniform and a band with more than fifty members, and although Brown thought it was a treat to see a large army corps, there was one thing she missed. Brown wrote, "We went in and sat through the service and got up and walked out without one soul speaking to us—that's not like being at one of our mountain churches, when we have a visitor we shake his hand, pat him on the back, find out who he is and where he is going before he ever gets out." Brown attributed the distance she felt to her street clothes, stating, "I felt like a sheep in wolves clothing sitting there in a private dress." The next night, in the full uniform of the Southern Gray, Brown attended the Sunday night service. Although Brown felt all eyes upon her from the platform, she did not get the welcome she expected.[27]

Brown eventually moved into the old family homestead on lower Hurricane Creek. Located on the remaining one hundred acres of her grandfather's farm, the community was isolated, with no utilities or telephones—without a store or a church. Water came from the spring, light came from an oil lamp, and mail was retrieved weekly. Brown had a sentimental attachment to the place and wanted to spend the rest of her days there. In her newsletter, Brown wrote:

> The winter has been severe and "This ole House" was like living in a barn. I took what newspapers I had (they are a scarcity here) and poked them in the largest cracks to keep out the cold and have spent many long days and evenings sitting close by the old fireplace—did somebody say, "didn't you nearly die of loneliness?" How can you be lonesome on a cold winter night with a big crackling fire in the room, sitting in an old rocking chair, watching all the shadows from the fireplace dancing across the old smoked up ceiling, listening to the wind blowing through

27. Brown, "Mountain Life" (n.d.), 4.

the trees and hear the trickling of the creek running over and under ice covered rocks—its music you don't get on TV or radio.

She died there of cancer on December 4, 1958. One newspaper reported, "In her twenty-two years of traveling through the mountains, Major Brown served as preacher, doctor, nurse, teacher, lawyer, farmer, and taxicab driver. She wore out eighteen cars, several horses, and more pairs of shoes than she could ever remember."[28]

Just as the Salvation Army as an institution adapted to serve the physical, social, and spiritual needs of the American working class, Salvationists adjusted to the geography and culture of the Appalachian Mountains. Urban Salvationists used commercial culture to attract attention and gain adherents, including traditional army bands with bass drums and tambourines, dramatic sermons, and open-air meetings on street corners. Tambourine collections and *War Cry* sales paid the rent on living quarters and Salvation Army halls. In order to succeed, Brown adapted her ministry to mountain culture, and much of the success Brown's mountain ministry experienced can be attributed to the fact that she returned to her own environment. Brown knew the people and the culture, and she also knew their needs. Family and friends supported Brown's efforts to establish a mountain corps, and their donations of land, supplies, and labor enabled the mountain missions to be debt free. Although Brown still needed to raise funds to maintain the missions, she always had a place to stay and food to eat.

Similarities between the Salvation Army and established traditions about the Holy Spirit in the mountain region also aided Brown. The army, like the traditions that characterized mountain religiosity, stressed the centrality of the Holy Spirit. Although the Salvation Army was Arminian rather Calvinist in its theology, both emphasized heart-centered worship and focused on the Bible and the Word of God. Mountain churches, like the Salvation Army, were nondenominational, and although they encouraged spontaneity and liberty in their services, they were conservative or "Fundamentalist" in doc-

28. Ibid., 7; "Maj. Brown, 51, Dies."

trine. They were also independent churches with no ties to a central body, and although the Salvation Army had world and national organization, the army gave its officers the utmost freedom in the conduct of their meetings. In Brown's case, this freedom was expanded by the remoteness of her corps, allowing her even more freedom than that of her fellow officers.[29]

The ministry of Brown, a mountain girl from a working-class family, both complements and complicates the image of mountain mission workers. Despite the army's reputation for doing social welfare work and its influence on the Social Gospel movement, Brown was not a middle-class reformer from the outside. In the mountains, the understanding of community, and the role of the church in that community, contrasted sharply with the definition of community in home missions and their decision makers from outside the region. Brown returned to the mountains as a Salvation Army soldier, but she had the mountain people's understanding of community and church.[30]

Mainline denominations that undertook mission work in the mountains often viewed mountain religion as something that "needed to be overcome" and in their reports often condemned local worship traditions and labeled mountain preachers as illiterate, overzealous, and "uncooperative." Due to lack of funding, the mountaineers often welcomed the home-mission schools, but that welcome rarely extended to the home-mission pastors and churches. Mountaineers often found them condescending of mountain traditions. In addition, their emphasis on individual churches and church doctrine also limited the appeal and success of mainline denominations.[31]

In contrast, Brown and Colton included mountain religious traditions in their services and often shared duties at funeral services and held revivals with nearby preachers. The Reverend Pete Hicks, one of their own mountain preachers and a friend of Brown's grandfather, not only held revivals at Timber Ridge but also spoke at Brown's funeral. The Salvation Army was inclusive and had no connections to any

29. McCauley, *Appalachian Mountain Religion,* 15, 221, 239–41.
30. Ibid., 436.
31. Ibid., 28, 415, 433, 436; Smith, *Experiences in Mountain Mission Work,* 96.

church. In fact, as part of its doctrine, it remained neutral on contro-versial issues such as baptism and communion that caused factional-ism and interdenominational strife.[32]

Perhaps the most interesting aspect of Brown's ministry, and her biggest obstacle, was that of gender. In the late nineteenth and early twentieth centuries, Appalachia was a patriarchal society where men took care of the family needs and participated in business and politi-cal affairs, while women were confined to a domestic sphere that included household duties and childbearing. Yet the lives and images of Appalachian women were full of contradictions. In this patriarchal society, women wielded great power and influence, particularly as they grew older. Local color writers alternately described a mountain woman's life as a sorrowful life of toil and childbearing or one that sustained mountain traditions and culture. Women themselves were haggard and worn or strong and enduring. The stereotypes that emerged portrayed mountain men as paternalistic, controlling men who forced mountain women into a life of work and suffering while they drank alcohol and slept. In actuality, mountain marriages were often partnerships, in which each person was necessary for the wel-fare of the other. Gender lines were often blurred, with mountain women performing tasks that, outside the mountains, were seen as "unsuitable" for women. Although women were limited by legal and cultural codes, with few wives working outside the home, women's labor frequently contributed to the family economy and survival. As a mountain native, Brown knew how to negotiate these boundaries. Perhaps the fact that Brown never married, although she did raise a foster daughter, helped her to gain acceptance in her work. In Brown's case, her ministry was her work, and as a Salvationist who was called by God, she had a spiritual authority that few questioned.[33]

32. *Mountain Circle News* (April 1955), CBF; *Mountain Circle News* (June 1955), CBF; Ivy H. Waterworth, "Maid of Mountain Called Home" *War Cry* (1958), CBF; Wisbey, *Soldiers without Swords*, 20.

33. Mary K. Anglin, "Lives on the Margin: Rediscovering the Women of Antebellum Western North Carolina," in *Appalachia in the Making: The Moun-tain South in the Nineteenth Century*, edited by Mary Beth Pudup, Dwight B. Billings, and Altina L. Waller (Chapel Hill: University of North Carolina Press,

As members of the middle- and upper-class society, female reformers engaged in the mountain mission work of mainline denominations probably experienced more divisions along gender lines. Like
Brown, they often served as superintendents, secretaries, librarians,
and nurses. They rode through the community on horseback tending
to the sick, opened Sunday schools, taught school, and "prepared the
way for the preacher." Whereas women dealt with daily problems,
most of the ministers traveled through the region, perhaps preaching
to various congregations once a month. Preachers recognized the
value of women workers, especially when few ministers were available.
Although mountaineers liked to hear preaching, it was the women
who taught the Bible, books, manners, and health and who visited
the sick. The women provided most of the services, but preaching
was still considered a "masculine preserve."[34]

Brown took on all the duties of the female reformers, but she also
served as minister. As a Salvation Army soldier, Brown's rationale
for engaging in mountain mission work contrasted sharply with that
of middle-class female reformers. Female reformers maintained that
women must act as "social housekeepers" because of their special qualities as women, while Salvation Army women claimed that they had
an obligation to help because as sanctified women, they were precisely
the same as sanctified men.[35]

Although a few of the residents may have been skeptical of a
"woman preacher," historically women in the mountains played a vital
role in religious life, constituting the majority of churchgoers, laying
the groundwork for ministers, and organizing new churches. Religious
historian Deborah Vansau McCauley observes:

> Women held a prominent place in religious culture, with limitations
> varying from one mountain church tradition to another. Their
> "liberties" ranged from freedom to voice their own spontaneous,

---

1995), 185–209; Emma Bell Miles, *Spirit of the Mountains* (Knoxville: University of Tennessee Press, 1994), 64–70.
   34. Smith, *Experiences in Mountain Mission Work*, 38–39; Walker, "Pulling
the Devil's Kingdom Down," 47.
   35. Taiz, "Hallelujah Lasses in the Battle for Souls," 84.

ecstatic expressions; to praying out loud and testifying; to minister-
ing to people under conviction of sin in the context of worship;
to preaching in many independent Holiness churches (as well as in
the rural mountain churches of the Church of God [Cleveland,
Tennessee]), or on local radio or at revivals.[36]

This history contributed to Brown's acceptance as a female minister.

The mountain missions of the Salvation Army never achieved the
recognition that the army achieved on the national level, but the
army did extend itself into the rural areas of Appalachia. The experiences of the women Salvationists in the region, particularly Brown's
work in the mountains of North Carolina, illustrate that the Salvation Army was "a faith transformed through its interaction with the
surrounding culture."[37]

Brown's ministry blended Salvation Army traditions with mountain culture and blurred the lines among home, community, work, and
religion. In doing so, Brown provided the community with needed services and, at the same time, established a Salvation Army mission that
gained both national and world attention. Her story not only provides
insight into the lives of rural women in the mountain South but also
reveals how gender is produced and reconstructed, provides new perspectives on mountain mission work, and examines the interaction
between religion and culture. In the mountains of Appalachia, religion
and culture did collide . . . and both were altered by the encounter.

36. McCauley, *Appalachian Mountain Religion*, 221.
37. Winston, *Red Hot and Righteous*, 5, 252.

Officers of the Mountain Mission District, Waynesville, North Carolina

COMMANDING OFFICER
October 1, 1936–September 1, 1954   Capt./Adj./Maj. Cecil Brown

ASSISTANT OFFICERS

June 14, 1937	Lt. Virginia Robbins
June 6, 1938	Lt. Thelma Colton
Mary 27, 1940	Lt. Lettie Henderson
May 28, 1945	P/Lt. Marguerite Morton
November 21, 1945	Capt. Lillian Blackburn
June 3, 1946	Lt. Katherine Paddon
June 2, 1947	Lt. Zeta Fleming
June 2, 1947	Lt. Mildred Kirby
June 2, 1947	Lt. Florence Wall
September 1, 1948	Maj. Dorothey Smith
May 25, 1949	2nd Lt. Mildred Gentry
October 5, 1949	S/Capt. Hazel Pownell
May 30, 1951	2nd Lt. Polly Combs
May 30, 1951	Lt. Mildred Birney
May 12, 1952	P/Lt. Marjorie Kay
May 12, 1952	P/Lt. Doris McQuay
November 26, 1952	P/Lt. Glenna West
June 7, 1954	P/Lt. Doris Gregory
June 7, 1954	P/Lt. Mary Williams
October 26, 1955	Capt. Yvonne Pinder[38]

38. "S/Capt." means Senior Captain. "P/Lt." means Probationary Lieutenant.
Source: Waynesville, N.C., Corps History, Mountain Mission District, SASH.

III.

Town and Country Come Together

KAREN R. UTZ

Goin' North

The African American Women of Sloss Quarters

If you stayed in the country, you didn't have nothing to eat. The only thing the people in the country had to survive off was the white people. We came to Birmingham because we'd heard so much about Birmingham. We used to call it "goin' North." My husband walked from Richmond to Selma. He rode a milk truck and worked his way by picking up milk. When we came here we didn't know anyone. We were absolutely broke. All we had was willpower.

—MRS. GEORGE BROWN, Sloss Quarters resident, quoted in
Like It Ain't Never Passed: Remembering Life in Sloss Quarters

The first major migration of African Americans occurred during the Civil War as thousands fled the war-torn countryside to seek safety in southern cities such as Mobile, New Orleans, Memphis, and Nashville. Black women constituted the majority of the rural-to-urban migrants. In New Orleans in 1870, for example, black women between the ages of fifteen and forty-five exceeded the population of black men of the same ages by 50 percent. Single mothers found themselves pushed off the plantations because they could not rent farmland and were seldom allowed to enter into the world of sharecropping. The majority of Alabama's African American women participating in the rural exodus of the 1870s and 1880s, however, were accompanying their husbands or fathers in search of greater opportunities in the growing iron and steel industries of the Birmingham District. To keep these industries well supplied with cheap labor and to keep control over their employees, companies such as Sloss Furnaces, one of Birmingham's largest iron-producing plants, often built company houses near their factories.[1]

This essay focuses on the rural traditions and customs that mothers, wives, and daughters of former sharecroppers brought with them to the urban industrial landscape of Sloss Furnaces and its company housing, Sloss Quarters. Excerpts from the Sloss Quarters Oral History Collection not only speak to the ways in which these remarkable women coped and adapted but also provide an in-depth look into the lives of African American women who realized that the way to make a successful transition from rural life to urban life was by making their long-standing customs and beliefs an integral part of this life-altering transition. Traditional domestic duties such as child rearing, housework, and gardening remained the primary responsibilities, while many women were determined to bring in additional income by becoming domestic workers, laundresses, or seamstresses or simply by selling boxed lunches from the stoops of their homes.[2]

Sloss Quarters did not become a successful and cohesive community because of the men who labored in the neighboring blast furnaces; it thrived and succeeded because of the women who were determined to make better lives for themselves and their families away from the desperate poverty of their previous rural existence. And like southern white hill farmers from the northern regions of Alabama seeking new lives in the booming textile mills, black sharecroppers embarking on their journeys from the depleted Black Belt region of the South brought not only their possessions but also the "cultural baggage" of their rural communities as they headed to the new industrial town of Birmingham.[3]

1. Randy Lawrence, "Story of Sloss," Sloss Furnaces National Historic Landmark, Birmingham (hereafter SFNHL), n.p.

2. Gertrude Jones, interview by Utz, October 20, 2002, Birmingham; Sloss Furnaces Oral History Collection, SFNHL (hereafter SFOHC).

3. Jacquelyn Dowd Hall and others, *Like a Family: The Making of a Southern Cotton Mill World* (Chapel Hill: University of North Carolina Press, 1987), 43.

❦

In 1871, seeking to diversify northern Alabama's economy, several prominent Alabamians founded the city of Birmingham with the explicit goal of exploiting the mineral resources of north central Alabama (Jones Valley), where every ingredient necessary for making iron and steel could be found within a thirty-mile radius. One of these men was James Withers Sloss, a northern Alabama merchant who had brought the Louisville and Nashville Railroad into Jones Valley in 1871, transforming Birmingham from a squalid jumble of tents, shanties, and boxcars into a thriving community. Anxious to tap the rich mineral areas surrounding Birmingham, Sloss and his fellow Birmingham promoters acquired thirty thousand acres and formed the Pratt Coal and Coke Company (named in memory of Daniel Pratt, an early antebellum Alabama industrialist). Pratt quickly became the largest mining enterprise in the district. Soon blast furnaces for processing the iron ore mined by Pratt sprang up all over Jefferson County, and pig iron production rapidly became big business in northern Alabama. By the 1880s, Birmingham was booming and, due to its rapid growth, had earned the nickname the "Magic City." Growth and prosperity continued into the twentieth century. The city seemed to embody the promise of the New South, and the Birmingham District became a magnet for thousands of settlers, both black and white. Nonetheless, as historian W. David Lewis notes, "The status that Birmingham attained as a leading symbol of the New South was paradoxical. The city was deeply rooted in the old plantation system." Whereas northern industry was based on free labor, these New South planter-entrepreneurs favored the old southern model of manufacturing built upon the institution of the earlier slavery years where whites had complete control and a dependent labor supply.[4]

The majority of the new workers flocking to Birmingham were former farmers and sharecroppers from Alabama and other southeastern states who hoped to escape the desperate rural poverty and find jobs and better lives for their families. They were frustrated and

4. W. David Lewis, *Sloss Furnaces and the Rise of the Birmingham District: An Industrial Epic* (Tuscaloosa: University of Alabama Press, 1994), 58, 82.

tired of being kept poor and in debt by landlords who devised a system of sharecropping that allowed them little more freedom than slavery had. Beginning in the 1880s and continuing well into the twentieth century, with numerous years of low cotton prices, many black farmers had decided that their only real freedom was to leave the farm and head to the mines and furnaces of Birmingham. Mary Harris recalled, "The reason we came to Birmingham was 'cause cotton went down to nothing. You couldn't get a real bale of cotton. Cotton was forty dollars a bale. Everything went to dropping. If you farming, you couldn't pay the landlords, you couldn't pay your bills."[5]

The move to Birmingham proved an enormous change to people accustomed to the simple rural life of an isolated farm. Although women seldom expressed a longing for the backbreaking hours spent in cotton fields, they missed family members, childhood friends, and church activities, as well as the familiar sounds and smells of rural life. Newly arrived blacks often stated that Birmingham contained "too many strangers in a strange place." Acrid smoke spewing from the smokestacks of Birmingham's numerous iron and steel mills meant economic progress for some, but frightened those used to gazing upon miles of open land and cotton fields.[6]

For many people, however, the prospect of life in Birmingham was thrilling. Clarence Dean, who arrived in Birmingham in the 1920s and eventually worked at Sloss Furnaces and resided in the quarters, remembered his first encounter with the city as a young child:

> When my daddy came to Birmingham, he got a job in the mines. We was still down in the country. Hopeville, Alabama . . . that's the country. He worked until he got enough money and sent for the family. My mother told me that we're going to Birmingham where all them bright light is. The Birmingham Terminal Station was lit like a big mansion or something. It was a sight to see. When I stepped off the train, they had to catch me because I'd never seen nothing like that before. I pointed and told them,

5. Harris, interview by Utz, October 20, 2002, Birmingham, SFOHC.
6. Ron Bates, interview by Utz, May 21, 2004, Birmingham, SFOHC.

"Pretty light! Pretty light!" They were beautiful. Being a little fellow, it looked like heaven to me.[7]

Although the majority of workers were African American and came from rural areas of the Southeast, other workers immigrated from outside the region. Skilled ironworkers from the North moved in to become the new plant and factory managers. European immigrants, often newly arrived in the United States, migrated to the Birmingham area to work in industry or provide services for those who did. Although dominated by black labor, the industrial workplace was rigidly segregated until the 1960s. At Sloss, for example, men bathed in separate bathhouses, punched separate time clocks, and attended separate company picnics. Most important was the segregation of jobs. The company operated as a hierarchy. At the top there was an all-white group of managers, accountants, engineers, and chemists; at the bottom, an all-black labor gang, assisted, until its demise in 1928, by the use of convict labor. Many southern states used the convict labor system, leasing the labor of local and state prison inmates to industrialists, planters, and other. Convict laborers, disproportionately African American, were not paid for their labor. They often faced physical abuse and inadequate living conditions, but they also provided southern employers with a source of cheap, easily controlled workers. As a result, convict labor provided an important weapon in the district's economic warfare with northern manufacturing. Slavery had not died but had merely been transformed.[8]

Between the skilled ironworkers, the managers, and the African American labor gangs, a racially mixed group of workers performed a variety of skilled and semiskilled jobs. Even in the middle group, however, whites held the higher-paying, higher-status "title" positions: stove tenders, boilermakers, carpenters, machinists. Black workers were restricted to such "helper" roles as carpenter helper, machinist helper, stove-tender helper. African Americans at Sloss often complained of

7. *Like It Ain't Never Passed: Remembering Life in Sloss Quarters* (Birmingham: Sloss Furnaces National Historic Landmark, 1985), 8.
8. Lewis, *Sloss Furnaces,* 90.

the discrimination they suffered in the workplace, the consequences of a Jim Crow society. A worker's race defined the type of job he or she was eligible to perform, creating a system in which there was a clear distinction between a "white person's job" and a "black person's job." Black women of the quarters realized early on the distinction between white and black work. One former resident recalled, "My husband just knew where to look for a job. He didn't even look for the job he thought he was qualified to do because he knew the white man would get it." Although blacks held 75 percent of the jobs in Birmingham's iron and steel mills, none of them were in white-collar positions.[9]

Segregation at the workplace mirrored living conditions away from the plant. As Birmingham's population exploded in the late nineteenth century, Sloss Furnaces, Tennessee Coal and Iron, and numerous other furnaces and mines built low-cost, segregated housing throughout the Birmingham area. Sloss Quarters, the forty-eight houses adjacent to the actual Sloss site, were designed specially for African American workers pouring in from the depleted lands of the Black Belt. They were typical shotgun-style structures, with two rooms set on foundation posts and, in the early years, no indoor plumbing. Until the 1930s, drinking and cooking water came from a faucet at the end of each row of houses. Rain barrels caught water for the laundry. Nonetheless, many of these homes proved an improvement over the sharecropper shacks supplied by landowners. Peacolia Barge recalled years later, "They were simple dwellings for simple people."[10]

Company housing, which became the standard pattern of residential development in the Birmingham area, was a concept that had been around for centuries. Worker housing had been built next to the first factories in the mid-eighteenth century in England. The first factory "masters" believed this was the best way to control and train their industrial workforce. The early American iron and mining industries also provided housing for their workers, as their furnaces and mines operated in remote areas without existing communities. This practice

9. *Like It Ain't Never Passed*, 8.
10. Lawrence, "Story of Sloss," n.p.; *Like It Ain't Never Passed*, 21.

continued in the nineteenth century. The early industrialists of the Birmingham District often found it difficult to keep their workers on the job; turnover and absenteeism rates were high. Providing housing for workers in company towns was a means of keeping the workforce available for labor and retaining the services of skilled men. As the U.S. Bureau of Labor Statistics stated, "A housed labor supply is a controlled labor supply."[11]

Housing in the quarters served two purposes: it attracted family men, thus lowering the rate of absenteeism, and it made available a ready supply of black labor in case of emergencies. It also made workers completely dependent on the company for everything from housing to household supplies. Sloss realized early on that one way of combating worker "instability" was to hire as many workers with wives and families as possible. Furnishing houses to workers at reasonable rents also helped promote stability. Sloss charged four dollars per month for a one-room dwelling, five dollars for two rooms, and six dollars for three. Although company housing was a definite improvement over dilapidated rural dwellings, life for Birmingham's black iron- and steelworkers and their families was far from idyllic. Families no more than five to ten years away from their rural southern existence may have been freed from the burdens of sharecropping, but they nevertheless felt the loss of a sense of place. The old church, the river, the trees, the cemetery where members of the families were buried—these and other reference points simply did not exist in this new city called Birmingham. Women missed their mothers, their gardens, and raising their kids in the places where they themselves had grown up. And they would do everything in their power to re-create this sense of place in their new urban communities. The men, furthermore, long accustomed to following the rhythm of the sun and the seasons, found it difficult to adjust to the "tyranny of the clock."

11. Marjorie White, *The Birmingham District: An Industrial History and Guide* (Birmingham: Birmingham Publishing, 1981), 81–82; Mark Nixon, "Leisure and Recreation in Late 19th Century and Early 20th Century Birmingham," 1996, History of Southern American Women's Collection, SFNHL (hereafter HSAWC), 12.

For newcomers as well as for those who had been in Birmingham for some time, life was harsh.[12]

African American women, believing that "goin' North" would provide better jobs for their husbands, found the system working against them in the city. Black labor was the last hired in good times, the first fired in bad. Education and skill counted little in a system that gave black workers only the lowest-paying, most physically demanding jobs: charging the furnace, breaking up and carrying out the pig iron. Until the late 1950s, with the rise of unions, there was little chance for advancement. Mrs. Alonzo Gaines, whose husband worked at the furnaces for years, recalled that he complained of the lack of advancement opportunities. Gaines said, "You knew in them days and times that a white man's job was engineer, foreman, and such. You knew you couldn't get a white man's job because you were a nigger." Clarence Dean, a Sloss employee for more thirty years, told a white Sloss administrator in the 1940s of his desire to be an iron pourer. The supervisor responded, "That's a white man's job. Ain't no going to give no niggers no white folks jobs." Although the union made efforts to correct this situation, equal job opportunities for blacks would have to wait until the 1960s.[13]

But what did not wait was the commitment on the part of the wives, mothers, and daughters of black workers to make the best possible homes for their families in a new and alien urban landscape. The majority of women in Sloss Quarters not only kept their individual shotguns tidy and organized but kept well-manicured gardens and large flower beds as well. As sharecropper wives and as the primary caretakers of their rural dwellings, farm women had had little time, money, or incentive to cultivate and maintain a home they would be leaving in a year or two. The size and crudeness of a sharecropper's home made it difficult to keep clean. Landlords provided shoddy homes lacking glass for windows, running water, shelf space, and ade-

---

12. Lawrence, "Story of Sloss," n.p.

13. Gaines, interview by Ron Bates, 1990, Birmingham, SFOHC; *Like It Ain't Never Passed*, 8.

quate insulation. Once arriving in the quarters and realizing this would be their home for many years, women, many for the first time in their adult lives, painstakingly sewed curtains, decorated, and saved money for a new piece of furniture often purchased at the company store. Mary Harris recalled the beautiful pinafores her mom would make her with the remnants of leftover material: "My mother used to go to the commissary to buy her fabric . . . then she'd make curtains and such. . . . [W]ith the leftover fabric she'd make my pinafores . . . all by hand and no patterns. She'd just put that material down on that bed and cut it."[14]

The primary roles of women, as wives, mothers, and homemakers, left them little time for themselves. Evelyn Howard's mother had been the key figure in their household when they lived in rural Greene County and continued to be when they moved to the quarters: "There was no such thing as an eight-hour work day for the women of Sloss Quarters. As on the farm, a woman's day began before daybreak and continued long after she had put her husband and children to bed." Howard recalled looking to her father for financial support, but in all other areas, she depended on her mother. Endless rounds of house-work were even more difficult and time consuming because of the lack of modern household conveniences.[15]

City life seemed easier, however. A number of Sloss families sent their children to relatives in the country in the summer. The parents of the children of Sloss had come of age in the country and wanted their kids to be aware of their ancestral homes, as well as the ways of rural life. They not only wanted their children to develop emotional ties with cousins, aunts, and uncles but also believed that they would be "watched to stay out of trouble." Claude Dailey, who grew up in the quarters, remembered staying with his aunt and cousins in Lime-stone County, Alabama. What most amazed Dailey was the amount of work demanded of his aunt: "My aunt would have to come home

14. Jacqueline Jones, *Labor of Love, Labor of Sorrow: Black Women, Work, and the Family from Slavery to the Present* (New York: Basic Books, 1985), 86; Harris interview, 21.

15. Howard, interview by Peggy Hamrick, February 20, 1984, HSAWC, 6.

from the fields to cook her meals on a stove that used no coal; they used wood. . . . [L]ife was harder in the country."[16]

Although many of the women in the quarters worked as domestic workers or laundresses for the white "over-the-mountain" elites, some African American men refused to let their wives work outside the home. Men grew up with stories of how male family members, while tied into the institution of slavery, had no control over working conditions and the responsibilities of the wives, mother, and daughters. Following the end of slavery, however, many African American males insisted that female family members confine their work to the home. This desire to keep the girls out of the fields left them free to attend school year-round, whereas young black males were still pulled out during harvest time. Jeffery Rush, a Sloss laborer raised on his family farm, recalled his sisters going to school for the entire year: "Girls didn't do nothing out there. In them days, we had to do everything, dig sweet potatoes and cord wood in the winter to keep us warm." This pattern continued as families migrated to the Birmingham area. Clarence Dean not only refused to allow his daughter to work after school but also refused to let his wife seek outside employment. Dean stated, "This is yours here, that on the outside belongs to me. I do all the providing. . . . if there ain't nothing here but a piece of bread, you cook it." In 1921, the majority of the graduating class of Birmingham's black Industrial High School contained eighteen males and sixty-five females. As was true in rural communities, many young black males residing in Sloss Quarters entered the workforce before finishing high school for economic reasons.[17]

Because of low wages for black men, few wives and mothers at Sloss could concentrate on their household tasks alone. Many of the wives of Sloss employees were forced, as they had often been in their previous rural communities, into the workplace (primarily domestic

16. *We've Come This Far by Faith: Black Migration to Birmingham, 1900–1940* (Birmingham: Sloss Furnaces National Historic Landmark, 1988), 12.
17. Lawrence, "Story of Sloss," n.p.; *We've Come This Far,* 7; *Like It Ain't Never Passed,* 9; *Report of Progress: Birmingham Public Schools, September 1, 1921 to August 31, 1931* (Birmingham: Birmingham Board of Education, 1931), 139.

work) to ensure the economic survival of their families. The beginning of the twentieth century brought an increased dependence on domestic work among black southern women. This trend proved particularly pronounced in cities like Birmingham because of the large influx of agrarian workers seeking economic and social advancements. Although they preferred to stay at home with their own children and take care of their own homes, many of the women of Sloss Quarters became domestic workers. Domestic work had its beginnings long before emancipation. Some slave women, the mothers and grandmothers of the women residing in the quarters, learned the art of washing, ironing, cleaning, and cooking for white people from their female relatives and to a lesser extent by working for white mistresses. After they received their freedom, rural black women found restricted the types of work available to them. They acted as family caretakers, worked in the fields alongside their husbands, and often earned the family's only cash. This much needed income came from either taking in laundry, selling hand-raised produce, or working as domestics. Like their rural counterparts, most of the women of Sloss Quarters were forced into domestic service jobs by the necessity of providing for the present and future needs of themselves and their families.[18]

The women of Sloss Quarters labored as laundresses as well as domestics. And though this type of work was hard, it could be done at home, solving the problem of child care. The husbands of laundresses preferred this job for their wives over working in someone else's home because it conflicted less with their family "obligations." Because they could work in their own homes, new mothers not willing to leave their babies or small children often preferred laundry work. Although laundry work provided a certain amount of autonomy from whites and allowed women to care for their children and the pay proved considerably higher than black women earned in rural communities, the pay was nonetheless low and the task grueling. A typical laundress collected laundry from several white families on Mondays. The clothing

18. N. Lynn Sullivan, "The Silent People: Black Women in Domestic Work, Laundry, and Industry from 1900–1950," 1996, HSAWC, 4.

had to be boiled in a large pot on the front lawn, and the children drew water for the pot. After the clothes were boiled, they were scrubbed on a washboard, rinsed, starched, wrung out, hung up, and ironed. The clothes were then delivered on the following Saturday, and the laundress hoped that the customer would approve of the work and pay the full amount owed. In many instances, the customer would not pay if there were complaints about the detergent or a missing sock. These women were not only overworked and poorly paid, but the fact that washing was a "black job" resulted in the relegation of wash-women to a lower position on the social scale than domestic workers.[19]

Not surprisingly, most of the women of the quarters preferred doing laundry for their individual families. By the 1930s, the management at Sloss, fearful that the women in the quarters might possibly burn down the housing with their "laundry fires," ran a pipe from one of the blast furnaces to a barrel located in the front yard of one of the homes in the quarters. Although thrilled with this new system, Mary Harris recalled the problems of the barrel being located in her family's front yard. "My mother sometimes hated washin' day. The neighbors would be wandering in and out of our yard all the day... tramplin' her flowers and such."[20]

World War II opened a few industrial jobs for black women in the South, but most of the women of Sloss Quarters continued to "labor in someone else's kitchen." Black northern women benefited from the increased opportunities created by the war economy and found jobs in manufacturing plants, but their counterparts in the South were still cleaning floors. Fannie Temple began working in the homes of rural white families at eight years old. At that time she received $1.25 a week for chores performed both in the house and in the yard. By the time she migrated to Birmingham in the 1920s she was elated to find that she could make $2.50 a week as a domestic. And because of the low cost of domestic workers, all but the poorest white families considered a domestic servant or laundress affordable. The average wage

19. Ibid., 15.
20. Harris interview, 5.

offered in Birmingham newspaper advertisements in 1934 was $33.34 per month for a live-in domestic.[21]

❧

Sloss Quarters was not a company town in the strictest sense, because it did not provide a company school or recreational services. There was a doctor's office, however, and a commissary that became the focal point of life in the quarters. W. B. McDanal, a maintenance worker in the quarters, fondly recalled the first Sloss physician, Dr. J. P. McQueen: "We had a real good doctor here. Ol' Doc J. P. McQueen worked here for thirty-five years. As soon as he got out of medical school he started working here. He worked here until he reached old age. He knew everybody. He knew my wife and children by name. He'd come to your house. Yeah, he knew everybody's name. The common laborer was just as important to him as supervisor or the president." McQueen not only nursed the injured furnace workers but delivered babies, both black and white, and made frequent house calls as well. George Brown remembered, "When the children were sick, he'd come out there to your house and tend to them. When my oldest child had pneumonia, Dr. McQueen was right there. He delivered my first baby at the house for fifteen dollars."[22]

Although midwives, country doctors, and older women wise to folk medicines were respected members of rural communities, having access to a local hospital and a doctor who made house calls proved a great comfort and convenience to the women of Sloss Quarters. McQueen delivered five of Gertrude Jones's mother's children. Jones, a resident of Sloss Quarters for more than twenty years, asked McQueen to deliver her infant before he retired: "He was getting ready to retire and I asked him would he deliver my baby and he asked me when it's coming and I said August...and he waited until my boy came to retire."[23]

21. *We've Come This Far*, 2; Temple, interview by Peggy Hamrick, July 21, 1984, Working Lives Collection, Samford University Library, Birmingham (hereafter WLC).

22. *Like It Ain't Never Passed*, 16, 17.

23. Jones interview, 7.

An equally appealing and equally convenient part of life in Sloss Quarters was the commissary. The company store served as both pay office and shopping center. Shoes, cloth, tools, seed, appliances, as well as a variety of foodstuffs could be purchased at the Sloss commissary. In the early days, workers paid for items with company scrip called "clacker." After the use of clacker declined, families continued to purchase goods at the commissary, but more often than in the past they bought on credit. Although some Sloss workers found the credit system helpful, others saw it as a way for the company to take advantage of its workers. One former worker contended that in the early years, Sloss purposely overdrafted some of the men: "They couldn't read or write and the company decided to overdraft them. When they overdrafted you that meant that you couldn't get no more stuff at the commissary and sometimes didn't get paid. Some people would work for months and never drew their money."[24]

Others found the credit system to their liking, particularly the lease-sell system. With the lease-sell system, an employee signed an agreement promising to pay a specific amount out of his weekly wages. As one worker explained, "All you had to do was put four dollars a week on an appliance at the commissary. At the other places you had to put down some big money." Unlike the majority of white-owned stores in the Birmingham area, where blacks were allowed to purchase goods only if they had cash in hand, company commissaries such as Sloss often allowed their employees the opportunity to put down whatever they could afford.[25]

The quarters provided a relatively cohesive community setting for workers and their families coming in from various areas of the rural South, a community where people had the same customs, shared the same beliefs, and shared the same problems. Social events that tied neighbors together on the farms became the typical neighborhood gatherings in urban settings. Watermelon cuttings, barbecues, chitlin suppers, and quilting bees were but a few of the social events organized by the women of Sloss Quarters. Gertrude Jones stated that you

24. *Like It Ain't Never Passed*, 17.
25. Ibid., 8.

knew you had come of age when you were invited to "pull up a chair next to your mama and join in at the quilt. . . . I was about thirteen . . . 'bout the same age as my mama was when she started piece quilting. . . . [I]t was a proud time . . . something I had waited for." As in rural communities, quilting brought young and old women together for an afternoon of chatting, socializing, and feasting. Jones recalled, "In less than two days they would have a big quilt. It would be so pretty and I didn't never thought that I could do something like that but I did. And we'd just give them away, give to different people so they would now have a cover."[26]

In addition to neighborhood parties and quilting bees, the residents of the quarters instituted a kind of "neighborhood watch" program to curtail crime. A stove tender at Sloss Furnaces and resident of the quarters recalled, "We kept those Quarters in shape; we didn't have no rowdies. We took care of those rowdies. We'd go to them. We had this committee and we'd go to them and talk to them, 'you have to shape up or ship out.' But it never came down to that." Another resident recalled that crime was not a problem because "everyone knew everybody. Children couldn't get into no devilment away from home because another adult might whip them and they'd get two whippings."[27]

African American girls growing up on farms and in rural areas of Alabama were taught at an early age to keep an eye on their siblings as well as the children in the immediate area. This workload did not lessen once the family migrated to the quarters. With mothers busy tending the gardens or chickens or working as domestic help for the wealthy over-the-mountain whites, oldest daughters were still considered caretakers to the youngest family members. Parents, however, attempting to steer their daughters away from domestic work, demanded their daughters receive an education. With Thomas School nearby, the black children of the quarters had access to educational opportunities almost unheard of in the rest of the South. Therefore, most of the babysitting of younger siblings by the eldest daughter was done after school and in the summer months.[28]

26. Jones interview, 12.
27. *Like It Ain't Never Passed,* 8, 17.
28. *We've Come This Far,* 12.

Whether in rural homes or urban company towns, women took great pride in the preparation of meals for families and friends. Gertrude Jones remembered the pride her mom took in her cooking, even when times were lean: "My mama used to fry up the chickens she raised in our yard, cook greens and peas and fried okra and stuff like that and make cornbread and sometimes she would have neckbones and pinto beans and turnip greens, stuff like that. We would have it a lot and other people around there would. They loved the neck bone 'cause at the time if you wanted steak you couldn't get it no way so we enjoyed what we had." Juanita Seltzer recalled her mother cooking dinners for the single men working at the furnaces: "They would stop by the house in the morning and place their orders. In the evening mama would get some of the neighbor kids to help deliver the meals to the men as they were getting off work." Seltzer also packed lunch baskets and sold them outside the gates of Sloss at lunchtime. It not only raised extra money for the Seltzer household but also allowed Mrs. Seltzer to stay home with her three children—a luxury not often experienced in the quarters.[29]

Accustomed to growing their own fruits and vegetables, black women residing in the country often refused to move with their husband to the city unless they were promised enough land for a chicken coop and a large garden. Recognizing this desire for land, James Sloss instructed the architects designing Sloss Quarters to section off tracts of land for community chicken coops and pig yards, as well as individual gardens where women could grow the vegetables and fruits necessary for recipes that had been passed down for generations. Abraham Williams worked as a sand caster at Sloss Furnaces and remembered the superintendent of Sloss, Jim Downey, marking off the gardens for each family: "My wife said she needed a garden.... [L]ots of the women said the same. The company garden ran plumb back to the railroads, but we wanted our own garden. The company went and had Mr. Downey to mark off a garden for every family. He'd lay off a spot for your family and other spots would be for other families. We'd

29. Jones interview, 16; Seltzer, interview by Utz, February 13, 2002, Birmingham, SFOHC, interview transcript W3A, 4.

raise what we wanted . . . okra, beans, peas, and greens. We had a good little spot too."[30]

Although not afforded much free time away from cleaning, cooking, and caring for the children, women sought out various activities for their precious spare time. They participated in sewing circles, piece quilting, social and civic clubs, singing organizations, shopping, and catching up on the latest news. Leola Harris recalled that everyone in her neighborhood knew each other and was "just as friendly and sociable-like as can be." Some of the women in the quarters joined or formed social clubs to help them adapt more easily to urban life. Though black women also formed social clubs for the same purposes that white women did (companionship and to share similar interests), proportionately fewer black women living in the quarters found time to participate or preferred to form their own more domesticated gatherings, such as quilting bees and sewing circles. Birmingham's Cosmos Club, founded around 1910, concentrated on civic and charity projects while also providing social activities for middle-class black women. This particular club, like the Zeta Phi Beta sorority, the Masons, and the Sojourner Truth Club, was primarily made up of second-generation urban black women who had obtained an education through the urban school system. The Zeta Phi Betas gave scholarships to young women to further their educations, and only women with certified teaching degrees could belong to the group. The majority of black women residing in Sloss Quarters did not feel comfortable socializing with the women of Birmingham's black middle class.[31]

Just as they had while living in the country, the women of Sloss used the majority of their free time in church-related activities. Churches provided for their spiritual needs and their desire for social activities. They also served as a means of control by the white employers. White-controlled mining and manufacturing companies such as Sloss Furnaces, already dominating large portions of the lives of their workers, realized early on the importance of religion in black communities.

30. *Like It Ain't Never Passed*, 5.

31. Harris, interview by Brenda McCallum, June 25, 1984, HSAWC, interview 1A; Robert Corley, *The Other Side: The Story of Birmingham's Black Population* (Birmingham: Birmingham Publishing, 1989), 15.

Perhaps as another way to control their workforce or to provide all the community's needs within the quarters, the company built a church for the African American workers. New Hope Baptist Church, located in Birmingham's West End district, traces its beginnings to a congregation that met in a building owned by Sloss Furnaces. Residents of Sloss also created their own congregation. Adrienne Dean, also known as "Sister" Dean, the wife of a Sloss maintenance worker, started her own church on Sloss property in 1927. Dean was an evangelist who sought permission from Sloss administrators to use an old building down by the company reservoir. Abraham Williams, a member of Dean's congregation at Sloss, reported that Sister Dean's church was called the Sanctified Church because the "sanctified folks don't sin or do nothing . . . no smoking, drinking, or hair straighten'. Mrs. Dean was a nice lady. She used to have a service. She'd teach us a lot about the Bible and let us sing."[32]

African American church life in Birmingham at the turn of the twentieth century reflected its origins in the rural South. City and rural churches held to similar doctrines as divine judgment and the need for repentance and salvation. This consistency allowed black families from rural backgrounds to assimilate more easily into a society in which the church was such a crucial part. Furthermore, since black families had little access to Birmingham theaters, parks, and public recreational facilities, church functions provided one of the few public places where African Americans could gather. In the move from the rural to the urban world, religion seemed to be the constant. Fannie Temple, a young black woman who moved to Birmingham in the early 1920s, joined a church before she had even unpacked her bags. "The first Sunday, I'll tell you what I did. I found my way to the closest Baptist church."[33]

Iola Jackson, a member of the New Hope Baptist Church, believed that women were the "core of the church," as they had been in rural

32. *Like It Ain't Never Passed,* 15.
33. Wayne Flynt, "Religion in the Urban South: The Divided Religious Mind of Birmingham, 1870–1930," in *From Civil War to Civil Rights: Alabama, 1860–1960,* compiled by Sarah Woolfolk Wiggins (Tuscaloosa: University of Alabama Press, 1987), 258; Temple interview.

churches, and she served as both a choir member and a Sunday-school teacher. The church as an institution provided women like Jackson with the unique opportunity to get involved in positions of leadership where they were otherwise restricted. Typical church work done by women ranged from teaching and singing to cooking, sewing, raising money, and cleaning. The role of education providers played by women in black churches was actually a much more important one than it was in white churches because of the neglect and restrictions of black children's education by the white-controlled public sector. Tasks performed for the church, no matter how menial, were not equivalent to normal housework in the eyes of the Sloss women. Acts such as preparing and serving food to members of one's faith community could symbolize, in the words of historian Jacqueline Jones, the "spiritual component of collective survival." Many of the women at Sloss considered serving and participating in the church both a responsibility and an opportunity.[34]

Choirs, glee clubs, and all-day singing events were among the most popular church activities for women of the quarters as well as for the men and children. Just as they had in rural communities, all-day singing events brought members of different black churches together, allowing Sloss families to interact with families from other sectors of the steel, iron, and mining industries. It was a time to share stories and workplace complaints, as well as local and national political and economic concerns. Most of these events occurred twice a year and were accompanied by "dinner on the grounds." The church ladies brought their most prized home-cooked dishes and laid them on a long table outside the church for the much anticipated meal. Such activities demonstrated the same spirit of cooperation and companionship brought from rural life into urban life.[35]

Churches organized and sponsored many social and recreational activities. Evelyn Howard recalled weekly youth functions at her church, as well as fish fries, bake sales, volleyball games, picnics, and hay

34. *New Hope Baptist Church: Centennial Celebration* (Birmingham, privately printed, 1992), 2; Jones, *Labor of Love*, 230.
35. *New Hope Baptist Church*, 2.

rides: "We just had us a grand time, socializing through the church." Another activity, referred to as "shoe-box entertainment," brought the young adult church members together from the various Birmingham black churches. Young women would fix a special meal, place it in a shoe box, and choose a "special" boy to share it. Years later, Ella Mae Hodges remembered this as being the "grandest events of all the church events." (White textile mill workers in North Carolina shared similar events. Millworker Naomi Trammel met her husband that way: "The families would have the thing. They'd fix boxes and sell them. And these boys would buy them, and then they'd go and get the girl they wanted to eat with.")[36]

Laypeople received valuable leadership training through church life. Black laborers, who submitted to demeaning white management all week, and women who spent most their time cleaning and caring for their children became deacons, choir members, or religious instructors every Sunday. Many workers' identities, as well as the identities of their wives within the Sloss community, came from their church roles rather than from their employment, allowing them to gain respect and social status in the same manner they had gained respect and social status in their rural churches. By allowing these normally oppressed people to lead themselves and each other at least one day a week and hold positions of authority and responsibility, the church "promoted a sense of self-worth among blacks and encouraged participation and development of leadership skills."[37]

Basically the only institution free from white control, the church was a haven from prejudice and the logical center of activism. In a Sloss mining camp near Birmingham, union organizers met in a church building, and the congregation occasionally allowed union organizers to speak in Sunday services. Despite the risk of angering white management or the local Ku Klux Klan, churches became politicized early in Birmingham's history, thus laying the groundwork for their pivotal role in the civil rights movement.[38]

36. Howard interview; Hodges, interview by Peggy Hamrick, August 7, 1984, WLC, 27; Hall, *Like a Family*, 142.

37. Corley, *Other Side*, n.p.

38. Ibid.

The young adults of the quarters found time for weekend recreational activities outside the church. Birmingham-area theaters proved to be the preferred hangout. Marcel Hopson recalled that the Carver Theater offered high school kids the opportunity to get their first taste of nightlife. Places like Carver were popular because most of Birmingham's entertainment center was off-limits to people under the age of eighteen. The Famous and the Frolick Theaters catered to an older crowd, featuring entertainers with names like Butterbeans Susie, Hot Harlem Review, and the Brown Skinned Models. Hopson remembers when she first moved from the country wanting to visit the Frolic, where *Gone with the Wind* was playing. This was a rare opportunity, for, according to Hopson, movies and shows normally shown at the Frolic were "what you might called the X-rated sort of thing now, and certainly not suitable for a country gal." Savoy's Café on Birmingham's Fourth Avenue was the largest black café in the nation. H. D. Coke, a Birmingham journalist, was a regular at the café and recalled that they sold more beer than "any other outlet in the state of Alabama." The Savoy was open twenty-four hours a day, seven days a week, and regularly featured bands like the Cats and Five Blind Boys.[39]

The majority of Sloss children stayed close to home, entertaining themselves as they had in the country, shooting marbles, playing checkers, climbing trees, and inventing all types of games and activities to pass the time. Fannie Williams, a resident of the quarters for more twenty years, raised six kids at Sloss: "It wasn't such a bad place for children. At Christmastime the company would buy all the children fruit, candy, and toys and Mr. Jim Downey [superintendent of the Quarters] would dress up like Santa. No, kids wasn't so bad off in them Quarters." Contact between mill management and the African American children, though friendly, was limited.[40]

Singing and dancing at one of the weekly Sloss house parties, or "platter parties," with a disc jockey hired for a few dollars, catered to both the young and the old and proved a popular and inexpensive

39. Hopson, interview by Steve McCallum, February 7, 1985, Birmingham, WLC, 12; Nixon, "Leisure and Recreation," 13.

40. *Like It Ain't Never Passed,* 6.

way to have fun. It was also a much anticipated event since most of the residents of the quarters had grown up surrounded by music on family farms. Ballads, spirituals, and fiddle music were an important part of the southern rural landscape and were a source of comfort and joy to both black sharecroppers and white hill farmers as they migrated to mill and factory towns. Music also brought back memories of the land, families, and better times ahead. Black gospel quartets, their roots in the rural communities of Alabama, became a popular source of entertainment in the 1920s and 1930s. Recording studios set up makeshift studios in Birmingham hotels and recorded such groups as the Golden Leaf Quartette and the Sterling Jubilee Singers. By the end of the 1930s, Birmingham laid claim as one of the two cradles of black gospel quartet music. Music tied the families in the quarters together just as it had bound families and neighbors together in rural communities.[41]

Another popular form of entertainment, also brought from rural communities, was baseball. A 1926 Bureau of Labor survey of 431 industrial companies revealed that 223 of them reported one or more organized baseball teams in their plants. Seventeen of these companies were in the iron, steel, and mining businesses. Companies like Sloss Furnaces and Tennessee Coal and Iron encouraged team sports. Sloss administrators believed that organized company team events, although segregated, not only were recreational outlets but also taught employees the importance of cooperation and encouraged pride and dedication in the company. Sloss resident Clarence Dean believed that Sloss had "one of the best baseball teams you wanted to see. They called themselves the 'Raggedy Roaches' 'cause they'd run so and scuffle so and keep their suits torn up."[42]

Weekend baseball games appealed to all family members residing in the quarters. Used to their husbands, fathers, and sons playing in

41. Archie Green, *Spirit of Steel: Music of the Mines, Railroads, and Mills of the Birmingham District* (Birmingham: Sloss Furnaces National Historic Landmark, 1999), xii.

42. Timothy Whitt, *Bases Loaded with History: The Story of Rickwood Field, America's Oldest Baseball Park* (Birmingham: R. Boozer Press, 1995), 37; *Like It Ain't Never Passed,* 9.

the "cornfields of the counties," the women of Sloss found comfort and familiarity in a game that had been an important part of their rural world. Slossfield, where the majority of the games were played, became a gathering spot for the women of Sloss to relax and socialize, as well as cheer on their favorite teams. Women and their families, whether white or black, interacted with other iron-industry employees through ball games. Louise Burns recalled that "when the white team would play, all the blacks would be there rootin' them on and when the black team would play, all the whites would be there rootin' for them."[43]

Although women of the quarters enjoyed attending baseball games, many preferred to spend what little leisure time they had shopping. Shopping as a form of female entertainment saw its beginnings in the early twentieth century. And the women of Sloss Quarters, the majority of whom never encountered a store larger than the local general store while living in the country, looked forward to their trips to the Sloss commissary to shop and catch up on all the latest news.[44]

Downtown Birmingham provided a whole new shopping experience. Department stores such as Birmingham's own Loveman's offered "Merchandise That Merits Confidence" as well as a diverse array of home accessories and appliances. Department stores also represented a shift from necessity shopping that took place at the Sloss commissary to a more relaxed style where the women might pause for a bit of lunch or a stop by a local beauty salon. Trips to beauty salons were considered a luxury by women raised on farms where the only "beauty accessory" consisted of a bar of soap and a corn-husk brush.[45]

Though many department stores in the city were open to black patrons, the stores put considerable restrictions on them. African American women were not allowed to try on items, nor were they allowed to return merchandise. Although these women had faced

43. Cleatus Burns and Louise Burns, interview by Brenda McCallum, June 12, 1984, WLC, interview 8A, transcript 7, 12).
44. *Like It Ain't Never Passed*, 18.
45. Marjorie White, *True Stories of Birmingham* (Birmingham: Birmingham Publishing, 1990), 43; *We've Come This Far*, 6.

certain segregation practices in their previous rural settings, they, like the white sharecroppers in the area, traded at the local furnishing merchants who charged exorbitant prices to both poor black and white families alike. African American women found the blatant form of segregation encountered in Birmingham's department stores offensive and disturbing.[46]

Shopping remained the primary responsibility of the women, nevertheless. Peggy Sparks, who grew up near the quarters, recalled that it was her mother who always organized the shopping and made it a teaching experience for her children: "We girls had to go to learn how to do it." Sparks also told of the prejudice her mother endured while shopping. "When Mom would hand the store clerk a fifty or one hundred dollar bill, they always looked strange at her." She noted that her mother would always save up their money before they went shopping, yet the clerks would "always take up to the area where the cheaper clothes were."[47]

When women ventured away from the quarters to shop and socialize in downtown Birmingham, it was necessary to take public transportation, a new experience for women who had grown up in rural communities where walking was the main mode of transportation. Gertrude Jones recalled how her mom often reminisced about the days "where we could walk to wherever we needed to be. Back home [in their rural communities] people could walk wherever they wanted . . . but people here [Birmingham] can't ride wherever they want." Although familiar with the ways of segregation, women nonetheless found it unsettling to have to sit in the backs of streetcars and, later, city buses. At the beginning of the twentieth century, there were no state or city laws mandating segregation on public transportation, yet the bus companies kept black and white patrons separated by partitions. In 1910, the city code included section 1413, requiring the owners or operators of any bus to make a clear distinction between the buses for black and those for whites by "clearly indicating

46. *We've Come This Far,* 7.
47. Sparks, interview by Steve McCullum, October 14, 1985, WLC, interview 7C, transcript 12, 8.

or designating by visible markers the area to be occupied by each race." One resident of the quarters stated that there "might be forty black people on the bus and two whites would get on and they'd move that partition back and all the blacks had to get up, stand in the aisle and lean against each other and there may be ten more seats up there, but you got to sit behind the partition." Not only the buses but also the facilities tied to the buses, such as waiting rooms, restrooms, and other accommodations, were segregated. Residents faced segregation in the city's taxicabs as well as by the railroads. The railroads were required by the city codes, section 1002, to provide "separate entrances and exits . . . to prevent intermingling of the white and colored passengers when entering or leaving."[48]

❧

The Great Depression that began in the late 1920s was an extremely stressful time for the families of Sloss, as it was for thousands of blacks throughout the South. Migration to the cities increased. Workers could no longer afford to eat out or have a special night on the town. Sloss and other Birmingham industries were unable to sponsor their annual company picnics and other employee functions. Getting food and fuel became a significant problem for most black families in industrial neighborhoods. The women of Sloss kept their families going by canning, preserving, and growing produce. Some residents, like Iola Jackson, did not remember the Depression years as being particularly hard on them: "We never had much before, so those years weren't too different." Jackson believed that whites felt the effects of the Depression more than blacks and recalled telling a young white boy, "Now you see how it is, lil' white boy; now you know what it's like to live like the black boy." During the Depression, Clarence Dean recalled the residents coming together, as they had when times were hard in rural communities, to help those who were even less fortunate. "Mr. Downey, he done all he could for the people in the Quarters.

---

48. Jones interview, 10; Pauli Murray, *State Laws on Race and Color* (Cincinnati: Women's Division of Christian Service, 1950), 615, 619; *Like It Ain't Never Passed*, 8.

The women who lived in the Quarters would make some of the clothes. My wife would sew lots of clothes. And we'd give then to the needy...just like my mama had done back home when times were hard."[49]

By the early 1940s, the majority of African American women of Sloss Quarters realized that the decisions their mothers and grandmothers had made by leaving the country and venturing into the urban black communities of the Birmingham District were, for the most part, the right decisions. The children living in the quarters between the 1940s and early 1950s were receiving a better education and, following graduation, were moving into the growing black middle class. Gertrude Jones stated that although it took her mom "quite awhile" to get used to city life, she never regretted moving and was "most proud" of the education her children were able to obtain. Will Prather worked for Sloss Furnaces for forty-two years and credited his wife, Anne, for being the "education pusher" in the family: "My wife just took care of them children. That's all she did. I got four girls and three boys. I had seven children. And all of my children got an education. They got a good education, too. Didn't none of 'em go to college, but I put my granddaughter into college. She's got her master's degree now and works in Huntsville."[50]

❧

African American women migrating to Birmingham in search of a better life for their families did find something better than picking someone else's cotton and living in abject rural poverty. Alongside the harshness and discrimination were some advantages. In 1925, a sharecropper might make 50¢ a day by working a twelve-hour day. In the same year, a black worker at Sloss Furnaces could make $2.80 for a ten-hour day. This was enough money, according to Mary Harris, to "buy enough material for Mama to sew me a new pinafore for

49. Jeanne Sullivan, *Segregation in Birmingham: The Impetus for a Strong Black Community* (Birmingham: Sloss Furnaces National Historic Landmark, 1996), 15 (held in publisher's History of Southern American Women's Collection); *Like It Ain't Never Passed*, 7, 8.

50. Jones interview, 16; *Like It Ain't Never Passed*, 34.

every day of the week." Rural domestics migrating to Birmingham realized that an urban setting would offer them a greater number of "prospective employers" than rural communities. Domestics laboring in the homes of large rural landowners were often paid only out of the commissary with food, material, or other items. Rural-born women remembered being paid wages as low as $3.00 to $3.50 a week during the 1940s.[51]

Despite the drawbacks, Sloss Quarters provided a relatively cohesive environment for rural black sharecroppers migrating into Alabama's industrial heartland. It evolved into a community where people spoke the same language, shared similar rural customs, and shared the same burdens. Sloss Quarters was dismantled in the late 1950s as maintenance and repairs became a drain on the company's resources. At the same time, higher wages, improved transportation, and environmental concerns encouraged residents of the quarters to seek better housing away from the plant. For residents such as Mary Harris, however, the destruction of the quarters was upsetting. "It wasn't so bad a place to live. It was a right neighborly place. I didn't think I'd ever have to leave."[52]

This study provides insight into the lives of a group of women determined to create their sense of place in "Sloss Quarters," one of the many company towns developed in the rising industrial city of Birmingham, Alabama. While their husbands toiled and labored in the surrounding mines and blast furnaces (and literally built the city of Birmingham), and they faced the sting of segregation and discrimination, these remarkable women built strong and lasting family foundations by adapting their rural customs, traditions, and faith to their new urban setting. Gertrude Jones recalled, "Mama missed her home in a fierce way, but she knew we'd have a better chance in the city. Yes, she got sad, but never complained. . . . [S]he weren't like that." Jones often heard her mother sing her favorite hymn, "Amazing Grace," around the house. One of the verses states:

51. Harris interview, 22; Susan Tucker, *Telling Memories among Southern Women: Domestic Workers and Their Employers in the Segregated South* (New York: Schocken Books, 1988), 105.
52. Harris interview, 22.

The Lord has promised good to me;
His word my hope secures.
He will my shield and portion be as long as life endures.[53]

Endurance, supported by faith, rural values and traditions, gave families residing in the quarters the ability to cope in unfamiliar and often hostile urban surroundings and to create a new way of life in the industrial world of the New South.

53. Jones interview, 12.

MICHELLE HABERLAND

"It Takes a Special Kind of Woman to Work Up There"

Race, Gender, and the Impact of the Apparel Industry on Southern Alabama, 1937–2001

The apparel industry arrived in southern Alabama in 1937 with the opening of the first Vanity Fair (VF) factory in Monroe County. Two years later, the well-known lingerie manufacturer opened its second factory in neighboring Clarke County. For more than fifty years, the number of clothing manufacturing employees increased across the state, and, at its height in 1987, the industry dominated the working lives of more than fifty thousand Alabamians. In that same year, apparel employment accounted for 17 percent of the state's total manufacturing employment, resulting in the highest concentration of apparel employment of any state in the nation. The industry's traditional proclivity for female labor redefined the social and economic dynamics of these rural southern communities, in particular those dynamics related to race, gender, and segregation. As white and black women in rural southern Alabama made the transition from agricultural and domestic work to factory labor in a rural environment, issues of identity, work, and community came into sharp relief. Dot Guy, a sewing machine operator in Jackson's Vanity Fair plant for thirty-seven years, summarized the impact of the apparel company in this way: "There wasn't any jobs here for women but [farming cotton]. . . . They all came out of the fields to work for Vanity Fair." Eager though the women may have been to join the sewing machine lines, the work at Vanity Fair was not easy. As Ann Brown, a longtime

257

Jackson, Alabama, resident, explained, "It takes a special kind of woman to work up there."[1]

In the annals of southern history, the much studied phenomenon of southern industrialization typically traces the trajectory of one particular industry, the textile industry. Most studies of southern industrialization tend either to ignore the distinct history of the apparel industry or to subsume any discussion of apparel manufacturing into a larger portrait of the textile industry. In giving the apparel industry such short shrift, historians have overlooked an opportunity to understand the development of a distinct working-class culture among southern women, both white and black, in the decades after the Great Depression. Desegregation also takes on new meanings when considered from the perspective of a female workforce. Ultimately, this study explores issues of identity, work, and community from Vanity Fair's first factory in Clarke County through its expansion into neighboring counties and its eventual decline in the 1980s. Although this is a local study, it is one with significant meaning for the broader analysis of gender, race, and work in the rural South.

In 1937, J. E. Barbey went south in search of a new location for his successful glove and women's lingerie manufacturing company in Reading, Pennsylvania. The lingerie division was successful enough to warrant its own brand name, Vanity Fair. Barbey made no secret of his reasons for leaving Reading, the place that had, in fact, made him a wealthy and successful industrialist. By the turn of the twentieth century, Reading had become a textile and apparel center, and in the three decades that followed, the city emerged as a leader in the manufacture of ready-to-wear clothing. As the apparel industry gained a foothold in the mid-Atlantic states, the apparel unions soon followed. A wave of strikes among hosiery workers in Pennsylvania in the early 1930s convinced Barbey to move the company. He vowed that Vanity Fair would never run a union shop.[2]

---

1. U.S. Bureau of the Census, *Economic Census of Manufactures* (Washington, DC: Government Printing Office, 1987); Guy, interview by Haberland, June 20, 2003, Jackson; Brown, interview by Haberland, August 10, 1998, Jackson.

2. Jeffrey L. Rodengen, *The Legend of VF Corporation* (Fort Lauderdale, FL: Write Stuff Enterprises, 1998), 32–34.

With the intention of escaping organized labor and the higher wages that came with unionization foremost in his mind, Barbey headed south in 1937 to search for a new home for his lingerie company. The long and intertwined history of Vanity Fair and southern Alabama follows the basic parameters of a now familiar tale in the history of the rural South. Desperate for salvation from the Great Depression, small-town boosters greeted traveling factory owners from the North with offers of free land and factories built to their specifications and promises of an eager, docile, and abundant labor force. Barbey's experience was much the same. Two rural towns in southern Alabama gladly promised to raise funds to purchase the land and build the factories that Barbey's company required. Boosters promised a pliant and abundant labor force, ready to work as soon as the doors to the factory opened.[3]

J. E. Barbey relished his decision to move Vanity Fair's operations to southern Alabama. Looking back on the decision, Barbey had no regrets. The rural location was a critical factor in the decision. Barbey told a crowd of well-wishers gathered on the first anniversary of the Monroeville plant's opening that he did not want his factories to be located in "big cities." Rather, he argued, he wanted "to be out where folks are folks, and where people are genuine and unsullied of too many city influences." The "city influences" that Barbey disparaged in his anniversary speech actually included the tendency of industries located in larger cities to compete for workers as well as the increased possibility of urban workers in the North developing unions. Vanity Fair workers were well aware of the reasons the company moved to Alabama. Former worker Elizabeth "Buff" McDonald explained Barbey's decision to move to Jackson as the direct result of union organizing in Reading: "Everybody felt that Vanity Fair knew they had it made here. That's the reason that Vanity Fair came to Alabama because the union was forming in Pennsylvania. . . . Now he got cheaper

3. James C. Cobb, *The Selling of the South: The Southern Crusade for Industrial Development, 1936–1980* (Baton Rouge: Louisiana State University Press, 1982); Mike Breedlove, "Jacksonians Raised Plant Funds," *South Alabamian*, June 8, 1989; Bill Stewart, "From Concept to Construction," *Monroe (AL) Journal*, June 11, 1987.

labor here and this area was eager for something to help the economy. They got just about anything they wanted."[4] Jackson and Monroeville were not quite company towns, but they came to rely heavily on the income brought by Vanity Fair. There were sawmills and a few public utility projects, but they employed mostly male workers. Besides agricultural work, there was little competition for women's labor in either rural county.

And so, in 1937, after all of the necessary funding had been secured and construction completed, the first Vanity Fair factory in the South opened its doors to the community of Monroeville, Alabama. Local residents remembered that day as cause for much celebration. Just two years later, local businessmen from nearby Jackson, Alabama, succeeded in selling enough municipal bonds to attract the industrial employer to their rural community as well. Vanity Fair's reliance on southern women's labor grew stronger as each new sewing plant opened its doors, and by the mid-1950s, Vanity Fair had moved all of its operations to Alabama and ceased apparel production in Reading, Pennsylvania. In 1972, thirty-five years after the opening of the Monroeville plant, Alabama governor George Wallace declared, "VF Corporation has long been one of our finest corporate citizens." Even before the addition of three facilities in the mid-1970s, Vanity Fair employed more than nine thousand Alabamians, making it one of the leading industrial employers in the state. Wallace predicted that the additional jobs brought by the opening of the new plants would "easily make VF the state's largest employer."[5] By 1987, Vanity Fair owned a total of seven sewing plants in Alabama. In these facilities women manufactured a wide variety of garments, including loungewear, daywear, sleepwear, panties, girdles, slips, bras, shirts, and scuffs.

As a result of the opening of the two initial Vanity Fair apparel

4. Barbey's speech of June 21, 1938, reprinted in "Barbey Toured the South, Picked Monroeville," *Monroe Journal,* June 11, 1987; McDonald, interview by Haberland, June 21, 2003, Jackson.

5. Patrice Stewart, "Vanity Fair to Celebrate Friday," *Monroe Journal,* June 11, 1987; Paula McLendon, "Time and Time Again: The Women, the Union and the Vanity Factory," *Southern Changes* 6:5 (October–November 1984): 10; for Wallace's comments, see *Monroe Journal,* August 10, 1972.

factories in Jackson and Monroeville, female manufacturing employment increased dramatically throughout the region. One woman
who began working at the Jackson plant back in the early 1940s
remembered the impact of the company on Clarke County. She joked
that the men worked to sell the bonds that brought Vanity Fair, and
then "Vanity Fair put the ladies to work and the men stayed home
and kept house." Whether or not the men of southern Alabama actually did stay home and keep house, and most certainly some of them
did, the identification of apparel production with women was hardly
a new phenomenon in the 1930s. Rather, sewing clothes had long
been considered women's work. Even as far back as the colonial period,
women sewed their families' clothing. The apparel industry simply
transformed women's domestic work into waged industrial labor. Thus,
it was no surprise that Vanity Fair would continue to rely on women
for its workforce just as it had done from the very beginning in
Reading.[6]

The coming of Vanity Fair to small towns and rural landscapes
throughout southern Alabama brought great changes in the nature of
work and the social fabric of those communities. From the perspective of the earliest workers at the first apparel plants in Monroeville
and Jackson, Vanity Fair was a good employer and a godsend during
the worst of economic times. For the southern women of the early
generation, the work in the Vanity Fair factories was an important
part of their lives. They worked for wages that helped them to feed
their families and paint their houses for the first time. Some even put
their children through college with the money they earned sewing
for Vanity Fair. But for women of a later generation, their memories
were much less positive. Their hopes for financial reward and even
for the promise of simple continuous work were dashed as the company slowly and painfully began to close its operations throughout
the region. Ripped apart by racial tensions and a bitter chapter of
unionization, the rural Vanity Fair communities of southern Alabama
today have little to show for their efforts to attract the company.

6. McLendon, "Time and Time Again," 9; Vivian Long, interview by Haberland, August 9, 1998, Jackson.

When Vanity Fair came to southern Alabama in 1937, the Great Depression had become a seemingly permanent feature of the southern economy. Life was particularly difficult in the small towns that dotted the southern half of Alabama as the plummeting price of cotton in the latter years of the Great Depression devastated the area. Families lived for generations in ramshackle structures that had never been painted. One of the men who worked on the bond issue that brought Vanity Fair to Jackson described the situation of the town in 1939: "When Vanity Fair came in here there wasn't a brick building in Clarke County, just old board shacks and pale faced women trying to make a living." There was little electricity, or reason for getting it, since few could afford the utility bill that would come with it. As one woman put it, "We had nothing." Even the families of the professional class suffered. As the daughter of a physician, one Vanity Fair worker remembered that during the Depression patients often paid in kind for the medical services offered by her father. "We loved it if they brought vegetables. We truly lived on that." In the years just prior to the opening of the factory, poverty was the norm for the vast majority of rural Alabamians.[7]

One year after Vanity Fair opened its first factory in Alabama, President Franklin Roosevelt's administration issued *The Report on Economic Conditions of the South* and famously labeled the South as "the Nation's No. 1 economic problem." As the New Deal encouraged the mechanization of cotton agriculture, the system of sharecropping and tenant farming collapsed, reducing both the required amount of farm labor and the price of cotton. It was in this context of desperate and persistent poverty that the white women of southern Alabama welcomed the chance to leave the cotton fields for factory work. Ted Hartmann, a supervisor in the early years of the Monroeville plant, described the transition from farm to factory as an improvement: "It was a change in environment for the girls who first came into the sewing plant, because they had been used to picking cotton and working outside. They were very grateful to get this type

7. Breedlove, "Jacksonians Raised Plant Funds"; Long interview; McDonald interview.

of work—even more so because it was steady work." Indeed, the women who found employment at Vanity Fair in the early years were appreciative, especially given the absence of alternative employment for women. Many of the first employees at Vanity Fair's plants in Alabama remembered that women in rural Alabama had few choices when it came to employment. Arcola "Cola" McLean, who began working as a sewing machine operator, felt most fortunate when she landed a job at the Vanity Fair sewing plant in Jackson in 1947. She explained, "I just thought that was great [to work at Vanity Fair] because there wasn't any jobs for women. You could farm, but you couldn't make any money. You couldn't sell what you made. Nobody didn't have no money." Alyne Sigler, a forty-six-year veteran of Vanity Fair, also expressed her gratitude for the opportunities Vanity Fair brought to rural Alabama in the Great Depression. She said, "We were glad we had jobs. Not many people had jobs in the late thirties." The poverty of the rural area, combined with the absence of nonagricultural job options for women who needed to work, meant that Vanity Fair rarely wanted for workers to run its sewing machines. Vanity Fair was understood by women in southern Alabama to be one of the few employers that actually preferred women to men employees.[8]

The desirability of a job at Vanity Fair could be measured by the lengths to which women traveled and the difficulties they endured to get to the factory. Vanity Fair often attracted women workers from communities quite a distance away. Commutes across one or two county lines were common at both the Monroeville and Jackson sewing plants. In that way, Vanity Fair's influence reached well beyond the small towns of Monroeville and Jackson, extending along country roads into farming communities throughout the region. The distance of workers' homes from factories created transportation challenges, however. An assistant manager at the Monroeville plant remembered a husband who would drive his wife to work every morning and wait for her in the parking lot until her shift was finished. He stayed

8. *New York Times*, July 7, 1938; Camilla Clay, "Hartmanns Found Mud Roads, Strange Accents," *Monroe Journal*, June 11, 1987; McLean, interview by Haberland, August 8, 1998, Jackson; Camilla Clay, "Mill Meant a Lot in Bad Economy," *Monroe Journal*, June 11, 1987.

because the cost of the gasoline to drive home prohibited him from leaving while his wife worked in the factory. A generation later, an African American sewing machine operator who lived one county over in Wagarville showed a similar dedication to her work. When her car pool failed to pick her up one morning, Buff McDonald recalled that the woman walked more than twelve miles along country roads to get to the plant. "She was coming to work," McDonald said. "It was that important to her." Car pooling was commonplace, especially in the early years when fewer workers owned cars. Cola McLean and Dot Guy, white women who worked at Vanity Fair's Jackson plant in the years before desegregation, both rode to work with other sewing machine operators. Guy remembered one man who earned a small livelihood by ferrying women to and from the plant. "He made a little bus out of the back end [of his pickup truck] and he hauled about ten women from there to Vanity Fair every day. We paid him two dollars a week."[9]

The majority of the rural women who worked at the sewing plants in Monroeville and Jackson were sewing machine operators involved in the actual production of finished garments. According to one count, in 1976 Vanity Fair's Jackson sewing plant employed "four hundred sewing machine operators, fifty-three examiners ... thirty-six packers, and seven mechanics (all male)." An operator from the early days remembered that the management at Vanity Fair frequently stressed that the sewing machine operator was "the most important person in the company." Managers at Vanity Fair believed that the future of the company rested on the careful work of the women sewing machine operators, for without their high-quality production, a garment would not sell. A typical day began at seven in the morning, as the women took their positions in one of eleven production lines of sewing machines. Every sewing machine operator had a single part of the garment to sew. The garments made their way down the production line, with each individual operator sewing in a seam or hem or piece

9. "Vanity Fair and WPA Provided Jobs," *Monroe Journal*, June 11, 1987; Long interview; McDonald interview; McLean interview; Guy interview.

of lace until, at the end of the line, there was a finished garment. Working together in this manner, the operators could finish as many as two hundred dozen slips a day. In the early years, the workday ended at four o'clock in the afternoon, but in later years twenty-four-hour operation was typical, with employees working one of three eight-hour shifts. Operating sewing machines was a fast and tedious job. Soon after opening the Monroeville and Jackson sewing plants, Vanity Fair began to require that prospective applicants take a timed dexterity test that involved threading nuts onto bolts. As Dot Guy explained, "If you didn't pass that test, you didn't get a job sewing." Sarah Phillips, who worked in the knitting department, held sewing machine operators in high regard. They were skilled workers, she believed, because only "certain women" could make it in the "fast, buzzing" sewing room.[10]

Although Vanity Fair did not pay its workers by the piece, as had been the tradition in the earliest years of the U.S. apparel industry, workers were encouraged to achieve maximum production with incentive pay and punished for falling below a standard level of "production." Workers referred to this minimum standard as "making production," and it was the only way to earn decent wages at Vanity Fair. Sewing machine operators who failed to "make production" earned only the lowest wages. If that failure to make production persisted, the underproducing workers were fired. Phillips recalled that the level of production was never easy. She explained, "If you got up to that amount [of production, the management would] raise it." With this seemingly ever-increasing level of production, some women just could not keep up. Guy remembered how she struggled early on to make production until her supervisor spent an entire day sitting next to her, showing Guy shortcuts and efficiency strategies. As she saw it, sewing machine operators "were on production and really had to be fast. To us, it was a challenge because we would be in a sewing line and back then people seem like they cooperated together so well.

10. McLendon, "Time and Time Again," 11; Guy interview; Phillips, interview by Haberland, June 19, 2003, Grove Hill, AL.

And if one got behind, we'd stop and help her. It was just a kind of team."[11] The first generation of sewing machine operators recalled those early days with great fondness, remembering how they worked together to earn their wages.

The transition from agricultural work to factory work was a welcome one for the early generation of women at Vanity Fair, but it also altered the nature of women's work in southern Alabama. No longer were domestic work and field labor the only occupations available to white women in these rural communities. For many women, the arrival of Vanity Fair brought an end to their lives as farm women. In 1947, Cola McLean went to work for Vanity Fair as a sewing machine operator. Like many other southern women of her generation and economic situation, McLean achieved only a limited education. As a young woman, she married and then worked alongside her husband in the fields for years. Agriculture was hot and difficult work in southern Alabama, and she hated it. But soon after Vanity Fair opened its doors, she saw a new opportunity for her life. The factory was clean and cool and paid wages that improved her family's standard of living. Going to work at the factory was different from working in the fields, and the attire of workers reflected that difference. In the early years at Vanity Fair, "dresses, shirts and ties were everyday attire." In contrast to the often isolated nature of farmwork, the cooperative nature of employment in the Vanity Fair factories led to the development of lifelong relationships among workers. Alyne Sigler was one of the first employees hired at the Vanity Fair plant in Monroeville. "Early on," she remembered, "it was more like a family. I used to know everyone's name."[12]

The work on the factory floor was conducive to the development of friendships. It was certainly not carefree, however. In sharp contrast to the rhythms of agricultural work, the production floor at Vanity Fair was run by the clock. Punctuality was important, and workers remembered the importance of the "three minute [warning] whistle

11. Phillips interview; Guy interview.
12. McLean interview; Clay, "Mill Meant a Lot."

and a seven o'clock whistle." Tardy workers were often not allowed to clock in and lost their wages for that day.

Even after beginning work at Vanity Fair, child care still accounted for a significant portion of women's daily labors, although it was more commonly a shared responsibility. Many of the earliest generation of women workers at Vanity Fair expressed gratitude for the African American women who took care of their children while they worked at the factory. Dot Guy recalled that she "had good luck getting colored ladies to take care of my children," but in less fortunate families, "the men stayed at home and kept the children while their wives worked." Farmwives often shouldered the double burden of field work in addition to domestic responsibilities like child care. Since farm women could rarely afford to hire child-care workers, they had routinely worked alongside their children in the fields. At Vanity Fair, women worked alongside other women, leaving their children at home.[13]

In contrast to work in the fields, however, the women at Vanity Fair had little control over their daily duties. Rather, supervisors determined the styles of clothing and production-line positions assigned to each worker. Moreover, the assignments themselves were incredibly repetitive, with each worker repeating the same maneuver hundreds of times a day, often for weeks or months at a time without changing positions in the production line. In all of these ways, the transition from farm to factory brought significant changes in the nature of work for the women of Vanity Fair.

The rise of the apparel industry brought about significant changes not only in women's work but also in the household economies of rural Alabama. The wages that women workers brought home from Vanity Fair's factories were rarely supplemental or nonessential to household incomes. In most cases, women worked because they had to. One worker recalled, "In the early years, you did find that most all of the people that went to work for Vanity Fair, they really needed to

13. McLendon, "Time and Time Again," 10; Guy interview; Christine "Big Momma" Blackwell, interview by Haberland, June 20, 2003, Jackson.

work. They had to work, a lot of them, to feed their families." The significance of women's wages to household economies did not fade with the passage of time. In March 2000, when Vanity Fair announced that it would close its sewing plant in Jackson and leave more than five hundred women unemployed, a local councilwoman lamented that some of the women soon to be dismissed from Vanity Fair were, in fact, the heads of their households. Buff McDonald, who worked in the personnel office and thus was in a position to learn of the personal details of workers' lives, recalled with sensitivity that "some of these women had unpleasant situations at home and this was their only means of livelihood." From her perspective, the wages these women earned made their difficult lives a bit more tolerable.[14]

In some situations, however, Vanity Fair's women workers brought home wages that afforded their families things a bit beyond life's bare necessities. For instance, some women were proud that their contributions to the household income made it possible to send their children to college. Dot Guy argued that Vanity Fair provided an opportunity for "women to work and buy their homes and paint their houses and send their children to college." Guy and McDonald remembered that their wages paid for school clothes for their children or the purchase of their families' first car and washing machine. As McDonald put it, women's Vanity Fair jobs "made all the difference in the world." The standard of living seemed to increase, as evidenced by the growth in the number of cars in these two rural counties. Whether utterly essential or modestly supplemental, women's wages were a critical component of the household economy and resulted in an increase in their families' standard of living. The wages that the working women of Vanity Fair contributed to the household economy were most certainly a source of pride for the women of southern Alabama.[15]

14. Phillips interview; Karen Tolkkinen, "Plant Closing Hits 543 Workers," *Mobile (AL) Register,* March 11, 2000; Karen Tolkkinen, "At Vanity Fair, Workers Wonder What to Do Next," *Mobile Register,* November 15, 2001; McDonald interview.

15. Camilla Clay, "Big Shears, Crank Calculator," *Monroe Journal,* June 11, 1987; Guy interview; McDonald interview.

The arrival of Vanity Fair also affected the local economies of the small towns in rural Alabama. The women workers of Vanity Fair spent their money in a variety of ways that sustained small businesses or even helped to establish new ones. The man who converted his pickup truck into a bus to transport women to and from the factory had, in fact, begun a small business based exclusively on the need of the working-class women of Vanity Fair to get to work. Vivian Long, who worked in the personnel office for more than thirty years, remembered that the number of stores in Jackson increased after the plant opened in 1939. Vanity Fair workers also remembered that Jackson and Monroeville shopkeepers in the late 1930s and 1940s were particularly eager to see them on payday. Longtime sewing machine operator Dot Guy recalled that the Jackson merchants treated the Vanity Fair women well. After all, "They were glad to see you coming." In Monroeville, the wages of the first generation of Vanity Fair workers had a significant impact on the local economy. The merchants of Monroeville asked Vanity Fair's managers, who in the early years paid workers in cash, to "please not give the employees any $10 bills, because they wouldn't be able to change them." On the occasion of Vanity Fair's fiftieth anniversary in Monroeville, the local bank also expressed its longtime appreciation of the wages the plant brought to the rural area. In a full-page newspaper advertisement, the bank boasted of a "50-year friendship with Vanity Fair," saying "it's easy to compare the economy before and after 1937 when Vanity Fair Mills moved here... IT'S SO MUCH BETTER!"[16]

In addition to the impact of working women's wages on the communities of Monroeville and Jackson, the opening of Vanity Fair's plants also stimulated the development of infrastructure. The company's demand for air travel brought Monroeville Aviation into existence and the first airplanes to Monroe County. Eventually, the private airstrip used by Monroeville Aviation became the county's public airport. In addition, Vanity Fair rapidly became the one of the largest consumers of water, gas, and electricity in Monroe County. In this

16. Guy interview; Long interview; Camilla Clay, "Hartmanns Found Mud Roads"; "It's So Much Better," *Monroe Journal*, June 11, 1987.

way, the labor of the working women of Vanity Fair, who constituted a majority of the company's employees, made economic development possible throughout this rural region. Without women's labor, Vanity Fair would not have come to Monroeville and Jackson.[17]

Vanity Fair was, by some accounts, a good corporate citizen in the rural communities of southern Alabama. In addition to the impact of workers' wages and the development of local businesses and community infrastructure, Vanity Fair won additional praises from the early generation of workers and white residents through the construction of community golf courses, tennis courts, swimming pools, clubhouses, and parks in both Monroeville and Jackson. The facilities were also a source of community pride. The company asked the citizens of Monroeville to raise thirty-three thousand dollars of the one hundred thousand dollars needed to build the clubhouse. Within seven short months, Monroeville residents and Vanity Fair employees had collected the necessary funds and construction was under way. In 1952, the community celebrated the dedication of Monroeville's Vanity Fair Park, which encompassed ninety-seven acres, including a lighted baseball diamond and grandstand and a five-acre lake. The Community House, as the clubhouse was known, was an impressive structure that included a ballroom, individual lounges for women and men, and a well-equipped kitchen. By the standards of the time, this level of welfare capitalism was unlike anything these rural communities had experienced. A similar process of local fund-raising and a donation from Vanity Fair funded the construction of Vanity Fair Park in Jackson in 1950. Never before had a local company gone to such lengths to win the loyalties of local residents. Dot Guy remembered that the park "made all the difference in the world" to the residents of Jackson. Community residents, workers, and their families were allowed to use the facilities whenever they wanted. The clubhouses in both Jackson and Monroeville were particularly popular among Vanity Fair employees as locations for family reunions and wedding receptions. The parks were also the location of the much anticipated annual com-

17. "County Airport, Utilities Benefit from Vanity Fair," *Monroe Journal*, June 11, 1987.

pany picnics. The early generation of employees in Jackson remembered the company picnics as delightful affairs, with workers and their families all invited. Sarah Phillips recalled that Vanity Fair "paid for everything. Then that night, we'd have this huge fireworks display." Taken together, the company-sponsored picnics and parks had their intended effect, as they engendered much support from the early generation of Vanity Fair workers.[18]

Beneath this corporate generosity, however, lay a grim southern reality. The rules of Jim Crow segregation prevented the African American residents of these rural counties from using the parks' facilities. In 1960, the populations of Clarke County and Monroe County were almost evenly divided, with African Americans and whites each accounting for around 50 percent of the residents. Yet the Vanity Fair Parks that were constructed with funds from both the company and the communities were off-limits to the rural counties' African American residents. As the achievements of the civil rights movement slowly chipped away at Jim Crow, Vanity Fair began to charge fees for use of the facilities. The white workers of Vanity Fair attributed this to a conscious effort to keep the facilities segregated. Guy remembered that although the Vanity Fair Park swimming pool was technically open to the community, "they had no problems with the blacks going . . . because the fee is so high that they can't afford it." Later, though, Vanity Fair decided to distance itself from the community parks. White women workers believed that the company's decision to sell the land and facilities to the Cities of Jackson and Monroeville was triggered by desegregation. Christine "Big Momma" Blackwell, a white woman who began working at the Jackson plant in 1950, argued that "Vanity Fair sold the community center to the city because of desegregation."[19] As African American women gained access to jobs in Vanity Fair's plants in the mid-1960s, their theoretical

18. Rodengen, *Legend of VF Corporation,* 54–56; "Foundation Has Helped Shape Area Recreational Facilities," *Monroe Journal,* June 11, 1987; "Knitting Plant, Jackson, Alabama, Events in History of Jackson Facility," Vanity Fair document, n.a, n.d, ca. 1997, original among Paula McLendon's personal clipping file in author's possession; Phillips interview.

19. Guy interview; Blackwell interview.

claim on the parks' facilities became more legitimate because they were now more than just community residents; they were employees. Although no white workers could remember a black employee actually trying to use the facilities, the mere threat implied by the desegregation of Vanity Fair's workforce was enough to warrant the implementation of tools of racial exclusivity such as daily-use park fees.

Back in the 1930s, when Vanity Fair moved its operations to the South, the company quickly accommodated the southern system of occupational segregation by race. For almost thirty years, the production jobs at Vanity Fair were open only to white workers, and the majority of those positions were for white women. Although some workers remembered that Cajuns from the nearby town of McIntosh did occasionally earn positions at Vanity Fair, no African American workers were hired until the mid-1960s. Both black and white workers at Vanity Fair believed that federal legislation was responsible for opening the factories to large numbers of African American women. Vivian Long, the white personnel secretary at the Jackson plant, explained that desegregation finally occurred "when the government required you to hire them." Prior to the 1960s, the great majority of southern apparel factories hired *only* white women for positions as sewing machine operators. Factories in Texas, however, were unique in that they employed Latinas in the early years of the industry. The passage of the Civil Rights of Act of 1964, prohibiting racial discrimination in employment, changed everything. Long explained, "We had some [blacks] apply. We didn't hire any until . . . that [federal] legislation came [in the 1960s], because most of the blacks were doing domestic work. They were maids and things." White women like Long resisted the employment of African American sewing machine operators because they envisioned another more appropriate race-specific *and* gender-specific role for African American women: "maids and things." New federal laws gave African American women a chance at positions within Vanity Fair, and Long resented it. Black women at Vanity Fair also credited the federal government, even specifically the Equal Employment Opportunities Commission created by the 1964 Civil Rights Act, with the desegregation of Vanity Fair. The memories of workers, both black and white, reveal the leading role that federal legislation like the Civil Rights Act played in initiating workforce integration at Vanity Fair and other apparel factories throughout the South.[20]

There were nonetheless changes and events at the local level in these rural communities that helped to create an environment that encouraged African American women to apply for positions at the once all-white Vanity Fair plants. Jackson was just ninety-four miles from Selma, Alabama, the location of the most dramatic episode in the struggle for African American voting rights. Whereas white residents were often silent about the civil rights era, saying that Jackson did not experience much formal activity, African Americans remembered the period differently. In sites ranging from churches to restaurants, African Americans in Jackson worked to achieve desegregation. In 1965, the same year in which Alabama police attacked six hundred civil rights marchers on the outskirts of Selma, seven African American men in Jackson formed a group called Men for Dynamic Action. These seven men decided, with very little forethought or formal planning, to challenge the power of Jim Crow by organizing a mixed-race group to enter a local restaurant, Ray's and Tom's, and demand service. Soon after they entered, police cars surrounded the restaurant. Although they were initially put off by the waitstaff while the owner called the mayor for advice, they were eventually served the steak dinners that they had ordered. When the men left the restaurant, they knew that they had achieved "the first official integration in Jackson, Alabama." Nearly forty years later, the memory of this incident still triggered strong feelings of pride for Richard Boykin, one of the original members of Men for Dynamic Action. Choking back

20. Long interview; McLean interview; Laurie Coyle, Gail Hershatter, and Emily Honig, "Women at Farah: An Unfinished Story," in *A Needle, a Bobbin, a Strike: Women Needleworkers in America*, edited by Joan M. Jensen and Sue Davidson (Philadelphia: Temple University Press, 1984), 227–77; Honig, "Women at Farah Revisited," in ibid., 425–52; Tera W. Hunter, *To 'Joy My Freedom: Southern Black Women's Lives and Labors after the Civil War* (Cambridge, MA: Harvard University Press, 1997), 108–11. For African American women's recollections of the causes behind the desegregation at Vanity Fair, see Vevelyn "Queenie" Gilchrist, interview by Haberland, August 12, 1998, Atlanta; and Sarah Boykin, interview by Haberland, June 20, 2003, Jackson.

tears, he said, "It's hard for me to talk about this." Around the same time, Buff McDonald heard rumors "that there would be some blacks to attend our church that Sunday." Although no African Americans did arrive that Sunday at McDonald's church, Vivian Long remembered that some African Americans attended white churches in 1965 without incident. White residents of Jackson often put a positive spin on the civil rights chapter of their local history. Dot Guy's assessment was typical. She said, "You had a few young [black] people to go into the restaurants. . . . Jackson handled that well. And they showed up at church a few times. Nobody made any moves. In the restaurants they just went ahead and waited on them." Sarah Boykin, one of the first African American sewing machine operators at Vanity Fair, remembered those times quite differently: "Life was hard."[21] The struggles that occurred in the churches and restaurants of Jackson, Alabama, laid a foundation on which African American women could stand and claim that they had a right to jobs at Vanity Fair.

White workers at Vanity Fair's Jackson plant had mixed reactions to the desegregation of the sewing room. Dot Guy remembered "the first two blacks that were ever hired sewed on my line. And they were wonderful." Whereas the two African American women "didn't seem to have any prejudice," Guy recalled, "some of the white girls on the line was kinda prejudiced." White workers often resented the demise of their once racially exclusive workplace community, and racial prejudices colored their assessments of the abilities of black workers. A longtime sewing machine operator hired in the early days, Arcola McLean, found racial integration simply intolerable. Vanity Fair "started hiring black people and that's when I didn't like it then. The black people didn't care if they done their work good or not." As African Americans began to join the ranks of white sewing machine operators at Vanity Fair, McLean quit her job of twenty-three years. "It wasn't a nice place to work anymore." Vivian Long, the personnel secretary of the same Vanity Fair plant for many years, also complained

21. Long interview; McLean interview; R. Boykin, interview by Haberland, June 20, 2003, Jackson; McDonald interview; Guy interview; S. Boykin interview.

that African American women had a poor work ethic. She went on to explain that the quality of production had been better when only white women operated the sewing machines at Vanity Fair. In the eyes of these white women, the nature of the work in the sewing plant reinforced the need for racial exclusivity. Sewing at Vanity Fair was a team effort, and individual operators relied on the quick, accurate work of other stitchers on the line to achieve the standard level of production and earn decent wages. A slower worker would mean that garments did not move down the line efficiently, and the whole line of sewing machine operators would fall short of the standard. McLean believed that African American women were inferior operators. "If you sewed next to [one of them], you just had to wait for work. You couldn't make nothing." Racial exclusivity, she believed, led to better cooperation between workers who depended on each other for their wages.[22]

Other white women remembered the integration of Vanity Fair differently. Sarah Blackwell Phillips, a white woman who worked at Vanity Fair's knitting plant in Jackson, remembered that her mother trained some of the newly hired African American women sewing machine operators. "There were a lot of the [black] ladies that learned well. They wanted to work. They wanted to put out a quality product just like [Mother] did."[23] Most of the white women workers did not leave their jobs after integration. Willing or not, they stayed on at Vanity Fair and worked alongside black women for the first time in their lives.

The process of desegregation was a difficult one for both white and black workers at Vanity Fair. Sarah Boykin, one of the first African American sewing machine operators hired at Vanity Fair, remembered, "When I went to work [in 1965] there were about five blacks. [Whites] were as nice as they had to be. A lot of them didn't speak to me." Buff McDonald, a white woman who worked in the personnel office at the time, remembered integration as a time of great uncertainty. "We didn't know what was going to happen." In addition

22. Guy interview; McLean interview; Long interview.
23. Phillips interview.

to problems on the production lines, white women workers were concerned about the integration of the restrooms at Vanity Fair. According to McDonald, a manager at the plant responded to this concern by mandating that the "first two stalls would be for the blacks. And the rest would be for the whites." McDonald thought that the manager did not really believe that this resolved the problem; he "was simply trying to relieve some apprehensions." Boykin remembered that when she started working at Vanity Fair, "prejudiced white person[s] wouldn't go in the stall behind you and stuff like that."[24]

Although the restroom facilities at Vanity Fair, like the production lines, were eventually integrated without substantial incident, African Americans still remembered the sting of discrimination. By 1965 the Jackson plant was technically integrated, in that African American women worked as sewing machine operators, but at the floor level, the categorization of occupations reinforced racial segregation. Vevelyn "Queenie" Gilchrist, a black woman hired shortly after desegregation, believed that she was unable to get certain jobs, especially supervisory positions, because she was black. After being overlooked for a promotion, she told a sympathetic white foreman, "I do think it was prejudice that I didn't get the job." Sarah Boykin also believed that white women had access to training and supervisory positions that black women were kept out of. In this way, the integration of Vanity Fair was incomplete.[25]

By the time African Americans joined the Vanity Fair workforce in the 1960s and 1970s, workers felt much less grateful toward the corporation than the earlier generation of women sewing machine operators. Workers hired in this later period offered a description of the work environment that contrasted sharply with the "team" metaphor used by white women who worked in the Jackson factory in the two decades after the Great Depression. One sewing machine operator complained that supervisors told the women workers to "keep their heads down" and ordered that there would be "no talking." Sarah Boykin recalled one supervisor that "would treat you worse than a

24. S. Boykin interview; McDonald interview.
25. Gilchrist interview.

dog. I saw so many people get up from their machine and go in the bathroom and cry. [The management] would give you so many days to get up to the production level or you would be fired."[26]

It was not simply a case of difficult supervisors and tough management at Vanity Fair. Sewing was difficult work, and the pressure to make standard production was enormous. The ever-changing styles of the women's fashion industry resulted in many complaints among sewing machine operators of this later generation. As the style being produced changed, the sewing machine operators would be forced to change jobs and machines, making it more difficult to achieve production. In addition, in the late 1960s and 1970s the U.S. apparel industry was under increased pressure to become more efficient as cheaper imported garments began to enter the market without tariffs. Clothing manufacturers like Vanity Fair that still employed American workers to sew garments had to find ways to compete with those companies that paid much smaller wages to foreign workers. The flood of cheaper imported apparel began in 1963 with the Kennedy Round of the General Agreement on Tariffs and Trade. The reduced tariffs on imported clothing that came out of those talks posed an enormous threat to the domestic apparel industry. From the early 1960s to 1976, the percentage of imported apparel in the United States grew from a mere 2.5 percent to more than 30 percent. Reduced tariffs encouraged apparel companies to import clothing that was assembled by lower-waged foreign workers. Apparel manufacturers would cut the cloth needed for the garments in the United States, using American workers. Then the cloth would be exported to a factory abroad where the clothing would be assembled by foreign workers who were paid much less than American sewing machine operators. The U.S. clothing manufacturers would then import the finished garment, paying tariffs only on the value added, or the cost of the foreign labor required to assemble the garment.[27]

26. Gilchrist, interview by Paula McLendon, November 1979, Frankville, AL, tape summary among Paula McLendon's personal clipping file in author's possession; S. Boykin interview.
27. Dana Frank, *Buy American: The Untold Story of Economic Nationalism* (Boston: Beacon Press, 1999), 148–50.

The additional pressure on the profit margin at Vanity Fair stemmed from a rapidly changing fashion industry, reductions in tariffs, and increases in cheaper imported clothing. Taken together, these factors brought about a decline in worker morale at Vanity Fair. In the early years of the factory, white women were grateful to have jobs, grateful to have an escape from the fields. But as time passed, some of the white women stitchers, many of whom had been with the company for decades, came to resent their low wages and minimal benefits. Other women, especially the oldest generation of white women employees, still felt personally connected and obligated to the company. As one of the women who later helped bring the International Ladies Garment Workers Union (ILGWU) to Vanity Fair put it, "A lot of the women in there have been there for years and years and years and they were under the impression that if it wasn't for Vanity Fair they'd just dry up and blow away and never be seen again."[28] As the older generation of women retired or quit and productivity pressures on remaining workers increased, however, the work atmosphere changed, leaving the company vulnerable to union organization.

In 1976, eleven years after the first African American women were hired at Vanity Fair, the ILGWU finally won a National Labor Relations Board election and earned the right to represent the workers at the rural factory. Some contemporary labor organizers believed that an interracial workforce was easier to penetrate than an all-white workforce in the South. In a 1963 interview with a business professor from Mississippi State University, Claude Ramsay argued that firms with a large number of African Americans were more receptive to unionism than those that were all white. The election's successful outcome was largely due to the union's commitment to interracial organizing. In fact, two white women at Vanity Fair, Cola McLean and Vivian Long, drew direct connections between the union and the desegregation of the sewing room. Long explained the ILGWU's organizing

28. Paula McLendon, "Union Turns Loners into Leaders," *Anniston (AL) Star*, n.d., reprint among McLendon's personal clipping file in author's possession; Rebecca Blackmon and Emily Woodyard, interview by Paula McLendon, December 16, 1979, Leroy, AL, original selected transcription among McLendon's personal clipping file in author's possession.

strategy as one that targeted African Americans. From Long's prejudiced perspective, the ILGWU organizers cunningly linked gullible black workers with disgruntled white workers: "You could take a black worker [and] much of them around here don't have too much intelligence. And [the organizers] could motivate them. And if they could find one white person that was dissatisfied, they stuck with that one." To her mind, the combination of black and white workers in a labor organization "festered" like a wound within the Vanity Fair community. From the beginning of the organizing campaign, the link between the ILGWU and interracial commitment was clear to unionists and antiunionists alike. Sarah Boykin remembered in the run-up to the union election, a white supervisor warned that Vanity Fair was the first employer in Clarke County "that hired black women out of the cotton patch and that if the union were voted in we would be back in the cotton patch." Especially at the local level, union organizers and officers were aware of the need to combat such divisive antiunion strategies and promote better race relations. After Vanity Fair workers requested union assistance, the ILGWU sent two women organizers to the factory, a black woman and a white woman. And the Vanity Fair employees themselves made their commitment to interracial unionism clear. By careful design, the original in-plant organizing and negotiation committee contained equal numbers of black and white women. When they traveled together to the regional offices of the ILGWU in Atlanta, the new unionists arranged to share hotel rooms, "one black and one white" per room. In an effort to combat the "race card" and the "black versus white" perception of antiunionists, the organizing committee conveyed an image of racial harmony under the banner of union activity.[29]

For many African American women workers, union activity and membership were a virtual branch of the civil rights movement. The introduction of African Americans seemed to signal, at least to some

29. Donald C. Mosley, "The Labor Union Movement," in *A History of Mississippi,* edited by Richard Aubrey McLemore, vol. 2 (Hattiesburg: University and College Press of Mississippi, 1973), 270–301; McLean interview; Long interview; S. Boykin quoted in McLendon, "Time and Time Again," 12; Gilchrist interview by Haberland; McLendon, "Time and Time Again," 14.

white Vanity Fair workers, the arrival of the ILGWU. They believed that African Americans would organize and seek collective action as they had done in earlier civil rights actions. In this way, the white women who opposed desegregation and understood unionism and black empowerment to be one and the same thing were correct. In 1975 Sarah Boykin, the central "ringleader," as she was often called, initiated the first request for union representation by workers at Vanity Fair. Her husband, Richard Boykin, had been an activist in the local civil rights struggle. In addition, he was also an active member of a United Parcel Service local of the formidable International Brotherhood of the Teamsters. Sarah Boykin came to see unionization as the solution to the way Vanity Fair mistreated workers. One evening Richard asked her, "Why are you crying?" She replied, "If you had seen [what I saw at the factory] you would cry." And then came the suggestion: "Well, don't cry. What you need to do is get a union." Another African American woman on the Vanity Fair organizing committee, Queenie Gilchrist, remembered that after she heard about the union's organizing campaign, she asked her father what to do. Gilchrist's father was himself a minister and longtime activist who had experience in collective and political organizing, and, as his daughter, she greatly valued his opinion. With his endorsement, Gilchrist joined the Vanity Fair in-plant organizing committee and helped lead the ILGWU to victory at Vanity Fair in 1976.[30] From the beginning of the campaign to organize Vanity Fair, civil rights and labor organizing were mutually reinforcing activities.

After winning the election by just sixteen votes, the new unionists at Vanity Fair quickly elected Sarah Boykin to be the president of ILGWU Local 118. Negotiations proceeded, and within a year of the 1976 election, Vanity Fair and the ILGWU signed their first contract. But the history of the ILGWU at Vanity Fair was destined to be

30. Michael K. Honey, *Southern Labor and Black Civil Rights: Organizing Memphis Workers* (Urbana: University of Illinois Press, 1993); Timothy J. Minchin, "Color Means Something: Black Pioneers, White Resistance, and Interracial Unionism in the Southern Textile Industry, 1957–1980," *Labor History* 39 (May 1998): 128–29; McLendon, "Time and Time Again," 9–11; S. Boykin interview; Gilchrist interview by Haberland.

short and embattled. Almost immediately after the union was voted in, antiunion employees began to work to decertify the union as the representative of the workers at Vanity Fair's Jackson sewing plant. After the results of two decertification elections were invalidated, the antiunionists finally secured a victory with a third election. With 188 votes against the union and 134 votes for the union, the ILGWU was officially decertified as the representative of the workers at the Jackson plant.[31]

In the meantime, the Vanity Fair factories in southern Alabama fell on hard times. Faced with an unprecedented increase in the amount of cheaper imported clothing allowed into the United States, the company began to close sewing plants and lay off workers. Like a number of apparel manufacturers, Vanity Fair secretly sought to produce its various lines of clothing in countries with lower labor costs. In 1984, the company announced that it would temporarily close its two Jackson, Alabama, plants as a result of "a business slowdown." At the same time, however, the company had already begun to shift those plants' operations to Latin American facilities. Announcing an "experimental" program in which workers in Panama would assemble garments, the company reluctantly admitted that it had established "agreements with companies abroad for about 20 years." Between 1996 and 1997, 600 workers lost their jobs at Vanity Fair's sewing plant in Monroeville. After announcements in March 2000, Vanity Fair finally closed the Jackson sewing plant on August 25, leaving the 543 mostly women workers unemployed. By November 2001, Vanity Fair had closed its last domestic sewing plant in Atmore, Alabama, at a loss of 510 jobs. In a bitter twist of fate, the company promoted Paul Parden, the leader of the antiunion decertification faction, to oversee operations at its new plant in Mexico.[32]

31. McLendon, "Time and Time Again," 14–16.

32. "VF to Shut Down for December," November 15, 1984, newspaper clipping from Paula McLendon's Vanity Fair file in author's possession; Karen Tolkkinen, "City of Jackson Struggles to Fill the Gap," *Mobile Register*, March 20, 2000; Jim Cox, "County Braces for Vanity Fair Closing," *Clarke County (AL) Democrat*, March 16, 2000; Tolkkinen, "Plant Closing Hits 543 Workers"; McLendon, "Time and Time Again," 15; Long interview.

The rural communities of southern Alabama that had once welcomed Vanity Fair's factories and its promises of jobs and economic salvation were now forced to confront a new reality of unemployment and empty factories. As civic leaders in Jackson and Monroeville scrambled to attract new employers, communities in Mexico and other Latin American countries welcomed U.S. apparel companies like Vanity Fair and looked forward to the fulfillment of the same promises of jobs and economic salvation that had once brightened the future of the rural South.

⚶

The story of Vanity Fair and the rural communities of southern Alabama is one that has significant meaning for the larger history of industrialization in the twentieth-century South. Over the course of more than a half century, the apparel industry profoundly transformed the lives of black and white women in rural Alabama. No longer relegated to lives of agricultural and domestic work, the women of Vanity Fair contributed significantly to their household incomes as well as to the economic development of the region. In addition, their individual experiences as industrial workers and, later, as unionists helped to both challenge and define new roles for women in the rural South. A focus on the history of Vanity Fair in southern Alabama helps to provide an understanding of the impact of industrialization, desegregation, and globalization at a local level. Although these processes are most often discussed at the macrolevel, they are forces that have the profoundest impact at the community level, for it is in this realm that the meanings of race, gender, and work are truly transformed.

Evan P. Bennett received his PhD in history at the College of William and Mary. His dissertation examines Bright Tobacco Belt farmers since 1880. His articles have appeared in the *Encyclopedia of Appalachia* and *Florida Historical Quarterly*. The recipient of the Archie Jones Fellowship from the North Caroliniana Society, Bennett has presented numerous conference papers.

Michelle Haberland is an assistant professor of history at Georgia Southern University. She received her PhD from Tulane University, and she is currently completing a manuscript on southern women's work in the apparel industry. Her article "After the Wives Went to Work: Organizing Women in the Southern Apparel Industry" was published in *"Lives Full of Struggle and Triumph": Southern Women, Their Institutions, and Their Communities*, edited by Bruce Clayton and John Salmond (University Press of Florida, 2003).

Lu Ann Jones is the author of *Mama Learned Us to Work: Farm Women in the New South* (University of North Carolina Press, 2002) and coauthor of *Like a Family: The Making of a Southern Cotton Mill World* (University of North Carolina Press, 1987; reissued with a new foreword by Michael Frisch and a new afterword by the authors, 2000). Her articles have appeared in the *Journal of Southern History, Southern Cultures,* and the *Oral History Review*. She is an associate professor of history at the University of South Florida.

Ann E. McCleary is an associate professor of history and director of the Center for Public History at the University of West Georgia. She earned her PhD in American civilization from Brown University. Her research has focused on rural history and material culture. She has published several articles on the vernacular architecture of the Shenandoah Valley and curated exhibits on rural women in the twentieth-century South. McCleary is currently working on two books, both of which draw heavily on oral history: one on the home demonstration club movement in Virginia and a second documenting change in rural life in the Georgia Piedmont in the twentieth century.

Lois E. Myers is a senior lecturer at Baylor University and associate director of Baylor's Institute for Oral History. She is author of *Letters by Lamplight: A Woman's View of Everyday Life in South Texas, 1873–1883* (Baylor University Press, 1991) and coauthor, with Rebecca Sharpless, of *Rock beneath the Sand: Country Churches in Texas* (Texas A&M University Press, 2003). With other Baylor faculty, she is editing the *Research Handbook of Oral History,* forthcoming from AltaMira Press.

Connie Park Rice is a PhD candidate in history at West Virginia University. Her dissertation examines African American political life in West Virginia from 1870 to 1930. Rice has given numerous conference presentations and published articles on African Americans in West Virginia and Appalachian migration. She is also collaborating with a colleague on a manuscript about women evangelists in Appalachia.

Lynne A. Rieff is an associate professor of history and coordinator of the Women's Studies Program at the University of North Alabama. She earned her PhD from Auburn University. She has published articles and presented numerous conference papers on home demonstration work in the South, most recently "Improving Rural Life in Florida: Home Demonstration Work and Rural Reform, 1912–1940," in *Making Waves: Female Activists in Twentieth-Century Florida,* edited by Kari Frederickson and Jack Davis (University Press of Florida, 2002).

Rebecca Sharpless directs the Institute for Oral History at Baylor University. The author of *Fertile Ground, Narrow Choices: Women on Texas Cotton Farms, 1900–1940* (University of North Carolina Press, 1999), she is president-elect of the Oral History Association.

Karen R. Utz is the curator at Sloss Furnaces National Historical Landmark in Birmingham, Alabama. She holds an MA from the University of Alabama at Birmingham and now teaches American history there. She has consulted on numerous exhibits and television documentaries.

Melissa Walker is the author of *All We Knew Was to Farm: Rural Women in the Upcountry South, 1919–1941* (Johns Hopkins University Press, 2000), a book that was honored with the Southern Association for Women Historians' Willie Lee Rose Prize. She is also the editor of *Country Women Cope with Hard Times: A Collection of Oral Histories* (University of South Carolina Press, 2004) and the coeditor of *Southern Women at the Millennium: A Historical Perspective* (University of Missouri Press, 2003). She is an associate professor of history at Converse College.

Staunton, Virginia. *See* Curb markets: Staunton, Virginia
Stewart, Martha B., 193
Stubbs, Florence Hamer, 89–90
Sue Bennett College, 198
Sykes, Maybeth, 190

Teass, Helen, 111
Technological change in agriculture, 11, 124
Temple, Fannie, 240, 246
Tenant system. *See* Crop-lien system
Thompson, Elizabeth, 201
Tilly, Dorothy, 199
Tobacco cultivation: "thirteen-month crop," 18; prices, 23, 78; processes, 25–26, 27; women's roles in, 69–73; harvesting and curing, 71–74; markets and sales, 74–76, 78–79; African Americans and, 81–82
Tobacco Growers' Cooperative Association, 67; importance of women's work in, 77–78; formation of, 80; membership, 81–82; support by Cooperative Extension Service, 82–83; support by Clarence Poe, 83, 85; masculine rhetoric in favor of, 83–85; gaining women's support for, 85–90; women's roles in, 90–92; women as local officers of, 91–92; discrimination against women in, 92–93; lack of membership, 93–94; women's opposition to, 94–95; African Americans in, 81. *See also* *Tri-State Tobacco Grower*
Tobacco prices, 78–79, 80, 81, 86
Townsend, Grace, 113
Tri-State Cooperative. *See* Tobacco Growers' Cooperative Association
Tri-State Tobacco Grower "Farm Women's Page," 87–90
Troll, Shirley Underwood, 72
Tuskegee Institute, 139, 141

U.S. Food Administration, 147
Urbanization, 11, 231–33. *See also* Birmingham, Alabama; Vanity Fair apparel manufacturing; Sloss Furnaces; Sloss Quarters

Van Lear, Hazel, 116, 125–27, 133–34
Vance, Rupert, 4
Vanity Fair apparel manufacturing; effect on women leaving agriculture, 257, 262–63, 266; anti-unionism, 258–60, 281; move to Alabama, 259–60; employment of women, 260–61; desirability of employment at, 263–64; sewing machine operators' work, 264–65; wages, 265; production quotas, 265–66; contrast with agricultural work, 267; child care, 267; worker control, 267; importance of wages, 267–68; impact on local economies, 260, 262, 269–70; community facilities, 270–72; desegregation, 271–72, 274–76; segregation, 272; racial discrimination in, 276; difficulty of work, 276–77; economic pressure on, 277–78; worker morale, 278; unionization, 278–80; impact of race on unionization, 278–80; plant closings, 281–82
Vocational education, 137

Wampler, Charles W., 112
Wampler, Fannie, 105–7
Wampler, Phyllis, 133
Wampler, Ruth, 112
Ward, Alleyne Holliman, 51
Ware, Louie, 116
Washington, Booker T., 137
Washington, Maggie Langham, 55
Water supplies, 27
Weathersbee, Susie, 51, 62
Weyers Cave, Virginia, 106
White, Bertha May, 190–91